D1554991

A Land Alone: Colorado's Western Slope

For Our Parents:
George and Ruby Vandenbusche
Stanley and Ila Smith

A Land Alone: Colorado's Western Slope

Duane Vandenbusche
Duane A. Smith

PRUETT PUBLISHING COMPANY
Boulder, Colorado

First Edition

1 2 3 4 5 6 7 8 9

Printed in the United States of America

Library of Congress Cataloging in Publication Data

Vandenbusche, Duane.
  A land alone, Colorado's western slope.

  Bibliography: p.
  Includes index.
    1. Colorado — History, Local. I. Smith, Duane A.,
joint author. II. Title.
F776.V36   978.8   80-23265
ISBN 0-87108-560-7

Acknowledgments

We owe a sincere debt of thanks to many people and agencies who helped make this book possible. It is not for lack of appreciation that someone's name may have inadvertently been left out.

The Boettcher Foundation generously provided a grant that assisted with travel, purchase of photographs, and other necessary expenses. The staffs of numerous libraries, including Western State College, Fort Lewis College, Library of Congress, and the Denver Public Library, as well as the Colorado Historical Society, Western Historical Collections (University of Colorado), National Archives, and local and county historical societies, provided information and assistance. So did numerous Western Slopers who kindly agreed to be interviewed about their times and themselves. Our thanks, too, to those people who provided photographs which add an important dimension to this study.

Individually, Cathy Conrad and Sharon Livermore typed numerous chapters of this manuscript in rough draft, and Gay Smith edited and typed. David Lavender was a special help through his writings, personal encouragement, and his continual enthusiasm for his home region.

Foreword

During the middle of the 1970's the National Endowment for the Humanities helped celebrate America's Bicentennial by subsidizing, at a cost of more than a million dollars, a series of small volumes, each outlining the history of one of the nation's states. The motivating force behind the experiment was a conviction that the country as a whole could not be fully understood until its dissimilar components were also comprehended. The theory hardly needs defense. Even our stereotypes recognize it. The Connecticut Yankee, the Georgia cracker, the Arkansas traveler, the California hustler all bespeak fundamental differences.

So great a diversity springs, of course, from many sources—a multiplicity of ethnic groups, clashing economic and moral views (the Civil War was a supreme example of such differences) and from a willingness, sometimes grudgingly given, to let young people develop for themselves, amid a kaleidoscope of opportunities, whatever legal modes of working and living suit them best.

Another shaper of destiny—some students call it the most powerful one—is the American land itself: the rocky coasts of Maine, the deep soil of the Midwest, the rain-soaked forests of the coastal ranges of the Pacific. Clearly, as the title of this book indicates, its authors include in the list the Western Slope of the Colorado Rockies.

Two factors, they say, make the region unique—its rich stores of minerals and the water that the tall peaks drain, mostly in the form of snow, from the northern hemisphere's eastward driving storms. Agriculture? Well, yes, but mostly as it has served the needs of mines and of towns, Denver included, that first achieved prominence because of their symbiotic attachment to the mines.

Excessive dependence on just two principal resource bases, the authors continue, has inflicted on the Western Slope a regional schizophrenia that both the inhabitants themselves and those outsiders who want to exploit (or protect) the area need to recognize.

First, Colorado's original creators, gold and silver, brought with them a permanent boom psychology that today burns hotter than ever, now that energy-producing minerals are in the limelight. Cash in quick! — but the trouble is that the necessary capital has always come from the outside, and as a consequence the outside reaps most of the profits. Now that water is as transportable as coal (in fact, water sometimes serves to transport coal) it too flows toward the sources of money and power. Thus though the Western Slope speaks proudly of "its" riches, it actually finds itself in economic thralldom to Denver and points beyond. The result is a prickly defensiveness among many Slopers and, often, a deep ambivalence about which way to jump next.

Should they join in the exploitation of the land for the sake of the jobs and other economic gains that accompany a humming business atmosphere? Or will the quieter amenities of clean air and water, unscarred hillsides, and uncrowded meadows be worth more in the long run than a high gross Western Slope Product? And, somewhere in the middle, lies this quandary: what impact will their choices have on the tourist industry, winter and summer, and the real estate developments that now loom so large in the Western Slope's sense of well being?

Of such questions, expressed and implied, is this book made. The authors do not agree with those savants who contend that history should be flatly objective. They hold strong opinions and at times express their convictions. That is to say, they do not heap up facts for the sake of facts alone. Their aim is to impart knowledge, not just information.

Presumably the National Endowment of the Humanities would approve: knowing a part is a prerequisite to understanding the whole. For anyone interested in comprehending Colorado and, indeed, much of the boomtime West, *A Lane Alone* is a good place to begin.

David Lavender

Contents

THE WESTERN SLOPE

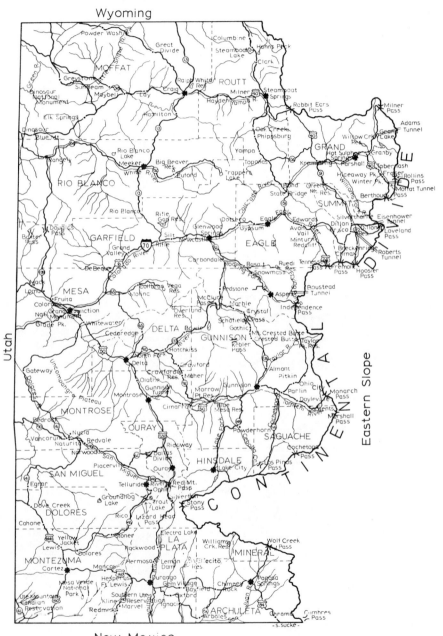

Introduction

The Western Slope of Colorado! The name has a special ring to it. It is as much a state of mind as it is a region of Colorado. When speaking of the eastern side of the Continental Divide, one uses the term "eastern slope," referring to the geography. That region west of the Divide by contrast is spelled with capital letters. "It is a human as well as a physiographic entity. It is also a mystique," wrote David Lavender in his *Colorado*. The people of the Western Slope feel that they are tougher than lesser mortals. They believe they have been shaped and hardened by the numbing cold, heavy snow, high elevation, and rugged terrain of the region. They often refer to outsiders derisively as "flatlanders" and laugh at their difficult transition to the seven, eight, or nine thousand feet elevation. Physically, the rugged Western Sloper is a myth; psychologically, he is real, even in the eyes of those who do not live there. Western Slopers are simply awed by the craggy terrain and elements.

The Continental Divide, which separates the Western Slope from the eastern slope, follows a snaking, confusing line from the Wyoming border in the north to New Mexico in the south. From north to south, the Western Slope stretches 276 miles. From the Utah border in the west to the Continental Divide in the east, the distance is not as easy to measure because the Divide meanders. In the north, the decider of waters, the Continental Divide, bulges far to the east to pick up the headwaters of the Colorado River near Grand Lake. From that point, it runs south by southwest, crossing some of the best

1

known high passes in the state—Rollins, Berthoud, Loveland, Boreas, Hoosier, Fremont, Tennessee, Independence, Cottonwood, Monarch, Marshall, and Cochetopa. At Cochetopa Pass, southeast of Gunnison, the Divide makes a big swing to the west to pick up the headwaters of the Rio Grande River near Stony Pass just east of Silverton. From there, the Divide snakes its way south and east into New Mexico, crossing Wolf Creek Pass en route.

Geography has always been the key to the history and development of the Western Slope, and still is today. The forbidding mountain ranges, bitter cold, inhospitable canyons and plateaus, and the paradox of heavy snow and little water have forced people to conform to the lay of the land and nature. And nature has blessed the Western Slope with magnificent scenery which has led to a billion dollar a year tourist industry, as well as some of the finest skiing in the world.

Nature has also given the Western Slope a great mining industry, one whose best days are still ahead. Great mineral wealth in the San Juan and Elk Mountains, and major coal deposits have always blessed the region. With the dawn of the 1980s, other mines are poised to open. This time production will center around oil shale, uranium, and molybdenum, as well as the ever-abundant coal.

The desperate need for energy in the United States has thrust the Western Slope into the limelight. In addition to the great deposits of coal, oil shale and uranium exist in abundance. The region is also a natural for solar and thermal energy if the government decides to move in that direction. One thing is clear: the Western Slope will never again be the tranquil, quiet, and pristine wonderland it once was. Its geography has already seen to that. The Age of Innocence is over; important decisions are being made today which will affect Western Colorado perhaps for the next century. Major change is on the way. The form and magnitude of that change is still unknown. Whatever the future holds, it will be molded and influenced by geography which, after all, has always been the key to the Western Slope.

It is our wish that this volume encourage interest in the heritage of the Western Slope and stimulate further research and writing about its past, present, and future. In this expectation, we call attention to the bibliography and the chapter footnotes, where primary and secondary sources will be found, and hope that they will lead the reader to other sources. The time to preserve the past is fast receding; the time to plan for the future is now. Senator Gary Hart challenged: "It's wrong to think that our future is totally out of our hands. The people of Colorado must not abdicate their responsibility . . . ." We ask here only that our efforts broaden and enrich the past and challenge and encourage thinking about the future.

History is people. Although it is impossible to discuss individuals thoroughly in this type of survey, we have included four mini-biographies of Western Slopers. These four symbolize them all — the people who opened, settled, and lived on Colorado's Western Slope.

I

A Land and Its
People—1874

Silence! The silence of centuries hangs over these ruins in the Ute Mountain Ute Park, as it does in scores of others scattered throughout southwestern Colorado. Archaeologists have been slowly unraveling the mystery of these ruins and their inhabitants, though much of their history will perhaps never be known. *Courtesy Richard L. Gilbert.*

Once the Western Slope was like a book of blank pages waiting to be written upon. First came the Indians and over the centuries they left their imprint. Then in increasingly rapid succession arrived the Spanish, the fur trappers, American explorers, and finally the miners, who stayed. By 1874 the introduction and several chapters of that book were completed.

1.
Once This Was Ours

The mesas stand empty now, the canyons silent where once they buzzed with activity. In times past the largest "urban complex" in North America flourished there, a prehistoric "megalopolis" that stretched far beyond the boundaries of Mesa Verde National Park. The Anasazi (Navajo for "Ancient Ones") developed an advanced agricultural society in the twelfth and thirteenth centuries that would not be reestablished in southwestern Colorado until 600 years later. When the Indians abandoned their homes in the late thirteenth century, they left behind the United States' most spectacular archaeological ruins and a tantalizing mystery.

Exactly when the Anasazi appeared on the Mesa Verde has not been determined. It was probably 2,000 years ago that they first walked into the canyons and climbed to the mesa tops. From the start, their life required adaptation to the environment and to the terrain. Their ancestors, a hunting culture whose remains can only be faintly traced in camp and kill sites, date back approximately 10,000 years. What distinguished these two cultures from one another was agriculture; the earlier Indians hunted and collected native food products. Among the Basketmaker people near Durango, sometime shortly after the time of Christ and as late as the fifth century elsewhere, corn was introduced, having been acquired from more advanced peoples to the south. Initially grown to supplement wild food, it became the staff of life, the basis of a new era. The roaming days of the hunter were replaced by the semi-sedentary existence of the hunter/farmer and finally by a subsistence agriculture and a culture, complete with villages, irrigation, and trade. The Anasazi were concentrated in what, centuries later, became known as southwestern Colorado, northwestern New Mexico, and northern Arizona. Evidence of their culture is also found in such peripheral areas as parts of the Colorado River Basin and the Yampa River Canyon in Western Colorado.

These people possessed no written language or calendar, which leaves the student of the Anasazi adrift in a mute, languageless void. To provide a chronological framework, southwestern archaeologists developed classifications and assigned dates, referring to the earliest Anasazi as Basketmakers. The Basketmakers evolved into the Pueblo period, out of which came the great ruins which fascinate tourists.

The Basketmakers, named because of their skill in that art (so finely woven as to hold water) and in manufacturing sandals woven from yucca fibers, are given the dates from A.D. 1 to 750. Within these centuries they advanced through several phases, moving from shallow, wind-formed caves to pithouses built on the mesa tops. As important as shelter and clothing are to humans, they remain subordinate to the more basic physical need for food. The Basketmakers shifted from hunting and gathering to cultivating corn, squash, and finally beans. In small fields beside the streams, Basketmakers wielding digging sticks, planted and weeded, hoping that the harvest would carry them through until the next planting season.

Agricultural expansion allowed these people to group together, something that hunting seldom permitted for any length of time. They climbed out of the damp, chilly caves to the warmer, healthier mesa tops. Their pithouses, dug partly underground and covered with a log-mud roof, gradually moved closer together to form villages. During the last two hundred years of the Basketmakers' era, they worked with pottery; the idea probably came from the south, like the introduction of corn, this time from Mexico, with its more advanced Indian culture. The Basketmakers also acquired knowledge of the bow and arrow, using them to replace the older, less efficient atlatl, or dart thrower. Obviously, hunting, which the Anasazi continued to do, was simplified; militarily, they gained potentially superior "fire power."

By the end of the Basketmaker period the wild turkey was domesticated. For warmth and fashion, feather robes supplemented animal skins. The dog was also part of the Basketmakers' life; its origin remains a mystery. Prehistoric Rover seems to have been primarily a pet, perhaps he came with the Indians to the New World.

8

No monumental event foretold the change from Basketmaker to Pueblo period, nor does even one moment in time mark the passage. The Pueblo improved upon its predecessor to achieve a golden age in southwestern Colorado. Architecturally, the pithouse evolved into a surface dwelling, or pueblo. It also went downward to an even deeper room which became the kiva, the underground ceremonial structure. Pottery shapes, designs, and firing methods were modified and improved. Different regions produced their own distinctive styles, making it possible to identify their origin and the Pueblos' trade contacts. Mesa Verde pottery, for instance, was of a black-on-white style, with a carefully polished, glossy surface.

Stone axes and hoes eased the work of the Anasazi farmer and builder. Baskets, grinding tools, and other items came from the Basketmaker heritage, although the simpler-to-make pottery vessels replaced baskets for many purposes. New varieties of corn, better able to mature in a short growing season, and, perhaps, cotton gave the farmers a better yield and the women a new fabric. Both most likely came from Mexico. In 1977 cotton pollen turned up at Hovenweep in a test excavation and may represent the most northern distribution of this plant.

During the early Pueblo period communal activity grew, as shown by the building of the great kivas and in the more numerous villages. Masonry structures made their debut, and before long the number of rooms markedly increased. The obvious cooperative work effort in building was not noticeable before these years. Finally, the great, or Classical, Pueblo period emerged. The remains of this period are most spectacular at Mesa Verde National Park and Chaco Canyon National Monument.

Dating from A.D. 1100 to 1300, architectural changes were the most notable. The Anasazi consolidated into fewer, but larger, communities. At first they built on the mesa tops; then, at Mesa Verde especially, they retreated to large alcoves in the canyon walls. There they constructed magnificent structures by accretion rather than by design. They moved into multi-storied "apartment houses," of a size that would be unmatched in the United States until the 1870s, when the modern apartment house appeared in New York City. The move to the canyon accentuated the communal trend and undoubtedly changed the life styles of the people crowded together in their closely confined communities.

The Anasazi had attained their cultural apex, shown not simply by their architectural achievements, but also by their increased agricultural production in response to such population concentration.

Centuries before the white man assumed he had introduced irrigation into Western Colorado, irrigation was giving life to Anasazi crops. Irrigation systems with ditches (some of them four miles long), check dams to catch run-off from heavy summer showers, and "reservoirs" to store the water criss-crossed Mesa Verde. The real purpose of these "reservoirs" is speculative. They may have been temporary impoundments or catchments but probably did not function very well for storage. All these things improved water reserves and allowed farming of more mesa-top land. The Anasazi, long burdened with a nearly total involvement with food gathering and maintaining food reserves, were granted more time to devote to other activities.

Excavations of sites from the Classic Mesa Verde period have given archaeologists the best picture of Anasazi life for the periods under discussion. Although it is beyond the scope of this chapter to examine in depth what has been discovered, the excavation of Mug House on Wetherill Mesa illustrates how these silent ruins have relinquished their secrets. A study of the skeletons from this site disclosed a number of ailments that plagued the residents, including the "nearly universal appearance of degenerative arthritis in mature adults." There is also abundant evidence that a dentist would have kept exceedingly busy. Apparently, grit from the grinding stones rapidly wore away the hard enamel tooth covering, promoting, or at least contributing to, decay. Abscesses and infected teeth caused further grief, leaving the Mesa Verdians with what might be described as a dental disaster. Few adults reached age forty; probably half the children died before age four. The many early deaths suggest that illness constantly menaced their lives. Although hard to prove, it may be that the mothers' malnutrition during the nursing period was directly related to infant mortality. The dumping of trash and human waste in front of the caves fostered growth of numberless microorganisms, and produced a distinctive addition to the odors already permeating the site.

Corn, squash, and beans, supplemented by seeds, meat, wild greens, and even cactus were diet mainstays. From evidence provided by animal bones, it can be deduced that the most important single source of meat may have been domestic turkeys, followed by rabbits, squirrels, wood rats, and deer. The concentrated population required more food storage space, and in Mug House over one-third of all rooms "were apparently assigned storage functions." People and garbage, plus stored food, proved irresistible to hordes of pests, including beetles, flies, rats, and mice.

Technologically, the Anasazi remained a stone-age people, their tools hewn from stone, bone, antler, and wood. Pottery was their finest handicraft, technically and artistically. In a more elementary fashion the residents of Mug House practiced basketry, weaving, and leatherworking. Available artifacts indicate some of them were master craftsmen, others only amateurs.

To the Mug House residents, as to their current neighbors in Cortez and Mancos, water was a precious commodity. They constructed a "catchment" near Mug House; when this dried up, the nearest source was at least a mile away. They made as good use of their environment as was possible without "a more advanced technology and without the benefits of extensive trade."[1]

At the peak of their development in the last half of the thirteenth century the Anasazi abandoned their homes. The first hint of difficulty came with the abandonment of the mesa-top communities and the move to canyon cliff dwellings. This major population shift made farming that much more difficult by adding the inconvenience of climbing up and down those cliffs. The study of Mug House concluded: "About the only important advantage to be gained from living in a Mesa Verde rock shelter is the ease of defense. It would be far more comfortable and sanitary to live in a house on the mesa top near most of the fields."[2] In fact, most people probably did live at least part of the year on the mesa top—the farm house for summer was comfortable and easily constructed, or one could walk from the cliff dwellings.

Why they moved is a question that has baffled archaeologists and others who cannot find a definitive answer. Several factors probably contributed to abandonment by 1300. A twenty-four-year drought began in 1276, although it was certainly not the first the Anasazi experienced. Over-population, or at least a too-high ratio of people to available land and water resources, may have necessitated a move. An outside enemy would seem to be a natural explanation, considering the defensive nature of the cliff dwellings. However, excavations show no evidence of warfare or the presence of alien people. It has been speculated that a religious upheaval also might have occurred, or that an epidemic of some kind caused widespread panic; perhaps internal squabbles forced abandonment. In their flight they left a silent monument to their civilization, as well as a fascinating mystery.

Centuries slipped away, and the Utes who came to claim this land did not resurrect the Anasazi way of life. In legend and story, today's Pueblo people preserve a hazy recollection of the Anasazi as a civilization that vanished completely. In the years following the 1859 gold rush, prospectors spread into Western Colorado where they dis-

11

covered some of the ruins. Amazed by what they found, they quickly concocted romantic theories to account for them. A well-known Colorado prospector, Dick Irwin, speculated in 1870, for instance, that the ancient ruins had been abandoned by "civilized Indians" rushing to the rescue when Cortez besieged Teotihuacan.

Not until the 1870s did intruders finally penetrate the canyons that carved the heart of Mesa Verde; one of them was William Henry Jackson, the photographer. The Wetherill brothers and Charley Mason are generally given credit for finding the spectacular cliff ruins in 1888 and 1889 that became the prime attraction of Mesa Verde and neighboring Ute Mountain Ute Park. No doubt, others preceded them; they simply did not display the same enthusiasm nor possess the promotional ability.

By 1893 a collection of relics enthralled visitors to the World's Fair in Chicago. In the 1890s tourists and scholars gathered at Mancos, a young, rough-edged farming community that only palely reflected the urbanization which once flourished at its back door. From Mancos the curious either hiked or rode up the narrow trails into Mesa Verde. Increased visitation, mounting vandalism, and enthusiastic, if misguided, relic gathering generated increased demand for preservation of the ruins. In the forefront of the fight stood a group of Colorado women, who were soon joined by others. By the turn of the century, six centuries after the Anasazi left, the movement was well under way. Following some setbacks, Mesa Verde National Park was established in 1906. A Federal Antiquities Act put a stop to the looting and vandalism, especially when rangers arrived to patrol the ruins and enforce the law. The Anasazi had come full circle, reemerging as a major tourist attraction. The peacefulness of Mesa Verde vanished forever.

In the quiet centuries following the Anasazi abandonment of southwestern Colorado, the people known as Utes slowly settled into the mountain valleys, eventually claiming all of the Western Slope as theirs. In truth, almost the entire state, as well as much of Utah, became Ute territory, and on their hunting expeditions the tribesmen roamed into the Texas Panhandle, south down the Rio Grande Valley, and north into Wyoming. Their beginnings are lost in the shadows of history. They spoke of the supreme ruler, Manitou, who created the earth, living creatures, and human beings.

Unlike the agriculturally oriented Anasazi, who crowded into villages, the Utes wandered over valley and mountain, hunting and gathering seeds, berries, and other foods nature provided. Traditionally pictured as short, stocky, and dark complexioned, they actually defy a composite picture; some grew tall and raw-boned, while others ranged in between. They lived in small family units, which joined together only on special occasions, or in winter when sheltered valleys provided a bit of relief from the snow and cold. Seven Ute bands formed a loose confederation (some might say they had no political structure whatever), each with its own leaders; the Europeans called them chiefs. Of these bands, the Weeminuche, Tabeguache (also called Uncompahgre), Grand River (later White River), and Yampa called Western Colorado home. The Capote, who lived primarily in the neighboring San Luis Valley, frequently crossed the Divide, and the Uintas drifted in and out from eastern Utah.

Once beyond the friendly confines of the mountains, the Utes faced opposition from other Indians, who claimed dominion over the land upon which they were trespassing. In all directions lived peoples whom the Utes threatened; warfare became a fact of life. Sometimes more a game than deadly combat, war could become a tribal vendetta, growing into a struggle for supremacy and honor. The Navajos, Apaches, Kiowas, Comanches, Sioux, and Snakes confronted Ute warriors in a hit-and-run series of skirmishes.

In their mountain sanctuary, where the Utes followed a seasonal life, occasional raiding parties kept them alert. When spring loosened winter's cold grip, the Utes moved from the valleys into the mountains to hunt and gather. Half-hearted farmers at best, they might plant a patch of corn, squash, or beans in the spring, let nature take its course, and harvest what matured. Late in the fall the families migrated to warmer valleys; many of the Western Colorado Utes drifted to Arizona or New Mexico. Americans were not the first to realize the benefits of those sun-kissed lands.

Thus the generations passed. The Utes adjusted to the Western Slope's environmental and climatic conditions and evolved a compatible life style. Solidifying their hold, they became masters of the land. Their Supreme God, whose power created all things for his people, had been good to them. Minor gods (some benevolent, some mischievous) entered into Ute life, including a number of animal gods, the coyote chief among them. The Utes were nature worshipers; they accepted what came their way, courting the favor of the deities as needed. The medicine man, as the whites named him, assisted if the magnitude of a problem or illness warranted his services.

Into this fairly well regulated world came a disruption, which completely upset the balance the Indians had managed to achieve. The Spanish rode northward into the Rio Grande Valley. More than just a strange people, they brought with them a totally different culture: energetic promoters of proselytizing Christianity, beneficiaries of budding industrialism, and possessors of superior weaponry. They were a double-edged threat to the very core of the Utes' existence. Sometime in the mid-sixteenth century, rumors of these strangers riding fearsome animals reached the Utes. No serious threat arose, however, until the Spanish permanently colonized the Rio Grande Valley, thereby bringing the Utes into fidgety contact. The impact proved lasting once trade was initiated. The repercussions that came with the introduction of metal items were immense; iron replaced stone, effecting a jump of industrial centuries. The novelty which most caught their fancy, however, was the horse. The horse revolutionized Ute life, even more than the car changed life in the twentieth century. The first horses, acquisitions of trading or raiding, instantly gave the Utes a mobility and freedom they had never known. Excellent horsemen almost as quickly as they mounted the animals, they soon were ranging far afield in search of game or raiding quarry. Beyond the foothills Ute hunting parties rode out to the buffalo range, where that shaggy, walking commissary supplied food, clothing, and even housing materials in an abundance they had never before relished.

The horse forged the Utes into stronger bands. No longer did the Indians have to scatter to find scarce food; they could live in central camps and send hunters far and wide. In truth, this wondrous new animal unlocked a new life for the Utes, one not without its tribulations, however. An expensive item in trade, the horse came at a high price when deerskins represented one's principal bargaining product. Their new, exhilarating mobility brought the Utes into greater contact with equally well mounted enemies and dangled the tempting possibility of raids upon the Spanish, the source of the horse. The Spanish, of course, objected to meeting force with force. Increased desires and pressures made the Utes more aggressive, and they found themselves contesting more aggressive neighbors.

The Spanish and Utes, uneasy neighbors, had trouble adjusting to one another. The Utes feared and needed the Spanish, whose power threatened them. But the sources of that power had to be acquired, if the Utes hoped to keep pace with other Indians ringing their territory. Periods of raiding and trading alternated, as the two factions sparred for advantage. Finally, in the mid-eighteenth century, peace came. The Utes traveled south to trade; a lively trade it was, even to the point of bartering slaves, particularly children, whom the Utes had seized in raids. At the same time, the Spanish pressed forward in Western Colorado; their day was beginning.

2.
The End of the Beginning

The Spanish achievement on the Western Slope of Colorado has forever been shrouded in mystery. A lack of written records, problems in translation, illegal expeditions across the Continental Divide and, until recently, a belief that the Spanish were not very important, diminished the achievement of Spain on the Western Slope of Colorado.

But the men of Spain were on the Western Slope and they were there in greater numbers than previously thought possible. Riding their tough little ponies or trudging along monotonously on foot through the arid canyon country of Western Colorado, they first appeared in the seventeenth century. The Spanish penetrated the Western Slope not from the east, but rather from the south—from the dusty little capital of New Mexico—Santa Fe.

They came to Western Colorado for many reasons. Conflicts with the Ute Indians led Spanish raiding parties as far north as the Uncompahgre Valley and the Gunnison country. Juan de Anza's expedition against the Comanche in 1779 over Poncha Pass is indicative of earlier and similar expeditions on the Western Slope. Then, too, isolated Spanish expeditions sought the black gold of the mountains— the pelt of the beaver—and came north and west from Santa Fe to examine the many streams beyond the Continental Divide.

More than Ute Indians and beaver pelts, though, Spain was interested in gold. Was it true that on the Western Slope lay immense deposits of gold waiting for those with the courage to mine that most precious of all metals? Was it true that another Zacatecus awaited its

15

destiny? There was only one way to find out — send expeditions into Western Colorado for a look. Long before Don Juan Maria de Rivera's 1765 expedition, many illegal Spanish parties (no doubt small in number) made their way into the darkness and danger of the Western Slope to find gold. Before Rivera, the mountains in southwestern Colorado had already been named "La Plata," or "silver," in Spanish. Old arrastres, forts, mining tools, placer diggings, and names carved on trees bear witness to Spain's early entry on the Western Slope.

In 1765, an official Spanish exploring expedition, led by Juan Maria de Rivera, moved north out of Santa Fe to the San Juan River and across the northern spur of the San Juan Mountains in search of gold. His quest led him down the Dolores River, across the Uncompahgre Plateau and River to the Gunnison River at the present site of Delta. After carving a cross, his name, and the year of his expedition on a cottonwood tree, Rivera began his return to Santa Fe, probably retracing his steps. Rivera's party returned with ore samples rich enough to induce other mining expeditions into Western Colorado. His historic journey was destined to have an epic sequel.

During the next decade, other traders from New Mexico, with or without government permission, made expeditions over roughly the same route Rivera had taken. In 1775, Pedro Mora, Gregorio Sandoval, and Andre Muniz went northwest as far as the Gunnison River, "where at the mouth of the Uncompahgre they examined the young cottonwood on which Rivera had carved a cross."[1]

That there had been still other expeditions into the cold north country of Western Colorado in the decade after 1765 is without question. Spaniards from Taos and Santa Fe frequently traded with the Ute Indians in violation of government orders, often remaining with the red-skinned warriors of the mountains for two, three, and four months at a time, trapping beaver and scouting the beautiful mountain country. Thus, by 1776, the Western Slope as far north as the Gunnison River and possibly farther was a favorite hunting and trading ground for Spanish men of adventure.

But for sheer drama and adventure, one finds it difficult to surpass the expedition of the two Spanish Franciscan friars, Silvestre Escalante and Francisco Dominguez, in the year of the American Revolution, 1776. Led by Juan Bautista de Anza, one of the great trail blazers, colonizers, and military men in the history of the American continent, Spain had colonized the southern half of California by that year. Now there was a need to link up the settlements of New Mexico with those of California. From California, blazing a trail east in an effort to link the mission stations, came Father Francisco Garces, a Western Ulysses. From the Colorado River in California to the Grand Canyon and Little Colorado River in Arizona, the Spanish padre, with only a few Mojave guides for company, made his lonely way through desert, canyons, and mountains until turned back by hostile natives at the pueblo of Oraibe in July of 1776.

Fathers Escalante and Dominguez, meanwhile, were working on the same problem but from the other end. In late July, 1776, driving cattle along for food, the ten-man Escalante-Dominguez Party left Santa Fe and headed northwest in an effort to avoid hostile southwestern Indians and the feared Grand Canyon. They swung west past rugged Mesa Verde and then headed north. They were already beginning to find out how challenging Colorado's Western Slope was. In mid-August, from their camp on the Mancos River, they crossed over a low spur of the San Juans and descended into the Dolores River Valley. Escalante and Dominguez left the Dolores River at Gypsum Canyon near the Paradox Valley and soon hit the San Miguel River just outside of present-day Nucla. From the San Miguel, the party worked its way east and ascended the rugged Uncompahgre Plateau; soon after, they descended to the Uncompahgre River by way of Dallas Creek.

As Escalante and Dominguez continued through the Western Slope, ever northward, they glimpsed one magnificent panorama after another. High, snow-covered mountains, clear mountain streams, great and open valleys, jagged canyons, and breathtakingly beautiful sunsets met their eyes. And still they went on. The expedition followed the Uncompahgre River to near its mouth (near present-day Delta) and then bent east along the North Fork of the Gunnison River near the orchard country of today's Paonia. From that point the trail ran north by northwest. Skirting the high Grand Mesa, the party dropped into the valley of the mighty Colorado River at the present site of Grand Valley. Crossing the Colorado, Escalante and Dominguez traveled north by northwest through the severe mesa and plateau country before hitting the Douglas Creek Canyon, which they followed to present-day Rangely on the banks of the White River. The Franciscan friars soon passed out of Western Colorado into Utah, where they saw the mighty Green River at the present site of Jensen.

Dominguez and Escalante got no farther west than Utah Lake, south of the great Salt Lake, when approaching winter sent them scurrying south and then east back to Santa Fe. Yet theirs had been an epic journey — a valiant effort to strengthen Spain's hold on its fading northern empire. But the two Spanish friars had also left their mark on the Western Slope. They had traversed the rugged canyons, hostile mesas, and plateaus, had forded the great rivers and had learned that this would not be an easy land to conquer. The trek of Escalante and Dominguez which zig-zagged throughout the breadth of the Western Slope opened up an immense new land to the forces of civilization.

Despite the efforts of Rivera and Escalante and Dominguez, along with other reported Spanish expeditions into the harsh land of the north, the Western Slope closed its doors in the face of Spain. Many were the reasons why the Spanish rarely appeared on the Western Slope after 1800. The harsh geography and fierce elements, protective Ute Indians not wishing further intrusions on their hunting grounds, and the failure of Spanish gold seekers to find any of the precious yellow metal—all contributed to the end of the Spanish drive into Western Colorado. But their philosophy lived on in the Spanish language and architecture, Spanish names of mountains, rivers, and towns, and the Catholic religion.

The Spanish era on the Western Slope was closely followed by an even more exciting era—that of the fur trapper, mountain man, or "knight in the wilderness." He came to the mountains of Western Colorado dressed in a buckskin shirt, leather britches, and soft, quiet moccasins. He asked no quarter from the Indians or elements and gave none; he was a man alone. And in the mountains of the Western Slope, the mountain man found a wonderland of towering mountains, fast flowing streams, and enormous numbers of the curious and very profitable beaver.

A limited number of early Spaniards had been the first mountain men on Colorado's Western Slope, but because of the mercantilistic policy of their government, they made little profit from the enterprise and the trapping of beaver soon came to an end. Not so, however, with the Anglo-American. This hardy and individualistic capitalist first appeared on the Western Slope prior to 1800, though very little is known about the early arrivals. Some were certainly Frenchmen, venturing into the mountains from their haunts along the Mississippi River. Others were Americans, psychological loners who wanted no part of civilized existence. Living with the Indians of the Western Slope and only occasionally venturing back to civilization, a scattered few in the late eighteenth and early nineteenth centuries became the forerunners of the later mountain men.

The real era of the mountain men on the Western Slope did not begin until 1821, when Mexico successfully broke away from Spain in the Mexican Revolution. Up until that time, the Western Slope was part of the Spanish empire and all trade with foreigners was illegal. The mountain man's place in the sun in Western Colorado was brief; the trade flourished only from 1824 to 1845. But during those two decades, the fur trapper did much to open the land to settlement. The mountain men were the shock troops of the Western Slope. They were the first to endure the numbing cold, tremendous snows, Indian dangers, and barren isolation. They found the headwaters of the rivers, climbed to the tops of the mountains, uncovered the high mountain passes, discovered the lush "hole" of the mountains, broke down the self-sufficiency of the Indians, and advertised the Western Slope. When the mountain man left in the mid-1840s, carrying his trusty "Hawken" rifle, he never looked back; yet he left behind a Western Slope that was now ready for settlement.

The Western Slope was a virtual bonanza for mountain men during the second quarter of the nineteenth century. The area was a haven for thousands of beaver who lived contentedly along the many streams which flowed out of the mountains. The eyes of the mountain men sparkled when they gazed upon such great beaver streams as the Colorado, Green, Yampa, Eagle, Blue, San Juan, Animas, Gunnison, Uncompahgre, and Dolores rivers. Some early mountain men, few in number, trapped on the Western Slope before and immediately after 1800 in much the same way as the hardy James Purcell, who worked the streams of South Park in 1805.

Trappers who followed Zebulon Pike's route into the rugged southern Rockies reached the perimeter of the Western Slope, but Ute Indians, isolation, and a very inhospitable Spanish government at Santa Fe kept them from gaining a toehold in the region. Notable expeditions were made by Jean Baptiste Champlain in 1811, Joseph Philibert in 1814, and Julius DeMunn and August Choteau from 1815 to 1817. Each party explored the Arkansas and Rio Grande rivers in Colorado and almost certainly scouted the territory west of the Continental Divide. None of the expeditions was successful because Spain still controlled the beaver country.

Then in 1821 it happened. Mexico threw off the bonds of Spanish imperialism and became master of its own fate. American fur men rubbed their hands with glee as dollar signs danced before their eyes. Now the beaver country of the Southwest and central Rockies was open. It did not take long. Almost before the bells of independence had stopped ringing during the late fall of 1821, American fur traders, their pack horses laden with supplies, trudged into Taos and Santa Fe, New Mexico. One of the first fur trading parties to discover the new opportunity at Santa Fe was the Jacob Fowler-Hugh Glenn party. In September, these two midwesterners had left Fort Smith, Arkansas, with eighteen men on an expedition to the Arkansas River Valley, after building a trading post at the future site of Pueblo. They trapped and traded in the area, pushing up the Rio Grande and into the San Juan Mountains near Wagon Wheel Gap. Some members of the Fowler-Glenn expedition may have made their way over the Continental Divide to examine the beaver streams of the Western Slope.

Other fur traders followed the Fowler-Glenn party into the beautiful, but isolated, Western Slope. Taos, New Mexico, rather than the closely regulated Santa Fe, provided the jumping off point. The major figure in the Western Slope fur trade was Antoine Robidoux, born into a large French family from St. Louis in 1794. Robidoux heard of the great profits being made in the fur trade, wanted a piece of the action, and thus came to Santa Fe in 1824. While in the New Mexican capital, he married a Mexican girl and became a Mexican citizen. In 1828, he built a trading post, Fort Robidoux, on the Gunnison River just below the mouth of the Uncompahgre River near present-day Delta. Located amidst the cottonwood trees which adorned the region, the fort was the first of its kind on Colorado's Western Slope and served as a supply and trading center for mountain men in the vicinity. It was also located on the north-south trailway which linked New Mexican settlements to the beaver-rich valley of the Green River in northwestern Colorado, Utah, and Wyoming.

Getting supplies to Fort Robidoux was a hellish venture. The route from Taos through the San Luis Valley, over Cochetopa Pass, and into the Gunnison country was not especially difficult, but the Black Canyon west of Gunnison was another story. To avoid the tremendous gorge where walls rose straight up from the Gunnison River for nearly 3,000 feet, Robidoux was forced to detour his wagons to the south and up and down one mesa after another. He affectionately named the twisting, rolling thoroughfare, "Son-of-a-Bitch" trail. But finally, near present-day Montrose, he broke into the open and followed a level road to his fort on the Gunnison. Fort Robidoux was in existence until 1844 when its founder recognized the inevitable and gave up. By then the Ute Indians had become hostile, the price of furs had plummeted to a dollar a pelt, and the streams of the Western Slope had been badly overtrapped. The remains of the fort were obliterated by incoming ranchers in the 1880s.

During the 1820s, many small expeditions of mountain men worked the streams of the Western Slope. The San Juan River from

Wolf Creek Pass to present-day Pagosa Springs was worked. In 1824, William Wolfskill and Ewing Young peered into the San Juan country. The Eagle, Colorado, and Roaring Fork rivers were trapped prior to 1830. Uncle Dick Wootton, a famous fur trader in Colorado history, told of one Calvin Briggs who worked for Nathaniel Wyeth in the Colorado mountains in the 1830s. Wootton stated that Briggs was one of a seventeen-man trapping party which left Bent's Fort in June of 1837 and trapped "pretty much all the streams of Colorado and Wyoming, wintered in Wyoming and returned to Bent's Fort in March, 1838."[2]

The center of fur trade on the Western Slope and one of the busiest trading points in the history of the West was Brown's Hole, lying in the extreme northwestern corner of Colorado. The hole, or valley, received only light snowfall and had been used by Indians seeking protection from winter storms. The mountain-walled valley through which the Green River flowed had a mild climate, plenty of grass, and was ideally located in the middle of the Rocky Mountain fur trade. William Ashley of Missouri was the first known white man to visit the park. In 1825, Ashley, looking for a convenient rendezvous where he might supply fur-traders for the next season and purchase their year's catch of beaver pelts, came to the mouth of Henry's Fork in northeastern Utah. In the spring of the year, in two boats constructed from buffalo hides, Ashley and his men ran the Green River, then called the "Seeds-kee-dee," hoping to make contact with fur traders to the south. "Running rapids, going six days without food [they were] in despair of ever escaping the canyon . . Then suddenly the mountain walls drew back, the river widened, and they shot out into beautiful Brown's Hole. Ten miles below was a great camping ground where thousands of Indians had wintered. . . ."[3]

There, in Brown's Hole (later named for fur trader Baptiste Brown), in the middle of a lush valley of grass and shining aspen trees, William Ashley had found his rendezvous. Starting the following year and continuing to 1840, Brown's Hole was the scene of active and extensive trading, "the volume of business done there annually exceeding even that transacted at Bent's Fort on the Arkansas and at Taos."[4] Into the park every July came mountain men from all walks of life: deserters from the Hudson's Bay Company, French-Canadians, Mexicans from the Southwest and Americans like Jim Bridger, Bill Williams, Joseph Meek, Jim Baker, and Kit Carson. They first asked for the previous year's news and welcomed old friends. Then the trading of beaver pelts for next year's supplies occurred. Only then did the mountain men partake of "Taos Lightning" and get roaring drunk. When the mountain man and his money were exhausted, he stumbled back into the wilderness of the Western Slope and surrounding mountains to once again resume his sole purpose in life—the trapping of the beaver.

During the winter of 1831–32, Prewitt Sinclair and members of the Bean-Sinclair trapping party from Arkansas wintered in Brown's Hole and erected the first cabins at the fur rendezvous. Four years later Sinclair, Philip Thompson and William Craig realized the commercial possibilities of the site and constructed Fort Davy Crockett, named after the famous frontier hero who was killed at the Alamo that same year. The fort was constructed of logs with three wings, a dirt roof, and no stockade and rested on the left bank of the Green River above the mouth of Vermillion Creek.

Isolated and constantly threatened by Indians, Fort Davy Crockett was called Fort Misery by those who visited it. In August of 1839, F. A. Wislizenus, a German doctor from St. Louis, stopped at the fort with an east-bound party from Fort Hall on the Snake River. Wislizenus was not impressed. He wrote: "The fort is the worst thing of the kind we have seen on our journey . . . . Instead of cows the fort had only some goats . . . . In short the whole establishment appeared somewhat poverty-stricken for which reason it is known . . . as Fort Misery."[5]

On August 12, five days before the Wislizenus arrival, T. J. Farnham, leader of an Oregon-bound party from Peoria, Illinois, arrived at the fort and left us the following impressions:

> Here . . . were the lodges of Mr. Robinson . . . who usually stations himself here to traffic with the Indians and white trappers. His skin lodge was his warehouse; and buffalo robes were spread upon the ground and counter, on which he displayed butcher knives, powder, lead, fish-hooks, and whiskey. In exchange for these articles he received beaver skins from trappers, money from travellers, and horses from the Indians. . . . When all the independent trappers are driven by approaching winter into this delightful retreat, and the whole Snake village, two or three thousand, . . . impelled by the same necessity, pitch their lodges around the Fort . . . there is no want of customers.[6]

By 1840, the fur trade in Western Colorado was fading fast because of overtrapping and competition from the silk hat in Europe. This, coupled with an increased Indian threat, forced the abandonment of Fort Davy Crockett in 1840. Even though some mountain men used the fort during the next few years, the era of the rendezvous and the beaver trade passed into history. The fort was burned to the ground in the late 1840s. An era had ended in the history of the Western Slope.

The demise of Fort Davy Crockett in 1840 signaled the end of the fur trade in Western Colorado for all but a few parties and hardy individuals. In 1841, mountain man Jim Baker joined one of Jim Bridger's trapping expeditions in northwestern Colorado, not far from Fort Bridger in Wyoming country. The Illinois native met Henry Fraeb and a band of forty men on the banks of the Little Snake River in the rugged canyon country where Colorado, Wyoming, and Utah come together. While camped along the stream, the trappers were attacked by 400 to 500 Arapahoe, Cheyenne, and Sioux Indians. In the bloody August battle from noon to sundown, the Indians killed ten trappers and over 100 horses, while taking heavy casualties themselves. The site of the desperate battle was the mouth of Battle Creek in today's Routt County, a mere half mile from the Wyoming border. The battle was further evidence of the Indians' reluctance to allow white trappers on their hunting grounds.

The last true mountain men on the Western Slope were probably Luther Simmons and Gus Lankin, who trapped in the Snake and Green River country in northwestern Colorado in the late 1870s. They dressed in buckskins of their own tanning, moving about with saddle and pack horses until a good number of furs had been collected. They then disposed of them at trading posts. By then, of course, the fur trading frontier in Western Colorado had long since passed. Simmons and Lankin were relics of an era gone by. But what an era it had been! The mountain men had laid the groundwork for settlement a mere thirty years away.

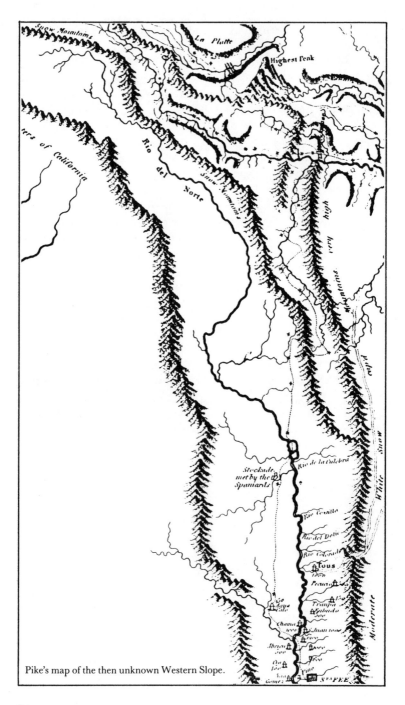

Pike's map of the then unknown Western Slope.

3.
Of Men and Mountains

From the end of the fur trade in the early 1840s to the coming of the placer miners in 1859–60, the Western Slope was in a state of transition. Heretofore, the region had been dominated by Ute Indians with scant numbers of Spaniards and mountain men leaving their marks. But now the Western Slope became involved in a maze of national politics. A transcontinental railroad was being discussed and Western Colorado seemed to be right in the middle of the central route. Then, too, the Army was interested in linking its forts in Utah to those in New Mexico with a good wagon road. Again, the Western Slope seemed to make up part of the route.

Even before explorers and surveyors set foot on the Western Slope they knew its dangers. The mountain men warned them of the rugged terrain and the terrible winters. They also learned from the experience of famed Oregonian Marcus Whitman, who became lost in heavy snows near Cochetopa Pass in 1842 and nearly perished. Three years later, the indefatigable William Gilpin, then a young man, passed through the Western Slope, returning to St. Louis from Oregon. Oblivious to the dangers of the region, Gilpin spoke of the Western Slope in glowing terms. The famed John C. Fremont traipsed through the Western Slope in 1844 on a return trip from California. From North Park, the explorer crossed Muddy Pass through the Rabbit Ears range near today's Steamboat Springs, continued through Middle Park, hit the Blue River, and followed it to its source near Hoosier Pass. Fremont left the Western Slope via the pass and descended into mammoth South Park. The following spring the tireless Fremont was on his way to California again, this time involved in a plot to take California from Mexico. While hurrying to the West Coast, he left the Arkansas River above Leadville, not over the pass which bears his name today, but rather over Tennessee Pass. Aside from Whitman, Gilpin, Fremont, and Ute Indians, only an occasional trapper and Mormon scouts looking for a homeland passed through the Western Slope until the early 1850s.

Fremont was again an exception, this time on an ill-fated expedition of 1848–49. John Fremont, already known as the "Pathfinder of the West" for his many expeditions, was on the trail again during the early winter of 1848 in an effort to test the 38th parallel as an all-weather, year-round route to the Pacific. Sponsored by St. Louis businessman and Senator Thomas Hart Benton, Fremont and thirty-two men, led by sixty-one-year-old guide Old Bill Williams, arrived in the San Luis Valley of Colorado in early December. Early snows and violent storms caused Williams to lose his way trying to cross a pass between today's Creede on the Rio Grande and Cochetopa Creek on the west side of the Divide. Alas, in the driving snow, Williams turned north away from the Rio Grande fifteen miles short of the true route to the pass and became hopelessly lost near Wannamaker Pass at the 11,000-foot level. During the next month the Fremont party took tremendous punishment from wind, snow, and below-freezing temperatures. By the time it was over, one-third of the 33-man expedition had perished, including Bill Williams, who was killed by Utes, while attempting to retrieve Fremont's baggage. Fremont's tragedy demonstrated the immense danger of the Western Slope and its environs in the wintertime.

The decade from 1850 to 1860 brought one exploring party after another into the Western Slope looking for railroad routes, overland trails, cattle trails, and just plain adventure. The indomitable Richens Lacy "Uncle Dick" Wootton was responsible for a little-known but significant trip through the Western Slope during the summer of 1852. The old mountain man bought 9,000 sheep at Watrous, New Mexico, and drove them to California, hoping to cash in on the hungry forty-niners in the Sierra Nevada Mountains. Employing fourteen Mexicans and eight Americans and using mules instead of horses, this immense drive began on June 24 and ended at Sacramento 107 days later on October 9 with the loss of only 100 sheep. En route, Wootton crossed Mosca Pass, Cochetopa Pass, the Gunnison country, and then followed the old Ute trail through northwestern Colorado. Wootton was enthusiastic about the new route and exclaimed: "I made the trip through to California . . . arriving there with my sheep in good order, having passed through some of the finest country I ever saw, had good camps, and plenty of wood, water, and grass every night during the whole trip. This route is at least 450 miles nearer than the route by Fort Laramie and South Pass. I recommend to emigrants by all means to take this route in preference to any other."[1]

In 1853, a virtual deluge of explorers and travelers descended upon the Western Slope. Lieutenant Edward Beale, heading west to become Commissioner of Indian Affairs for California, led the parade. Beale and his cousin, Gwinn Harris Heap, had been induced by Senator Thomas Hart Benton to examine a possible central railroad route to the Pacific. Traveling with pack animals and unencumbered with wagons, the Beale expedition of twelve men left Westport, Missouri in May 15 and, just over a month later, crossed Cochetopa Pass, which brought them to the Western Slope. Making good time, Beale passed through the beautiful Gunnison Valley and looked with awe at the Black Canyon before coming to the Uncompahgre River. The rustling aspen were still green as the Beale party crossed the Colorado River near today's Grand Junction and passed into Utah. Ninety-seven days and 1,852 miles after leaving Westport, Beale and his party arrived in Los Angeles. As a result of the uneventful trip, Beale and Heap produced a report which made the Cochetopa Pass route and the Western Slope seem almost incredible in their economic possibilities. The report was distributed throughout the country and further whetted the appetites of railroad magnates.

Following closely on the heels of the Beale expedition was forty-one-year-old Captain John Gunnison of the Army Topographical Engineers. Secretary of War Jefferson Davis had placed the New England–born army captain in charge of surveying a railroad route between the 38th and 39th parallels. Gunnison, an experienced surveyor, was elated with the assignment; this might be a chance to make a name for himself. On June 15, 1853, Gunnison left Fort Leavenworth, Kansas with thirty-two mounted riflemen, sixteen six-mule wagons, an instrument carriage, a four-mule ambulance, and a scientific staff. The aspen leaves were already turning bright orange as the Gunnison expedition crossed "the pass of the buffalo," Cochetopa Pass, on September 2 and descended into the Gunnison country on Colorado's Western Slope.

Gunnison's route along the Tomichi and Gunnison rivers was beautiful and uneventful until he reached the Lake Fork and Black canyons. The deep Lake Fork Canyon was crossed with difficulty but the expedition was forced to detour south around the fearsome half-mile-deep slit of schist called the Black Canyon. Around the canyon, Gunnison was forced to cross some very tough rolling hills and mesa country before crossing 7,909-foot-high Cerro Summit and descending into the Uncompahgre River Valley near today's Montrose. From that point, the Gunnison party had easy going, following the Uncompahgre and Gunnison rivers until the latter emptied into the mighty Colorado near present-day Grand Junction. Gunnison then crossed into Utah and into history. A month later, in southwestern Utah, he and seven of his men were killed by Paiute Indians and horribly mutilated. Gunnison's expedition through the Western Slope showed that while wagons could be taken to the West Coast, a transcontinental railroad was out of the question. The deep and rugged canyons, along with continuous mesas and rolling sagebrush country, proved that.

Like Marcus Whitman and John C. Fremont before him, Captain Randolph Marcy of the United States Army got a taste of how tough the Western Slope could be when he embarked on what would become a desperate journey during the winter of 1857–58. Marcy was under the command of General Albert Sidney Johnston who was trying to put down a Mormon rebellion in Utah in 1857. Johnston was holed up for the winter at Ford Bridger in southwestern Wyoming and was desperately in need of livestock and supplies to feed his men. To Marcy and sixty-four men he entrusted the task of bringing back supplies from Fort Union, New Mexico, a tough winter's journey away.

The relief expedition made its way through Utah and Brown's Park in northwestern Colorado in late November without incident, but the onset of an early winter soon put them in mortal danger. They crossed the Colorado River near today's Grand Junction in early December and on the eighth day of that month arrived at the site of old Fort Robidoux, where the Gunnison and Uncompahgre rivers came together. There, Marcy was warned by Ute Indians that it was suicide to continue through the Gunnison country. The captain had no choice; the survival of the men at Fort Bridger was in his hands. And so Marcy pressed on.

Soon, drifting snow deepened up to the men's waists and even snowshoes tried by scout Jim Baker sank through the powdery, loose snow. Near the top of Cochetopa Pass, with most of the sixty-six mules dead and twelve men with frozen feet, the desperate soldiers ran into powder snow so light that the three or four in the lead were forced to lie down and crawl so that the snow would pack for the men behind to walk. For twelve days the Marcy expedition lived off the meat of starved horses and mules sprinkled with gunpowder. In early January, unable to move any farther from near the summit of Cochetopa Pass, Marcy sent two men with the remaining three mules to Fort Massachusetts in the San Luis Valley for help. Eleven days later the rescue party came into sight; Marcy and his men broke down and wept. Wiser now, and with complete respect for the rugged winters of the Western Slope, Marcy, after getting supplies from Fort Union, returned to Fort Bridger along the base of the Front Range to the Overland Trail and then west through South Pass.

The first major wagon train passed through the Western Slope during the summer of 1858, only seven months after the Marcy expedition. The wagon train was made up of a military detachment under Colonel William Loring and included 50 wagons and 300 men. When the Mormon rebellion ended in Utah in the summer, Loring was ordered to take a wagon train from Camp Floyd, southwest of Salt Lake City to Fort Union, New Mexico. Making his own road most of the way, Loring came into Colorado via today's Green River, Utah and then followed the usual route from the "grand junction" of the Colorado and Gunnison rivers through the Uncompahgre and Gunnison valleys, over Cochetopa Pass, through the San Luis Valley and on to Fort Union. He arrived on September 13, completing a fifty-six-day trip and proving that large wagon trains could manage the rough terrain of the Western Slope.

In 1859, the "Rush to the Rockies" came with the discovery of gold in Colorado. Thousands of miners streamed into the territory looking for gold nuggets in every stream and under every rock, especially up Clear Creek Canyon, west of Denver. The future looked bright and Colorado yearned to be on the new transcontinental line being discussed back in Washington, D. C. But where would the railroad cross the mountains between Denver and Salt Lake City? While some men wondered, William Byers of the *Rocky Mountain News* and other men from Denver acted. In March of 1861, they hired a young, dapper, goateed miner from Golden to search out and find a good pass which could be used by the transcontinental line. The miner's name was Edward Louis Berthoud, born in Switzerland but raised in New York. Berthoud was an engineer, and a good one, who had worked on the railroad across the Isthmus of Panama.

In May of 1861, Berthoud and old Jim Bridger of fur trade fame rode up Clear Creek from Golden. At Georgetown, Berthoud sent Bridger to South Park to look for a pass while he moved above Empire to investigate a gap which had been seen by four prospectors the year before. On May 12, 1861, Berthoud and his men, scrambling, jumping, and climbing over ridges of snow, reached the pass that today bears his name at 11,314 feet in the clouds. From there Berthoud gazed upon stunningly beautiful Middle Park on the Western Slope. Unlike most other passes, this one showed no signs of having been used by buffalo or Indians.

From July to September, 1861, Berthoud and Bridger forged a road to Salt Lake City. Their route took them from Middle Park over Gore Pass to Egeria Park and from there along the Yampa River to present-day Craig. From there the trail dropped south to the White River at today's Meeker and then continued west to Salt Lake City. During this 1,000-mile exploration, much was learned about the virgin Western Slope, but, alas, Berthoud Pass proved to be too high, the weather too bad, and the grade too steep for a transcontinental railroad. But civilization was continuing in its effort to break down the door to the Western Slope.

As the tragic, war-filled decade of the 1860s came to an end, the Western Slope of Colorado, along with the rest of the territory, still lay dormant and undeveloped. The Ute Indians still owned the land west of the Divide. The great silver mines had not yet been found and no roads or railroads had yet penetrated the veil of secrecy put up by the rugged mountains. Yet, there was always the suspicion that there were great riches on the Western Slope. Rumors of lost Spanish mines, Indians with gold nuggets, and maybe even diamonds, were told and retold. Other rumors further whetted the imagination. One heard of cliff dwellings, long deserted in the walls of canyons in southwestern Colorado, of a "Holy Mountain" deep in the Rockies displaying an awesome cross of pure white snow and, finally, from one Sam Adams, of a navigable Colorado River from its origins on the Western Slope to its mouth in the Gulf of California. Despite the mountain men, railroad surveyors like John Gunnison, pathfinders like John Fremont, and army men like Randolph Marcy and William Loring, the Western Slope remained a mystery as the decade of the 1870s opened. What lay out there anyway?

If someone did not answer that vexing question, the Western Slope would remain untouched and unwanted. And then suddenly, like the legendary three musketeers, three great surveyors rode to the rescue. Their names were Ferdinand Vandeveer Hayden, Clarence Rivers King, and George Montague Wheeler. What was needed was a good geological and geographical survey of the Western Slope complete with reliable maps, a study of the flora and fauna, and some idea of the climate. Hayden, King, and Wheeler, along with the brilliant John Wesley Powell, headed the great surveys of the American West which covered much of that vast section from 1867 to 1879. During their surveys, the first three men extensively studied the Western Slope and told the nation what was really out there. When they finished, mining engineers, road builders, railroad men, cattle barons, investors, town builders, and timber barons were not far behind.

Ferdinand Hayden covered the Western Slope like a blanket. A medical doctor by training, Hayden soon turned to his first love — geology. During the three years the team spent in Western Colorado, the Hayden Survey was never a single unit, but rather was made up of different parties working widely apart, always according to a co-ordinated plan. Hayden believed in a realistic approach to his work, hoping to publish information about the Western Slope that would be of immediate use to miners, businessmen, and farmers.

Beginning in 1873 and continuing through 1876, the Hayden Survey walked through every major valley, gazed at or climbed every major mountain, and followed every major river on the Western Slope. With Hayden were some of the most brilliant scientists who ever set foot in a virgin land. They included famed photographer William H. Jackson, geologists William Holmes and Albert Peale, topographers Henry Gannett and Terry Gardner, the brilliant land-scape painter Thomas Moran, Hayden's guest, who first painted the Mount of the Holy Cross, and writer Ernest Ingersoll.

Working with transits, barometers, and cameras which used glass plates, and braving Indians, electrical storms, treacherous mountains, and unexpected changes in the weather, Hayden's men were indefatigable in their work. And they loved every moment of it. They surveyed in northwestern Colorado around Brown's Hole and the Yampa River, the San Juan country, Middle Park, the Gunnison country, Paradox Valley, the Elk Mountains and Roaring Fork coun-try, Grand Mesa and the Uncompahgre country, and along the banks of the Blue River. Perhaps the highlights of the Hayden expedition came when William H. Jackson became the first man to photograph the mysterious Mount of the Holy Cross in 1873 and the Mesa Verde ruins in 1874.

It was with a sense of sadness, nostalgia, and depression that the men of the Hayden Survey left Colorado following the season of 1876. Their work was finished on the Western Slope as they came off the Grand Mesa, a beautiful land of lakes and wildlife and forests high above the Uncompahgre Valley. Now the Western Slope's veil of secrecy had been torn away. Hayden's famous *Atlas of Colorado* covered over 100,000 square miles of Colorado, including all of the Western Slope. It was a job well done and the Western Slope would not forget Ferdinand Hayden and his hardy men.

The early 1870s found another government expedition on Colorado's Western Slope, albeit a minor one compared to Hayden's. This was a military expedition led by young George Montague Wheeler, who was to map sections of the country west of the 100th meridian, a rather considerable undertaking. The most practical achievement of the entire survey was caused, unbelievably, by an excruciatingly painful toothache.

It was in the late fall of 1873 that one of Wheeler's men, Lieutenant William Marshall, was holed up deep in Baker's Park in the San Juan Mountains on the Western Slope. The snows of winter were already falling and Marshall, in great pain from a toothache, was a very long distance from a dentist; yet it was essential that he get to one, and fast. His jaw was swollen nearly shut and he was living on thick soup that he could suck into his mouth without moving his jaws. The nearest dentist was in Denver, 300 miles away over rugged mountain terrain, but to Denver he must go—quickly.

Cochetopa Pass was the obvious crossing of the Continental Divide, but Marshall dimly recalled a pass through the mountains he had seen in the summer that might speed his progress to Denver. With a packer named Dave Mears, he headed for the depression, found it, and in spite of his wretched condition, he and Mears remained a day and night on top of the pass taking thermometer and barometer readings. Satisfied with their readings, Marshall and Mears descended to the eastern slope and made their way to Denver, far in advance of their main party which came in via Cochetopa Pass. Marshall and Mears had found a route that cut 125 miles from the trip between the San Juan country and Denver. Soon, the pass, 10,846 feet high, was named for William Marshall and before the end of the decade was used as the Divide crossing for Otto Mears' Marshall Pass Toll Road. In 1881, Mears sold his road to William Jackson Palmer. It was later used by the Denver and Rio Grande Railroad to enter the Gunnison country—the first railroad ever to arrive on the Western Slope.

The Western Slope, like much of the rest of the American West, was a virgin land in the early 1870s. Many were the men who tramped the untamed lands of Western Colorado in an endless search for riches. The land was still a mystery and who knew what riches it might yield? It was in this charged atmosphere that the greatest fraud ever committed in the West occurred—the great diamond hoax of northwestern Colorado.

Philip Arnold and John Slack, two dirty, bearded prospectors, appeared at a bank in San Francisco one foggy morning early in 1872. The two men stayed only long enough to deposit diamonds with the stunned bank clerk and then disappeared into the misty streets of San Francisco and let human nature run its course. The excited clerk showed the diamonds to the officers of his bank and they, in turn, contacted a number of the most prominent men in San Francisco. The diamonds were real all right and a massive search was launched for Arnold and Slack, who soon reappeared to claim their diamonds.

Playing the role of ignorant country prospectors, Slack and Arnold let themselves be included in the New York and San Francisco Mining and Commercial Company—after agreeing to accept nearly $600,000 from wealthy members of the company. Before agreeing to the deal with Slack and Arnold, the company investors insisted that the diamond fields be examined by an expert. They were examined by one of the top mining engineers in the nation, Henry Janin, who pronounced the fields real.

The spot chosen by Slack and Arnold for the diamond fields was one decided on only after careful study. The conditions had to resemble a country where real diamonds might exist. In addition, the fake diamond field had to be in inhospitable country, susceptible to great heat in the summer and howling blizzards in the winter, to give investors less time to check their investment. The site selected by Slack and Arnold was on a 3,000 acre mesa on the edge of Vermillion Creek at the foot of Diamond Peak in extreme northwestern Colorado. The Wyoming line was just to the north and the Utah line was only a few miles west.

Only the lack of knowledge about diamond fields, incredible luck, and the overpowering greed of the diamond investors allowed Slack and Arnold to get their wild scheme off the ground. Because of their great diamond hoax, twenty-five companies, capitalized at $223,000,000, were spawned. The names of the investors included William Ralston, Sam Barlow, George McClellan, and William Byers. Slack and Arnold's success was limited because of the efforts of geologist Clarence Rivers King.

Since 1867, King and his men had been engaged in the United States Geological Exploration of the fortieth parallel from the plains to the Pacific. If the diamond fields had been in Arizona, New Mexico, or southern Colorado, they would have been of no concern to King and he would have left them alone. But when it became increasingly obvious that the fields were somewhere along the fortieth parallel, King's ears picked up. Now the professional reputations of him and his men were in jeopardy, because nowhere along the fortieth parallel had they found diamonds or rubies.

Thus it was at the end of the surveying season, in late October of 1872, that King and some of his men undertook a scientific investigation of the diamond fields. Discussions with Henry Janin, their great knowledge of the fortieth parallel, and deduction led them to believe that the diamond field was in northwestern Colorado. From Fort Bridger, Wyoming, it was a five-day, 150-mile ride to Diamond Peak near the borders of Wyoming, Colorado, and Utah. The following morning in the biting wind and cold, the King party searched the barren mesa land near Diamond Peak and did indeed find diamonds. Samuel Emmons of the King party later recounted: "that night we were full believers in the verity of Janin's reports and dreamed of the untold wealth that might be gathered."[2] The next morning told another story. It did not take King long to find that the diamonds and rubies had been salted, dwindling rapidly as his men worked away from the wind-swept mesa.

Hurrying to San Francisco by mule and then by Union Pacific train, King exposed the diamond hoax to a stunned Henry Janin and the newly formed mining companies. Slack and Arnold got off scot-free, keeping most of their shady money and never serving a day in jail, but Henry Janin and the big investors like William Ralston were never forgiven. The diamond hoax of northwestern Colorado was the greatest fraud ever attempted in the West. It was, however, typical of the exploiters of the Western Slope. Be they mining men, cattle barons, shady stock speculators, or diamond field discoverers, they all wanted something for nothing and they all played on the ignorance of people who knew precious little about a new land ready to open its doors.

The passing of the great surveyors of the Western Slope—King, Hayden and Wheeler—marked the end of the age of innocence for that virgin land. Now the Western Slope was known and ranchers, town promoters, miners, and speculators were on the way. The place would never be the same again.

4.
"Hurrah for Georgia Gulch"

Before the great surveyors of the West had even dreamed of traipsing into Western Colorado, gold fever ran rampant in part of the foreboding Rocky Mountains. The land would be named Colorado and its promise was gold by the bucketful. The date was 1859. In the year of the fifty-niner and the Pike's Peak gold rush, people came by the thousands, walking, riding, and driving patient oxen, in an impatient race to capture a dream. A very few tried a wind wagon, to their grief. They came because gold beckoned, to escape their past, or for an infinite number of personal reasons. Almost incidentally the horde founded Colorado in the haste to find gold. One could hardly pan a week's earnings before mining camps emerged and people talked politics. Farmers dared to settle and plant on land once labeled the "Great American Desert," as high priced local markets challenged them to take the risk. Sooner than anyone realized, settlement had taken root along the eastern slope and pugnaciously advanced into the mountains. Still farther beyond lay the Continental Divide and the "terra incognita," the Western Slope of the future—a silent, "gloomy" wilderness of unknown potential.

The year 1859 was tumultuous once the existence of gold had been confirmed beyond a doubt. Prospectors and other would-be miners scurried over hills and down canyons, convinced they would uncover another fabled California bonanza. From the Gregory and Jackson diggings, better known as Central City and Idaho Springs, they moved out beyond the next ridge, and the next, to see and to test. "Gold fever" took them into South Park, to Tarryall, and Fairplay, once home of the trapper and Ute. From there a day's hike put them across the Snowy Range and into the valley of the Blue and Swan rivers.

May brought the rush to Central City; by mid-August the Continental Divide had been crossed and Western Slope streams were being prospected. Rumors of "pound-diggings" (an ounce or better was a good day's work in the "older" Gregory diggings) lured men to the beautiful Blue River Valley. Rumors abounded that year. None could be discounted because they had a way of becoming reality—reality measured by gold in the pan.

The adventurers rushed in and most stampeded back out. No "pound diggings" were to be found, and reports of hostile Utes left them all uneasy. A very few braved the winter, and others returned permanently the following spring. That gold in the pan overcame fear of Utes, isolation, and disappointment. But it was still not enough, and prospecting parties were off again in search of the "mother lode," where it was said enough gold existed to fulfill any man's dream. A strange breed of men these; dissatisfaction with present discoveries, restlessness, and determination sent them far out into Western Colorado. Not the solitary prospectors of mining legend (their day was yet to come), they traveled in groups for protection and support. Some ventured into the depths of the San Juans, where they found the Spanish had preceded them; others roamed far to the northwest. David Collier chronicled the travels of one exceptionally large party, initially 100 men, that spent nearly two months in the field. In a series of articles in the *Rocky Mountain News*, Collier traced their adventures from the Colorado River Valley (called the Grand then), southward past the San Juans. In his October 17 comments, Collier concluded that the gold belt passed from Boulder, through the Blue River, "southwesterly . . . for several hundreds of miles, and that in all probability grows richer as one goes in that direction." That was what people wanted to hear.

By late fall of 1860 prospecting parties had pried open some of that "terra incognita." Much of its potential remained only rumor; the odds were long against those who cast their lot there. Yet permanent settlement had come to the valley of the Blue, the beginning of American settlement in Western Colorado. This was, however, a special type of settlement related to placer mining. During the years 1860–62, Summit County, the Blue, Swan, and Snake rivers, and intersecting creeks and gulches came to be Colorado's greatest placer district, establishing a claim that has held up and scarcely been rivaled since, except by Lake County's California Gulch.

Placer mining is the search for free gold—gold that can be easily recognized and is not in combination with any other mineral. This gold may be found in or along stream beds, on the ground's surface, or as deep as bedrock. Technically, the nineteenth century miner defined it as a deposit of gold not in place in a lode or vein. It appeared that the recovery of this kind of gold required little work; this illusion furnished the basis for the 1849 California rush and the Pike's Peak stampede. All that was needed was a shovel, a pan, and a strong constitution, and wealth would surely accrue. Gold could be panned that way, albeit slowly and tediously. Being innovative Americans, however, these men turned to other methods that would work more gravel faster. Thus were developed the colorfully named rocker, long tom, and sluice box. No matter what method was used, it was cradled on the premise that the weight of the gold would cause it to sink to the bottom where it could be recovered. The belief that one could get rich without really working bedrocked them, but the fifty-niners, like their California counterparts, discovered that they had never worked so hard to make money without working. Placer mining—hard, long hours wading in cold mountain streams, moving rocks and gravel— soon killed any illusions. The scenery might have been spectacular, but the miner hardly had time to notice as he labored six to seven days a week during the short June-to-October season. Hope sustained him: hope that his claim was rich, that he had enough water for the season, that some misfortune would not befall him, that winter would hold off long enough for him to work his claim profitably.

The story of Summit County's placer mines can be told simply enough. The year 1859 was one of discovery, 1860 one of exploration and opening, and 1861–62 ones of exploitation. By 1863 the "palmiest" days had passed and placering gradually receded. It continued for decades, but never again like those exciting early sixties when fortune beckoned from every gulch. We will never know exactly how much gold was recovered; the records simply are not available. Charles Henderson, in his *Mining in Colorado*, gives the best estimate. After weighing the production claims, he conservatively concluded that through 1867 $5,150,000 appeared to be a reasonable figure. With this figure as a basis, and keeping in mind that probably 90% of this production came before 1864, it can be estimated that these early peak years grossed more than $4.6 million. By Colorado standards, it was a bonanza. It brought a large measure of fame and fortune to the Western Slope that undergirded settlement and hastened exploration.

Except that it seeks gold, placer mining is unlike the more common lode (quartz, or underground) mining. In the first place, it affords more individual opportunity, regardless of one's financial status. Food, pan, shovel, pick, and bedding suffice; what experience is necessary can be quickly gained. Hence the rumor of a rich placer discovery immediately attracted large numbers, who, by the very nature of the game, drifted on at the hint of even better discoveries if they did not find profitable diggings. Some did not even need that incentive — they just wandered off. Dan de Quille, Mark Twain's Comstock compatriot, put it this way: "every spring [there is] a kind of unrest — men of all classes feel as if they should go somewhere. This feeling is particularly strong among miners, . . ."[1]

As a result, the Summit County miners were forever dashing hither and yon. In 1860 they were off to Gold Run, Georgia, French, McNulty, and Illinois gulches; the next year Humbug, America, Galena, and Negro gulches, not to mention Buffalo and Delaware flats. By then it was said that French and Georgia gulches and Gold Run were "dull" — and so it went. Each season produced its own favorites and last year's has-beens, although the latter might simply have been suffering from lower production and too high expectations, rather than total abandonment. Not satisfied with what they saw in the core district, these prospectors went over to work Ten Mile Creek (which was longer than that and rich), and on beyond, to the Eagle River. But the farther afield they went, the more isolation and poor transportation hampered them.

Such transience caused problems. These miners worked in a territory far distant from its seat of government; until the organization of Colorado Territory in 1861 they were appended to Mormon Utah. Consequently, they improvised their own mining districts, mining law, and extra-legal miners' courts to handle disputes. The first miners into a gulch established the rules, with which the late-comers might not agree. Young Daniel Conner recounted his experience in the Miners' District in 1860. Everyone was nearly unacquainted with each other. Once the news of the discovery leaked out an "unruly population" drifted in, "who immediately became savage on questions of ownership of mining claims." A miner could hardly leave his pit long enough to eat without finding someone jumping his claim. As a result, the miners banded together to oust the intruders, which, Conner noted, led to conflicts and even lost lives. This confrontation finally brought both groups to their senses, but not until news of the Gold Run discoveries skimmed off the surplus of men was there permanent peace.[2] With the establishment of Colorado and the standardization of mining laws, such disputes as Conner witnessed eventually declined. Unfortunately, these incidents gave the placer districts a lawless image, both here and in California.

Like their quartz mining counterparts, what the placer miners wanted was a civilized image. Adventurers were not welcomed; honest, hard working miners only need come. As early as August 8, 1860, a Breckenridge correspondent to the *Rocky Mountain News* mentioned how surprised he was to see so many women and children. Families, he proclaimed, should not hesitate to emigrate to the Blue River for fear of encountering a "lazy set" of "uncivilized beings"; such was not the case there. Despite that glowing report, a year later on August 21 another correspondent to the same paper noted how few ladies or families resided there, with few amenities of social life.

Somewhere between these two opinions lay the truth. This was an urban frontier, though not the same type that evolved where quartz mining took root. Placer mining's transitory nature militated against permanence. Not only did people rush off to new discoveries, they tended not to winter in the mountains, where expenses ran high and shortages threatened once the snows came. As soon as the mining season ended, many descended to lower elevations with less harsh climates.

As a result, the fledgling mining camps struggled for existence. Jerry-built to begin with, they faced a precarious life without plan or purpose, except as dictated by the surroundings and immediate needs. Wagons and tents gave way to log cabins, which in turn surrendered to frame construction once sawmills appeared — if the camp survived that long. Such haste ruled out architectural esthetics, but few miners worried about that.

The scramble gave birth to Lincoln City, Parkville, Breckenridge, and even more fleeting claimants to camp status scattered along many of the gulches. Of the placer camps, Breckenridge endured, though even here the nature of settlement was shown by the fact that the first newspaper did not appear until 1880, two decades after the camp's establishment. Contrast this with Pitkin, Aspen, or Silverton, where newspapers came to stay within a year of the community's start.

Other outward signs of "civilization" also found it difficult to gain a foothold, the church, for example. Methodists tramped in with the first miners. The Rev. William Howbert, "with a shirt in one pocket, a Testament and hymn-book in another, bread and beef in a third," arrived on July 7, 1860 and preached to small congregations at Gold Run and Breckenridge. Howbert thought he did remarkably well, considering the disturbed state of the country, the population's transient nature, and the fact that he could not recall any who "expected to make this country their permanent home." Better known, John Dyer preached in the district the next two years, on a circuit that exhausted even his enthusiasm. The people stopped so short a time in one place that there was little profit in starting a permanent "class," he confessed. "I tried to adapt myself to the situation, neither showing that I felt above anyone, nor ever compromising with sin or with transgressions . . . ."[3]

The miners may not have wanted newspapers and churches; opportunities for "sin and transgressions" were another matter. Saloons, embellished with drinking, gambling, and billiards, lay well within Dyer's definition, and they appeared everywhere. A couple of "theaters" and dance halls were launched, although what kind of productions the former featured remains a matter of conjecture. As one man observed, the latter advertised "free and easy" dances, including about a score of "females." A general store or two and a hotel (using the term loosely) made up the corporal's guard of the business district. Breckenridge had, in addition, a meat market and post office to give it class.

Being a merchant was no easier than being a miner, perhaps even riskier, because it required a larger investment. Not only did the businessman face the usual problems of freight charges, volume, credit, and customers, compounded by mining uncertainty, but he could also be confronted by all types of unexpected miseries. The bottom must have been plumbed in the summer of 1861, when peddlers from over the mountains and people leaving for the states (nicknamed "pilgrims") so glutted the market with all types of items that prices plummeted. This left the poor merchant in a horrible bind. He persevered despite such trials, and a camp such as Parkville could point with pride to its own brewery and "excellent lager beer."

This masculine world was almost exclusively white. Women were in short supply throughout Colorado in the early 1860s, but the Western Slope suffered even longer odds. An older lady and her daughter came into the gulch where Daniel Conner was working to set up a "deadfall" (the mountain parlance for grog shop). The daughter waited upon customers, attracting miners from quite a distance. "Boys, there is a gal in the gulch . . . Hurrah! Hurrah for Georgia Gulch; come, let us all go see her." And they hurried over, Conner remembering they looked upon her with as much curiosity as boys who went to see a monkey.[4] Not many men would risk taking their families into the world of placer mining; the cost, inconvenience, and danger were too great. A few prostitutes drifted through, mostly on seasonal demand, since business was too scarce in the winter and spring.

Though isolated from the rest of the territory and nation, these early West Slopers kept up with current events through newspapers shipped from the outside. July 4 was the holiday most miners celebrated. The Fourth of 1861 was particularly poignant — the Civil War had just broken out. French Gulch observed the day with small arms fire, several flags, and in the evening a large bonfire, patriotic address, and three cheers for the Union, then groans for Jeff Davis and the Confederacy. Sentiments were not unanimous; for Kentuckian Conner the unhappy war spirit converted "Rebel and Federal friends" into "Rebel and Federal enemies." Breckenridge promoted the Union spirit by changing the spelling of its name, which *had* honored John C. Breckinridge, late Vice President and soon-to-be Confederate general and Secretary of War.

Urbanization generally fought a losing battle, but back in the gulches and along the streams the miners kept busy. All they wanted was for those camps to last long enough to satisfy their wants while their current claims paid. Then off they went to find others, with few second thoughts about what was left behind.

What they left behind was complete disarray, the hallmark of placer mining. Despite the brevity of their stay, placer miners littered and tore up the land at a fearful rate. The pan and shovel started it and, before they finished, the land was pitted and the streams murky. Add the rockers (which looked like a baby's cradle) and the long toms and sluices (imagine wooden boxes with riffles to catch the gold, sometimes stretching over 100 feet), and the pace of deterioration was quickened. More men shoveling, more gravel and rocks being moved meant more water used, more streams polluted, and gulches torn up.

The miners were not content to use simply a pan, a pick, and a shovel; they had to find faster and better ways. In September, 1859, amazingly early, a group banded together to build a dam across the Blue River to turn the water down a different channel and open the riverbed for working. The next year they constructed ditches to carry water from the Blue to gulches where the supply was inadequate. This took time, labor, and capital, yet digging persisted until an 1868 visitor, Samuel Bowles, could ride along the Blue all morning and be continually in sight of ditches.

Those ditches allowed more area to be worked; they also indicated more capital had been invested than ever before. Companies with no direct interest in mining came to own them, simply selling water at so much per miner's inch (a unit used to measure water, approximately 2,274 cu. ft. per 24 hours). This marked a new turn of events for Summit County placer mining, foreshadowing the appearance of corporate control. Having to pay someone else for water aggravated the miners. In 1863 their resentment boiled over; miners at Buffalo Flats struck for a lower water price, complaining that neighbors paid less (which in truth they did). The strike worked and within a few days the two sides had reached a compromise.

Even the longest sluice and plenty of water were not enough. There had to be a faster way to find the gold; it was called hydraulicking. For a slightly higher initial cost and more water, hydraulic systems could use pipe and hose to shoot water out of a nozzle under great pressure. Aimed at a bank or the ground, this pressure eroded and washed large amounts of gravel through a sluice in a short period of time. Two men could do the work of thirty laboring with pick and shovel. The ultimate answer had been found; no one cared, for the moment, that the debris was also greater.

The Blue River district can claim to be one of the first, if not *the* first, to use the hydraulic method in Colorado. Correspondent "Sea Pea" wrote to the *Rocky Mountain News* on July 18, 1860 that several "hydraulic apparatuses" were ready to wash "rich banks." In September, 1861, a Humbug Gulch visitor painted a realistic picture of both the miners' greed and determination, and their environmental impact: "hydraulic and otherwise, they are tearing up 'Mother Earth' at a fearful rate, undermining houses, and removing every obstacle to their progress in searching for the precious ore."[5] Two years later, a local complained about the great scarcity of hydraulic equipment and urged Denver merchants to have it on hand, because "we miners must have it, let it cost what it may."

Hydraulicking demanded more ditches, more flumes, and more capital; still it gained popularity because it paid better and conserved labor. Not until August, 1863, did some begin to question its advantages — and not because of the devastation of "mother earth" — but because it took too much water at the going rates.

While some men panned and others sluiced and hydraulicked, still others prospected. The cardinal leaven of the placer districts was this continual search for new and richer deposits. Victim of a romanticized legend, the real-life prospector lived a strenuous life that more often than not went unrewarded. One group's journey of several weeks was recounted for readers of the *Rocky Mountain News* on April 26, 1862. The previous August a party of five men had suffered through miserable weather ("rain, rain, our bedclothes have been wet for a week"), hard traveling over fallen timber and steep mountains, and lack of food when the victuals ran out several days before they reached a ranch. Hardship and exposure were their only rewards. Yet men were attracted to this never-ending search as moths to a flame. Not until 1863 did prospecting start to slacken, a sure sign that the first period of placer mining was drawing to a close.

The decrease in the value of recovered gold, the failure to find new deposits, the mounting cost of mining, and the lure of newer discoveries drained people away. Now the isolation, long winters, and primitive conditions started to take their toll. Bayard Taylor estimated in the mid '60s that fewer than 500 miners remained where there had been 5,000 in 1860. High on both figures, he nonetheless accurately pictured the trend.

The Western Slope's first mining boom was finished. Many of its characteristics would reappear time and time again — rush, boom, and decline, exploitativeness, and lack of concern over environmental issues. This last, not uncommon throughout the West, appeared to be at its worst in the wake of placer mining. What had this unconcern done to the once beautiful valley of the Blue? The Blue was not blue anymore, noted Samuel Bowles, as he rode along its banks in '68, "its waters have been troubled by the miners, and it gives its name and mud color to the combined stream." Gulch mining, he remarked further, "leaves a terrible waste in its track." If this were not bad enough, these early Western Slopers also burned mountainsides of timber to make prospecting and travel easier. At least one horrified local suggested "hanging" the guilty parties, yet the practice continued. In his 1870 report Rossiter Raymond, United States Commissioner of Mining Statistics, severely criticized Western miners who left in their tracks "lifeless, desolate looking hillsides."[6]

The trend from simple to complex mining methods and the continual need for more money was also typical. Only on a small scale, however, did corporate control rear its head, and absentee ownership proved to be no major concern. An uneasy truce prevailed with the Utes, one which fortunately precipitated no battles, although the '59ers built a crude fort and little scares flared now and then. Many were caused by nerves, such as when Daniel Conner and friends fired at what they assumed was a Ute brave late one evening. On reaching a nearby settlement the next day, they found that a white man had raced through reporting he had been attacked by "at least twenty" Indians. Other Blue Riverites proved equally quick on the trigger; one hunter shot and killed a miner he thought was a bear.

As placer mining peaked and declined, interest in quartz mining increased. The faithful *News* correspondent "Sea Pea" reported that lode mining was underway in 1860. The time, effort, and expense

43

were simply too great, however, when compared to placer gold mining. Placer miners also exhibited a certain animosity toward lode mining, based primarily on economics and emotions. It would take something innovative and intriguing to stimulate much underground work.

Silver was the answer. As early as 1860, reports of amazingly rich silver ore deposits appeared. Inexperience and enthusiasm grossly exaggerated the reality of these claims. Then, in 1864, silver was found in payable quantities in Summit County (Snake River district) and also in neighboring Clear Creek County, across the Divide. No question about it this time—as one editor described it, a "silver mania" took hold. Despite the fact that Summit County could claim to have the first silver lode discovered in Colorado, only expectation and disappointment were mined.

Silver never got a fair chance in the sixties. Developmental capital, an extremely scarce item on the Western Slope, was necessary. Meanwhile, investors' money went to more famous silver mines in Nevada, or to Georgetown, Colorado's first silver queen. Transportation over mountain passes was also too costly, slow, and uncertain. Had it been possible to resolve the capital and transportation problems, there would still have been the one of smelting. Milling silver ore from complex minerals had not yet been mastered. So, although some people became "Snake Bitten" over promising silver mines (mostly just prospect holes and hope), silver remained a potential for a future day.

Gold and silver discoveries proved there were minerals on the Western Slope. If they were found in one place, then surely they would be found in another, and the search went on to find those districts.

The first mining thrust into the Gunnison country was a spinoff of contemporary activity in Summit County. Prospecting parties traversed the Gunnison area and then miners came to Washington Gulch. That ubiquitous Methodist, the energetic John Dyer, took his ministry there in September, 1861, visiting the young camp of Minersville. A couple of days and Dyer was on his way; the miners stayed a bit longer. Lasting settlement might have come sooner, if the Utes had not been so hostile, the district so isolated, and the placers so quickly played out.

Prospecting parties moved in and around the Gunnison country for the rest of the decade and into the 1870s. The Utes stubbornly continued their hostile ways, correctly surmising that if the miners stayed, the land would eventually be lost to them forever. The Gunnison country, in the words of early Colorado historian Frank Fossett in 1880, "until recently [has] been an unknown land to the world at large and even to the people of Colorado."[7]

Far down in southwestern Colorado rose the jagged San Juans, some of the most magnificent and forbidding mountains on the Western Slope. Isolated by hundreds of miles from the nearest settlement, in the heart of Ute domain, they nevertheless attracted adventuresome prospectors. The Spanish had mined in the area in the eighteenth century, quickly gutting shallow deposits. They left behind melodious names for the mountains and rivers, and even more romantic legends. Fur trappers also crossed the San Juans. Some Colorado prospectors wandered in surprisingly early (1860), considering the hardships and distance involved.

Charles Baker and a small group reached what became Baker's Park (today's Silverton) that fall and, thanks to his promotion, a small rush developed in the spring of 1861. Astutely promoting his discoveries, Baker awaited the miners with a toll road and town site. Nothing went well, and the bubble burst, thanks in no small part to the mountainous environment, isolation, and Ute menace. Primarily, however, Baker's gold placers simply did not pan out and by fall the mining rush ebbed away, leaving only a season's litter behind.

Despite such a setback, enthusiasm did not abate. Mining's lure is amply demonstrated by the fact that interest in the San Juans persisted. Rumors and legends would not die, somewhere in the San Juans was the "mother lode." In 1869 prospecting parties returned, moving into the Dolores and Mancos valleys and the next year back into Baker's Park. It was a seasonal migration, in after the snows melted and out before winter closed the passes. For a while Colorado newspapers debated whether this was another San Juan "humbug"; those early San Juaners did not debate — they dug.

This time they sought quartz mines, not the fleeting placer deposits. Gold brought them in, but silver soon won their allegiance. They staked claims on mountainside and canyon bottom, everywhere and anywhere that held promise. By the end of 1873, the transformation from wilderness to settlement was well underway. Trails were being improved, mines and districts promoted, and communities planned. A few hardy San Juaners wintered in the mountains.

A melancholy outlook characterized the spring. Developmental money was almost non-existent; even improved transportation facilities were abominable, living conditions primitive, and the mines undeveloped. The Utes, mightily upset at this trespass onto land promised them forever, threatened trouble. The Utes went first; the other problems proved harder to resolve. Nothing stopped those San Juaners, they matched the mountains. Permanent settlement had come to the San Juans.

By the early 1870s the only Western Slope mining district to have shown any lasting potential was Summit County. Development lagged even there, but high hopes held fast. A Breckenridge writer to the *Rocky Mountain News*, back on May 2, 1867, had optimistically forecast, "We feel that from our present indigent position, we must soon awake. . . . in two years hence we will be 'out of the wilderness' and can 'paddle our own canoe.'" It was not to be. By 1873 placer mining had dropped off and lode mining had not taken up the slack. To stimulate the former, "booming" was introduced. This environmental nightmare involved collecting water in a reservoir, then discharging most of it in one rush to flush great amounts of gravel through a large flume. Booming tore up a few more gulches.

Western Colorado's big three "metropolises," Breckenridge, Montezuma, and Saints John, totaled 144 people, according to the 1870 census. Breckenridge's population of 51 embraced 37 native and 14 foreign born (northern Europeans predominated). Women were outnumbered better than 2½ to 1. The business district housed two retail grocers, a butcher, blacksmith, and carpenter. Urbanization had not yet achieved a major foothold.

In a Colorado just starting to improve mining production in the early seventies, after the doldrums of the late sixties, the Western Slope languished. Transportation, isolation, financial support—problems which had shadowed it from the start—continued unresolved. Hence, investors shied away and money went elsewhere. An adventuresome investor with a few spare dollars might have gambled in Summit County mines, thinking that they offered the best record and potential on the Western Slope. He would have bet wrong.

While interest centered on mining, the Western Slope tourist industry limped off to a start. Miners, seldom noted for their appreciation of nature's beauty, worked in some unsurpassed scenery that was more an obstacle than a joy to them. Posthaste they developed a penchant for the hot springs, where the aches and pains of a shift in the wet, cold placers or the damp quartz mines could be soothed. The Utes had visited the springs for centuries for their medicinal and therapeutic values; now the miners did the same.

Hot Sulphur Springs got off to the earliest start. "The old grew young and the young joyous," rhapsodized Samuel Bowles after an August, 1868, visit. Bowles, who found the whole area delightful and the high mountain raspberries "intoxicating," was swept off his feet.

46

The springs for bathing and the rivers for fishing were the great attractions. "They are a considerable resort already by Coloradians [sic]," and Bowles counted 20 or so visitors there during his stay. Three years to the month later, Isaac Beardsley and a party of fellow Methodists found a two-room log cabin at the springs and a "toll" for bathers. After bathing, fishing, and holding religious services, the group returned home, "invigorated and strengthened, . . . healthier, wiser and better."[8] Such praise gladdened the heart of William Byers, owner of the *Rocky Mountain News* and the springs. Byers envisioned this resort as a great tourist attraction long before most of his fellow Coloradans saw much use for the Western Slope. No heartier booster of Western Colorado tourism than Byers existed at the moment.

Even less noted at the time was the introduction of skiing. Ruben Spalding, who wintered on the Blue in 1859–60, said two Norwegians in his group made "snowshoes" (nineteenth-century term for skis) that were 9 to 13 feet long. These allowed them to get around once the snow fell to great depths. In their snow-locked camp they could hardly have imagined the significance of their improvisation.

An untapped paradise, Colorado's Western Slope — a land of unspoiled natural beauty for the tourist but one that begged exploitation by those with dreams and money to develop it. From the outset of Western Slope settlement, this predominant and crucial conflict emerged — tourism *vs.* development.

To Byers, Western Colorado promised one thing, to the miners of Summit County yet another, but what was its image during these years? Three words would probably have sufficed for most people: unknown, wilderness, and potential. Even with all the prospecting and other exploration, much of the Western Slope remained a mystery. Bowles described it as having "no especial history," and the *Rocky Mountain Directory* (1871) referred to it as yet "so little known."

Even the "well known" spots were only a step away from wilderness. Beardsley shuddered when coyotes and wolves made the night hours "hideous" with their howling during his visit to Hot Sulphur Springs. Almost everyone who stopped there had seen the Utes or just missed them. Considering this rated as one of the more frequently visited spots, one did not have to let imagination roam to picture the rest of the Western Slope.

If a land possessed only a fleeting history, and a tenuous present, then its future shouldered the burden of unlocking its potential. Bowles spoke of "untold" wealth and "unnumbered" beauties, and Rossiter Raymond of "magnificent grazing country and an abundance of fish and game." The *Rocky Mountain Directory* (1871) praised the "great" inducement it offered to all classes of settlers. Natural beauty, a wilderness, and an unexploited land—interwoven contradictions that beckoned diverse development. A tourist's delight, a miner's bonanza, cattleman's mecca, the urban developer's dream—there was something for everybody.

Already the Western Slope was a place to come, to see, to marvel at, and if a living could be secured, a place to make a home. If not, Bayard Taylor echoed the thoughts of many visitors when he wrote of his short sojourn, "I shall always retain a very pleasant recollection of Breckenridge."[9]

12. Monte

II
When Mining
Was King
1874-1914

Red Cliff. *Collier photo courtesy First Federal Savings.*

The age of mining came to the Western Slope as the 1860s gave way to the '70s and '80s. Mining was king and heady optimism was in the air. But ahead was the terrible silver panic of 1893 which brought despair and depression. Only then did Western Colorado realize that silver could not permanently sustain the region. On the horizon, however, were gold, coal, and a great cattle industry.

5.
"Waiting for a Boom"

In the two decades after 1873, the Western Slope was transformed. What once had been a seldom visited wilderness, home of the nomadic Utes, became the promised land for the miner, farmer, town builder, rancher, lumberman, merchant, and tourist. Railroads curved through its valleys, the lonesome whistle echoing deep into mountain canyons of the San Juans and Gunnison country. Miners scrambled everywhere; nothing stopped them. Nor did anything deter the lumberman, who cut down trees to satisfy the appetite of mushrooming settlement. The Utes had been driven away by the relentless pressures of onrushing settlement. Only a remnant remained, huddled harmlessly on a reservation in Colorado's southwest corner. The rancher and the farmer came to replace them with their settlements, such as Cortez, Montrose, and Grand Junction. Water that once rushed unimpeded to the sea was channeled into irrigation ditches. Land which had nourished only scrub grasses and sage now grew wheat and corn; some of it was carefully cultivated into orchards. It was Christmas every day for the town promoter/builder. A person could hardly take a step without stumbling over someone else's plat. With reference to mining, but applicable to the entire Western Slope, a journalist commented:

> New mining camps spring into existence so rapidly and in such great number in Colorado that it is almost impossible to keep correct on our geography or remember the names given the prospective cities. A correspondent of one of our exchanges writes that he entered one of these camps in the morning, when there were two houses, and by night there were sixteen.[1]

53

Towns sprouted on canyon floors and mesa tops, crowded into mountain meadows, and spread along river banks. Over the Western Slope, Colorado's last unexploited frontier, swarmed pioneering Western Slopers in search of their share of the promised land.

Tourists began to arrive in larger and larger numbers, the railroads carrying them with an ease and comfort that belied the fact that this had so recently been a wilderness. They tramped, camped, and rode out to see nature's handiwork; most stayed close to those railroad cars and civilization. They came to view the magnificent scenery, to partake of the "vanishing" frontier, to dip into the hot springs' curative waters, and to "see the elephant," as the miners liked to refer to it. They snapped pictures (the Kodak camera was coming into popularity), "oohed and ahed," purchased a souvenir or two, gathered a rock or something else that struck their fancy, and went home to tell their friends. Some, captivated, stayed, as their tourist descendants have been doing ever since.

The big attraction was still mining, Western Colorado's foundation stone and principal inducement for settlement. This region, which produced approximately $139,000 in gold and silver in 1874, by 1893 had yielded nearly $13,000,000, primarily in gold and silver, with some copper, lead, and zinc thrown in. If coal is added, the magnitude of the increase is staggering. Where once Summit County had been the foremost district, with only a struggling outpost in the San Juans, now miners dug in hundreds of locations. Indeed, Summit County no longer even ranked as one of the top five producers. The previously quoted reporter had this to say: "A very large number of promising districts have been discovered during the present year [1879] . . . Although all of these are not likely to 'pan out' to the expectations of the prospectors, yet the work that is being done must add vast sums to Colorado's wealth."

Wherever one looked in the mountains somebody was burrowing into the ground to promote or speculate in mines. Mining, once it gets into a man's blood, becomes an addiction. He cannot go "cold turkey" and take the cure. Dan O'Connell, who spent nearly fifty years prospecting in the Colorado mountains, came as near as anyone can in attempting to describe the feeling in words:

> There is a lure in the great out-of-doors, in the broad vision which the hills afford, in the quest of something which is ever evasive but which may be turned up with the next strike of the pick, and above all in being able to come and go when you please — in being your own man amid surroundings of your own selection.[2]

"Come and go as you please" well described the prospectors' way of life. On their heels came the miners, then the denizens of the camps, and finally the loggers, farmers, and others. They soon overran the San Juans and the Gunnison country, both of which claimed their day on the mining stage. The former enjoyed a long mining career, the latter wrapped its boom and decline cycle into two decades.

The San Juans, Ouray, San Miguel, Dolores, La Plata, San Juan, and Hinsdale counties and, to be technically correct, Mineral and Rio Grande (both east of the Divide), were being prospected by the mid-seventies. Mining and settlement grew quickly. Silverton, Ouray, Lake City, Rico, and Telluride (initially called Columbia) date from the 1870s, as do a number of smaller camps, now abandoned sites: Animas Forks, Henson, Parrott City, Tellurium, Gladstone, and others. Intra-San Juan rushes continued into the eighties. Red Mountain, with its silver in pillars rather than veins, prompted a large ripple of excitement; so did Rico when the "second contact" was tapped and high grade ore discovered. Silverton benefited mightily by the coming of the Denver and Rio Grande Railroad in 1882. The railroad's arrival ushered the San Juans into Colorado mining society. Before the 1880s expired, Ouray, Red Mountain, and Lake City had gained connections, and rails were on the way to Rico and Telluride.

The railroads brought tourists, settlers, and investors and gave birth to the San Juans' major metropolis, Durango. Durango was never truly a mining town, although coal miners dug within its city limits. It was a railroad, business, and regional smelting center. So great was the San Juans' attraction that Durango was urbanized in the first months of its existence, leaping from zero to 2,500 population from mid-September to the end of December, 1880. At that time, Durango's mining laurels rested with its smelting complex. With plenty of available coal of the good coking variety and the railroad to ship various types of ore needed for flux in smelting, it was king of the district. No matter how hard it tried or how much it wanted to, each little mining camp or town could not hope to maintain its own smelter.

Around Durango, in the Animas Valley, flourished the first successful San Juan ranching and farming ventures, which actually predated the town by a decade. A milder climate and water were the keys to agricultural development; the Anasazi would have approved.

In the mountains, mining went on unabated. By the 1890s some districts had already been abandoned, either mined out or devoid of hope. Low grade ore, and not much of that, will drench even the hottest flame of optimism. Foreign and eastern investment increasingly undergirded San Juan mining, and with it came those accouterments of the new mining era—corporate control and absentee ownership. The San Juans, never a poor man's district to begin with, now moved well beyond that classification.

By 1893 attention focused on the district's big three: Silverton, Ouray, and Telluride. While they had not garnered many headlines outside Colorado, thanks in no small measure to the Leadville, Aspen, and Cripple Creek excitements, they stood on the threshold of making the San Juans a first-ranked national mining district.

The ill-defined, rather unwieldy, Gunnison country drew a second breath in the late 1870s. Then, after Aspen took away part of its territory and the opening of the Ute reservation carved several new counties, it shrank to present Gunnison County. For a moment Colorado's mining frontier paused and Gunnison stood in the spotlight.

Transportation flamed the spark, as it had in the San Juans. Prior to the coming of the railroad, travel was over trails/roads rated abominable to passable. Mary Jane Matlock remembered: "After we left Lake City, we traveled over some of the worst roads I have ever seen. Only the trees, stumps and rocks which would make the road absolutely impassable had been removed, but no thought had been given to the comfort of the traveler."[3] Steep, uneven grades, mud holes remarkable even for that day, and bridgeless streams harassed the traveler but did not stop him.

As in the San Juans, little intra-district rushes kept the search alive. In 1879 White Pine, Pitkin, Ruby, Hillerton, and Gothic got started, though most of the rushers retreated that fall in the face of winter's storms. The exodus proved brief. When the warmth of spring brought them back, Crested Butte, Pittsburgh, Tin Cup, Ohio City, and Crystal became familiar names. Six-year-old Gunnison blossomed as the major trade and railroad center and served as a jumping off point to the surrounding camps. Like its contemporary, Durango, Gunnison was destined for greater things than its neighbors.

One who observed Gunnison during its growth pangs might have questioned such predictions. Young New Englander Clarence Mayo tried to picture it for his parents and sister back in Warwick, Massachusetts: "Gunnison is a tough place, now full of strangers of the worst type. Railroad men and all sorts, I carry my pistol in my hand ready for use, if I go to town after dark." If this provided little reassurance, he commented a few months later, in November, 1881, after a "thundering cold night," that he could sleep very comfortably under "7 double blankets, 3 overcoats, 4 comfortables, two rubber blankets and 4 or 5 boards."

The West changed Clarence, as he tried to explain. The East, he told his mother, was full of "little petty jealousies," but the West was different. "I believe I am changed"; things that used to be annoying now had no effect and "I enjoy life better." Following the shooting of President James Garfield, he observed, ". . . there is little said about the assassination here, it is too common for men to get shot here to cause much comment, Gunnison will forget it in a week." Mayo, apparently a steady church-goer back home, backslid: "It has got so you meet women on every corner begging for the churches, as far as I am concerned they can all go to the D---. I don't go to church any more much, found it was fast braking [sic] my health going so much, I won't be bothered singing." Regarding his old home in Warwick, Clarence conceded things must also be changing there, but "we western folks care very little about it, we have to drift along and as a rule don't worry and fret much." Pleas to return home brought this stubborn response, "I will never go home a step till I have made some money." In a later letter he summarized his disenchantment with the East. If he had the money he would like to be home, but to be there and have to work every day, then not earn anything "would never do. I shall hardly ever visit Warwick unless fortune favors me."[4]

There were thousands of young, eager Clarence Mayos on the Western Slope in the late nineteenth century, all just as determined to make their fortunes and not have to return to what they saw as the static East. As Mayo changed, so had they all. And, like Mayo, many sought their livelihoods in the communities. Clarence, who worked in a lumber yard, carpentered, and took other jobs, often found himself unemployed and would then try his hand at prospecting.

Gunnison owed its prospering existence to the Denver & Rio Grande, which reached there in the fall of 1881, and to the tributary mining districts. And there were many — Quartz Creek, Elk Mountain, Gothic, Ruby, Tomichi, and Gold Brick, to name a few — dotting the landscape. Their small camps bloomed and withered within a short time. George Root recalled White Pine as a one-street town, "not quite crooked as a dog's hind leg, and at the time of my arrival was about as rough as the traditional 'road to Jordan.'" On that March day in 1883, when he arrived to help start the *White Pine Cone*, the camp's residents numbered 250 to 300, with a "floating population" of 100.[5] The most the census taker could ever find was 170. A score and more of "White Pines" gave color and life to the Gunnison country before night closed in for them.

Even with all the exuberance and the "hoopla," the Gunnison country never developed into a major mining district. The neighboring San Juans and Aspen far outdistanced it in the ultimate test of production. Primarily a silver region, its best years were 1890 and 1891 ($900,000), thanks to lead, which accounted for nearly half of the total produced, though mined as a by-product.

The whole Western Slope was waiting for a boom, perhaps no more so than the Gunnison country. The adage about living on hope applied here, as it had decades before. A few of the more forthright individuals admitted it. Helen Hunt Jackson, while visiting Schofield, encountered a discontented lady who confessed:

> Waiting for a boom; that's what's the matter with this town. I've got no patience with this boom business. It's the ruination of this country. It just spoils everything. There isn't a decent house in the town, and there won't never be.[6]

The Western Slope lived on boom fever in the nineteenth century, and as yet had not seen the error of such shortsightedness.

Other smaller rushes carried miners to the Western Slope. Hahn's Peak, far north in Routt County, had been prospected in the mid-sixties. No permanent settlement dared that isolation for the next decade. These placer mines finally achieved some notoriety in the second half of the 1870s when companies gained control of the thousands of acres and started hydraulic operations. Tiny camps served as homes for workers and supply points for prospectors working the area. Hampered by a continual scarcity of water, isolation, and small returns from low grade deposits, the Hahn's Peak placers left stockholders with far more expenses than dividends. Even less successful were the silver discoveries made in the Gore and Rabbit Ear Ranges and near Steamboat Springs and Craig, and the Yampa River's short-lived gold excitements.

Old reliable Summit County far outstripped such upstarts and claimed some very good years in the 1880s and 1890s, thanks to Leadville and the railroad. Miners from Leadville revitalized the Ten Mile District, building the new camps of Kokomo and Robinson. Other discoveries followed, and Summit County's production climbed to new heights, though never quite escaping Leadville's shadow. Old-timer Breckenridge revived, rejuvenated by the quartz and placer operations at its doorstep. Like the rest of the county, however, it suffered slumps along with the boom years.

Regardless of which Western Slope mining district one selects, it is obvious that this was a man's world. One feminine stronghold held fast, though, that hallowed institution of camp and mine, the boarding house. Few miners preferred their own cooking for long. Constant baking, remembered one woman, was her mother's fate. She and her mother worked together; the former diluted and mixed Eagle Brand Condensed Milk for every meal. Hungry boarders devoured bread, biscuits, cookies, and pies, especially her mother's famous soda biscuits and "tasty" vinegar pie. Years of hunting depleted game near the camp of Chihuahua over in the Snake River Valley, so beef, supplemented by pork, was the steady diet. Winter supplies were generously laid in; beef was stored in nearby snowbanks for easy retrieval when needed. With relish, she recalled the delicious nutty flavor of "steel cut oats," a cold winter morning's delight. Homemade ice cream was another treat for any season of the year, so long as the snow lasted.[7]

In spite of such obvious culinary inducements for staying in Chihuahua, or the promises of a Telluride or Pitkin, the miners and prospectors tarried only briefly. They drifted in search of their own personal Eldorado. Most of them, at one time or another, succumbed to the mining sensation of the Western Slope — Aspen.

Aspen! Long before the first skier found this village or the jet-set drank in its charms, the name wove silver magic. Colorado was "high" on silver in the 1880s and no higher than in Aspen, Colorado's newest "silver queen."

Colorado needed another mining bonanza to promote it, and Aspen provided one. The 1860s had Central City; the 1870s, Leadville; and now the 1880s, Aspen. The Western Slope, always before a bridesmaid to such fame, now demanded its share of glory. Suddenly investors flocked in and found owners willing to deal. Fame came in a rush, an avalanche which benefited the whole Colorado West. Aspen did it all and more, but not without a price. Investors went first to Aspen, then elsewhere, leaving the San Juans, for instance, still short of cash and recognition.

The Roaring Fork River Valley, once part of the Gunnison country, was prospected in 1879, probably earlier. Prospectors, who knew Leadville deposits, erroneously assumed that Aspen ore zones were in similar geologic conditions. Sharp observation and insight served the prospector as well as the pages of a geology textbook, which very few had ever turned. But here, as elsewhere in Colorado, experience could be unreliable. As an example, twelve miles from Aspen, Ashcroft seemed to offer more promising conditions, grabbing early attention and, for a while, appearing destined for greatness.

Regardless of potential, Ute troubles in 1879 drove nearly everyone out of the district. Not for long, however; in the spring of 1880 they hastened back, joined by others, and the Ashcroft-Aspen saga began.

"New sensation" in Colorado mining camps, crowed Aspen's *Rocky Mountain Sun*, July 16, 1881, as the editor went on to explain how his camp was improving and building rapidly. He even found time to welcome a competitor, the *Ashcroft Herald*. Rival Ashcroft prospered, freighters, residents, and visitors crowding the streets in a community served by two daily stages. Within a year it was being hailed as the "mining wonder of the West," not just Colorado. No parochialism restrained those early promoters.

The surrounding mines had to prove themselves equal to Ashcroft's bombast. The future looked promising, thanks in no small part to Colorado's best known mining man of the day, Horace Tabor. He invested in the Tam O'Shanter Mine, a combination of several of the best claims in the Ashcroft section. Where Tabor went, others were sure to follow. He planned to invest large sums of money to build a smelter, improve the roads, encourage a railroad, and develop his property. Tabor was going to give the region what it desperately needed: improved transportation, a local smelter, long-term development of a promising property, and a generous influx of capital.

The silver-lined dream of '81 turned into a nightmare when the Tam O'Shanter became ensnarled in a debilitating lawsuit contesting its sale. Vultures lurk around every mining district, waiting for prey; the wealthier the mine or owner, the more likely it is to become involved in litigation. The case dragged into 1888, Tabor emerging with only a Pyrrhic victory. Court costs negated small mining returns and left Tabor holding an expensive white elephant. When he did work the Tam O'Shanter, labor disputes and two brief strikes dogged him. Finally, the bank holding the final $95,000 payment in escrow failed, and that money was lost. Tabor's bad luck held, the Tam O'Shanter never became a steady producer.

Ashcroft succumbed to rival Aspen in 1884. Aspen had much richer mines, which had taken longer to develop. But it did not enjoy an easy victory; the problems which plagued Ashcroft also hindered Aspen. Initially, goods and smelter ore were shipped by mule train, then by wagon over high, tortuous passes, with costs that matched. The *Aspen Times*, May 9, 1885, complained about Independence Pass, "Three jacks in a pack train coming over the range yesterday fell in the mud and were trampled out of sight by the rest of the train. . . . What kind of condition must the roads be in when this is the case?" Not until 1887 and 1888, with the arrival of the Denver and Rio Grande and Colorado Midland railroads, did conditions improve. The significance of railroads to mining is clearly shown in Pitkin County, which produced $600,000 in 1886, $4,000,000 the next year, following the advent of the rail.

Local smelters to work the ore were also needed; shipping ore to Leadville was costly and time consuming. Tabor voiced a commonly held belief, when he predicted in 1882 "that Pitkin County had the mineral of the grade that make rich and permanent mines. . . . All the young county wants is smelters . . . ."[8] That very year a smelter was built, though it and its rivals faced tough times, with high expenses and shortages. In the end, the railroad solved the problem, but for the price of the Aspen smelters' eventual closing. Competition from Denver and Pueblo proved too great.

Rare indeed was a new mining district blessed with abundant financial resources, explaining why men like Tabor were so welcome. The Aspen District attracted outside capitalists early, particularly from Ohio, then later New York, in the person of energetic Jerome Wheeler. Wheeler purchased mines (silver and coal), founded a bank, built an opera house and hotel, and invested heavily in the Colorado Midland. Aspen also produced its own homegrown wealthy, D. R. C. Brown and Henry Cowenhoven, as well as enriching men like Wheeler.

Aspen was notorious for its mining lawsuits. They made lawyers rich, investors hesitant, and owners infuriated, thereby serving to retard Aspen mining. At issue was control of the apex, or top of the vein. According to United States mining law, the claim containing the apex controlled the right to mine that vein's entire length, regardless of claim boundaries. Vertical sideline boundaries had no bearing, nor did date of entry. Instantly questions arose; the paramount one, where was the apex? Expensive apex litigation consumed months, sometimes years, as both sides brought in the "ablest mining lawyers," "experts," exhibits, and reams of testimony. Pity the poor jurors, asked for a nearly impossible decision that would have been difficult even for a judge learned in mining law.

A couple of examples will suffice. In November, 1883, the Spar Mine struck a valuable ore body that was, unfortunately, in the neighboring Washington claim. Immediately the Washington owners brought suit. The Spar people defended themselves on the point that they owned the apex and simply followed it. The dispute was resolved before trial by the Spar's purchase of the Washington.

The Durant and Emma were less fortunate, their dispute ended in court with a trial, retrial, and a final out-of-court settlement. All these proceedings cost a small fortune (reportedly $1,000,000), and two years. To ward off such legal entanglements, consolidation and purchase of all possible neighboring claims, regardless of cost, became the primary goal.

David Hyman, formerly a Cincinnati lawyer and now an Aspen mine owner, found himself and his properties ensnarled in these apex cases. Although he emerged a winner, he later wrote in his memoirs, "Having a knowledge of law and litigation I can say truthfully that no litigation equals a mining litigation in its intensity and bitterness." The expenses, as mentioned, had been staggering, including, Hyman recalled, $3,300 paid to detectives for checking the backgrounds of prospective jurors.[9]

The prizes were well worth fighting over. The Mollie Gibson, itself a product of litigation, hit ore pockets running to 20,000 ounces of silver per ton, and for several years it claimed the honor of being the "richest silver mine in the world." A "nugget" taken out of the Smuggler in 1894 weighed 2,063 pounds and contained 93% silver. One "pocket" in the Emma Mine netted its owners half a million dollars. Not all mines, of course, produced such bonanzas, but their names at least indicate what their discoverers/owners thought of them: The Best Friend, Empress of Aspen, the Justice, Bushwhacker, Mineral Farm — and so on and on.

Aspen's great years were the late 1880s and early 1890s. Then, as the respected New York *Engineering and Mining Journal*, March 9, 1889, reported, "the excitement in Aspen is said to be akin to that of California in El Dorado days." Leadville no longer reigned as silver queen; Aspen inherited the crown, and from 1888 through 1894 she produced $41,000,000 in gold, lead and silver, 87% of it silver.

Ambitious owners equipped their mines with the best and most up-to-date machinery money could buy. Aspen, as a result, was a mining showcase for the state and nation. Electricity gained immediate acceptance, and Aspen pioneered in plugging it into mining. The abundance of water in nearby streams, plus rapid fall down the canyons slicing the valley floor, offered unusually fine sites for power plants. With high fuel costs a problem even after the coming of the railroads, electricity was a natural answer. The Roaring Fork Electric Light and Power Company, incorporated in April, 1887, furnished power for electric hoists by July, 1888, and soon thereafter pumps and tramways joined the ranks. The town was only a step behind. In a twinkling, electric lights brightened store and home, and lamps lighted the main streets.

If the mines were the heart of the Aspen District, the town was its soul. Soul is something Aspen has always had. From languishing in the Ute Reservation in 1880, Aspen officially grew to 3,374 in 1885 and 5,108 in 1890, with all the "handsome, substantial and attractive" ornaments associated with a Colorado "silver queen" in the flush of her youth.

Her start, like the mines, was slow. The season of firsts came in 1880 — the first business, the first lot jumping, the first lawyer, the first subdivision, and the first hotel. Several women braved the isolation and wintered there. Warren Root remembered Aspen's first Christmas. The ladies invited the men to supper, "it most certainly can be said to the credit of the ladies that a more bountiful feast was never spread amid the wilds of the Rocky Mountains." The men returned the compliment on New Year's Eve.[10] Amid that winter's snow came a glimpse of the future: culture, in the form of a literary society, and skiing, the "snowshoes" handshaped by a couple of Swedes.

After the initial spurt, town activity subsided until the railroad chugged in, then it, too, took off again. In the 1880s six weekly and five daily newspapers chronicled local happenings. By decade's end five had found the competition too stiff and closed their doors. Their local news and mining columns enthusiastically reported typical stories for a major Colorado silver mining town. Aspen, of course, thought there was nothing quite like her and, without quibbling, Aspen was the largest, most significant Western Slope community.

Aspen suffered its share of lawlessness, which was totally disdained because of the civic image it projected. Except for excesses creditable to "John Barleycorn," and urban-related disturbances, the "wild west" vanished posthaste. More threatening to Aspen's future was fire; in 1884, for instance, the fancy Clarendon Hotel burned to the ground. Other threats proved more emotional. The Chinese elicited no welcome; when one appeared, he was firmly asked to leave by a delegation of seventy-five locals.

Uneasy rested the crown of a "silver queen." Judged against the dowager claimant and upcoming challengers, the holder either measured up or was dethroned. Aspen did its "darndest." A large and varied business district offered everything from the ever-present general merchant to jewelers, from confectionary stores to banks. A photograph of Aspen from the late eighties shows substantial brick and stone construction, buildings several stories high, and fine Victorian homes in the residential areas. It had three schools by 1893. The first one, completed in 1882, received praise as the best building in the county. Ministers came, continuing their never-ending fight to save souls. Soon steeples and church bells enriched Aspen's sights and sounds.

The red-light district, from saloons to "soiled doves," did justice to Aspen's claim as the "silver queen," growing with the prosperity of the mines and town to become one of the state's most notorious. Prostitution flourished. The 1885 state census taker interviewed the girls, six of whom unabashedly told him their occupations; the rest were more discreet. Mollie, Eve, Gertie, Frankie, Ursa, and Molla ranged in age from 17 to 35; two were married, and one divorced.

Aspen's social whirl rivaled Denver's, and may even be said to have matched that of the ski season today. In snowy February, 1884, roller skating was the "popular amusement." The less athletically inclined sat and watched the Congregational Church's children's concert, or the "children's jubilee," listened to a temperance lecture, or participated in a literary social. The GAR, Musicians, Mask, and Catholic Church balls, and a leap year party kept the dancers amused. The ever-ready saloon and red-light district beckoned those in search of more worldly entertainment. In the summer, baseball and other outdoor sports occupied the few leisure hours. In all seasons joiners could choose from numerous fraternal and other lodges for both men and women. Aspenites were especially proud of their fire companies, which fulfilled both a social and a utilitarian function. In 1888 the annual state firemen's tournament took place in Aspen. Races determined Colorado's fastest company, as money feverishly changed hands in the process; local pride demanded backing the "boys." A parade, foot races, and a grand ball concluded the tournament. The crown jewel in Aspen's social and cultural world, the Wheeler Opera House, mirrored the aspirations of those times. Opera seldom graced its stage; nonetheless, it provided the place for entertaining the middle and upper classes. They pointed to it with pride; few rivaled its grandeur in Colorado, none west of the Divide. Aspenites had the money to indulge themselves with the best.

Aspen's population in 1885, according to the state census taker's report, was typical of a Colorado mining community in those years. Mostly native Americans, Aspenites generally hailed from the midwest; the foreign contingent was predominantly English and Irish, with a smattering of other northern European nationalities. A fair cross-section of families had settled there. The very few Blacks found themselves locked into menial jobs.

Already Aspen promoted itself as a "sportsman's paradise" and a "haven of rest," with scenery "grand beyond description." The editor of the *Rocky Mountain Sun*, in the August 18, 1888, paper, puffed

Aspen as one of the most picturesque and peaceful valleys in Colorado: a town with very bright prospects and a winter season as "pleasant as an eastern fall." Tragedy and death accompanied the joy and prosperity. The newspapers recounted it all—marriages, business failures, high school commencements, mining accidents, births, deaths, socials, mining news, church notes, patent medicine ads, school honor rolls, editorials, reviews of plays, and even a column of wit and humor. The following are samples of the humor that "left 'em laughing" from 1888 to 1890. They tell much about Victorian attitudes:

Irish nationally won't stand—it's founded on a sham-rock.

Women, like diseases, always search out our weakest points for an attack; and they generally find them.

'Pa, what is a blanket mortgage?' asked Johnny. 'It is one that keeps a man warm working to pay it.'

Physician. 'You wished me to call, madam. What is the matter?' Lady reclining on sofa. 'Nothing doctor, but that is just what alarms me.'

In the early nineties Aspen's future development looked limitless. No one doubted a prediction that the population would double by late in the decade. The newest of the great silver towns, "naturally the most progressive," was unmatched in Colorado.

The prediction was never to be fulfilled; in 1893 a severe depression gripped Colorado and the nation. With the silver price collapsing, almost all Aspen's mines closed July 1 without notice. "The once flourishing mining camp of Aspen is now badly prostrated by a crushing blow to its great industry. It has been a complete knock-out," moaned the *Rocky Mountain Sun* in that day's issue. Idle men, "hopeless in their despair," lined the streets, adrift in a depression the likes of which they had never seen. Credit had helped keep Aspen and all its rivals afloat, now it collapsed like a deck of cards. Businesses failed, others were "crowded to the wall" in desperate attempts to stay open.

Management offered to reopen the mines, with lower wages based upon a sliding scale, dependent on the price of silver. Union leaders balked but finally conceded, when they saw no alternative. Jobs were scarce, and for the first time in twenty years in Colorado, no new mining districts opened to absorb the labor surplus. It was a bitter pill for the *Sun* to swallow; its masthead proclaimed, "A Journal Devoted to the Growth and Prosperity of the City of Aspen and the Mining Interests of Pitkin County." The world seemed to have turned upside down.

Good years still remained for Aspen. Production stayed above $2 million annually until 1908, thanks to an increase in lead mining. Silver mining tonnage also stayed high; it had to — the price per ounce of silver was half or less of what it had been when the district opened. But Aspen's mining boom had ended — the spark that gave life to the eighties flickered out. Vacant stores, abandoned homes, and declining population plainly showed a fading community. Less easy to see were the subjective changes in attitude and outlook. Aspen's mining youth was gone; old age set in almost immediately. The queen was dead, long live the queen. Aspen had been a great mining district, but she would not be the Western Slope's greatest.

Aspen, a hardrock town and district, was quite different from the previously discussed Blue River placer diggings and Breckenridge. It is perhaps unfair to compare the two communities, since Aspen was a mining town and Breckenridge a camp. This might seem to be only a question of semantics, but to the residents of each, it was a real distinction. The mining town, richer and larger, sustained a more commanding business district, was blessed with substantial buildings, examples of the latest architectural styles and the ornamentation of Victorian America, and evidenced a different spirit. The last, hard to define, could only be felt. This was the significant difference between Colorado placer and hardrock districts; the former had only camps of one kind or another, the great districts and towns were all hardrock.

Inherent within an Aspen-Breckenridge comparison are differences that need not be elaborated upon — transportation systems, newspapers, schools, churches, city government, businesses, and social life. The predominantly masculine world of the placer district vs. the more cosmopolitan nature of Aspen produced communities farther apart than mere chronological decades could justify.

The mining industry itself displays equal differences inherent within its framework. The methods and equipment used in underground mining differ from placering. The skills and techniques needed by underground miners are greater than for those above, with a correspondingly higher degree of physical danger. To mine at Aspen cost more; outside capital, therefore, had to be found to establish and maintain the mines. The attraction was such that it was easy enough to achieve, especially so when one examines the troubles Summit County encountered. Though both districts faced mountainous isolation, Aspen did not have to wait or to beg for a railroad, they raced each other to tap her silver bonanza. Corporate control came quickly to Aspen; it was never a poor man's district. Placer mining offered more individual opportunity, but fewer rewards. Corporate control was destined to intervene in lode mining, where it produced a more impersonal, industrialized life for the miner. Placer districts avoided this intervention much longer, and also avoided unionization, which arrived in Aspen during the nineties.

Both mining methods endangered the environment, though hardrock mining did less obvious damage. Dumps and buildings scarred the mountainsides, and tailings polluted the streams, but the disfiguration was less than in placering Summit County. Without doubt, had one visited both districts in their peak years, he would have found that Aspen appeared much more stable and permanent. That certain air was there in Aspen. The Blue River diggings could not evoke it.

The Western Slope was becoming home to more people each year, the first fruits of this new settlement were demonstrated by county births and amputations. An area that once had been primarily three counties — Summit, Lake, and Conejos — changed in 1874 with the introduction of La Plata, Hinsdale, and Grand. The Colorado legislature changed county boundaries in the years that followed. By 1889 the job was finished; nineteen counties were established. Only Moffat (1911) waited to be carved out of Routt County, which at the time contained all of northwestern Colorado.

Having projected a rural image for so long, the Western Slope now became strongly urbanized, a reflection of mining's dominance, which concentrated people in and around the camps. Urbanization was more expansive and regionally significant in the 1880s and 1890s than it would be for the next sixty years. Those little camps, now beloved by jeepers, hikers, and bottle collectors, relished their heyday.

Population growth patterns varied from county to county between the 1880 and 1890 census. Mining fluctuations caused most of the variations. For instance, Gunnison County lost nearly half its population, thanks partly to stabilization of its boom; primarily, however, the loss was caused by carving Pitkin and other counties from it. Ouray County jumped nearly 2 ½ times, while neighboring San Juan grew by only 44%, a large percentage only because of the initially small base. Summit County lost nearly two-thirds of its people, and Hinsdale declined by 40%. A strictly agricultural county is hard to evaluate, because most originated after the 1880 census. Routt comes as near as any to being an agricultural county and shows a tremendous jump — from 140 to 2,369 residents. Before assumptions are made about the attractions of ranching and farming, it should be kept in mind that this was Ute reservation until 1881.

Politically, the Western Slope carried little clout. First the San Juans, then Aspen, gained what little attention was received. A Republican fief most of the time, Colorado was divided politically into areas roughly defined as southern, mountain, and Denver, each with its own subdivisions. Backroom brawls over division of spoils enlivened election years, especially when the mining millionaires started throwing their gold and silver around. Tacitly it was agreed by the Republican leadership, the majority party, that the "loaves and fishes" would be split and not monopolized. Thus the two senatorships were not held by one group, and the governorship and lesser state offices were passed around.

Ouray's Frederick Pitkin was twice elected governor. Pitkin, a member of the "one-lunged" army which came West seeking health, was a walking testimonial to the curative powers of the "salubrious" climate. Aspen's newspaper editor and homegrown radical, Davis Waite, started a tumultuous term as governor in 1893. None of the senators, by far the most sought after office, held strong ties to the west and only Thomas Bowen, who made money in San Juan mining, could be classified as a part-time resident. With a few other candidates, the Western Slope, considering its relatively minor political significance, received its fair share of political attention.

In the eighties, Western Slope voters leaned strongly toward the Republican column, giving the GOP's presidential nominees a decided edge. Such Republican loyalty did not save the Western Slope from becoming a political colony of Denver, which controlled the largest block of votes and gained most of the prizes when it wanted them. Jealousy of Denver was only partially concealed by state and party loyalty.

The elections, part serious, part fun, were all partisan. Cornetist Clarence Mayo organized a band in 1882 to play at the rallies. "I have a band now and we do some playing outside, but you may be sure we are paid for it, no playing for fun." Nearer the election his group performed at torchlight and other processions for $3 an evening. Before the campaign was over, he made "some $50" playing for the "fools." Apparently Clarence did not think much of either party. Most Western Slopers got serious only around election time, and local contests often aroused more passion than state or national ones.

By the 1890s Western Colorado had won a tourist reputation for itself. The Denver and Rio Grande promoted the "Circle Tour" from Denver to Durango, Silverton, Ouray, and back. Hot Sulphur Springs now had its rivals for relief and recovery from all those ailments. Glenwood Springs, Ouray, Pagosa Springs, Waunita Hot Springs near Gunnison, and Durango's Trimble Springs promised near miracles from a dip in their waters.

68

The two decades ending in 1893 closed the pioneering period for Western Colorado. They exhibited all the ingredients so beloved by "westerns"—Indians, cowboys, miners, soldiers, conflicts, and romances. Ahead lay a time of trial, a testing to see if today's hopes would be tomorrow's blessings.

Caroline Romney. *Courtesy Rocky Mountain News.*

A Little Lady in a Man's World
Caroline Romney

> In making its first appearance on the shores of time, the *Durango Record* will be expected in accord with custom, to give some account of itself, some reason for its being.
>
> First and foremost, it will be devoted to Durango and its interests and service. . . .
>
> Next to the town, the *Record* owes allegiance to southwestern Colorado, a land not only 'flowing with milk and honey,' but seamed with silver and gold and floored with coal. (January 10, 1881)

Thus wrote Caroline Romney, editor of the *Durango Record*, as she surveyed the barely five months-old community. In a day and time when it was unusual to find a woman newspaper editor, Mrs. Romney was exceptional. A cheerful, witty disposition complemented a versatile, energetic, and talented personality. The combative, personal journalism of her generation did not faze Caroline Romney; she proved more than a match for her male contemporaries.

From Leadville she had come through winter snows, freighting her Gordon hand press by wagon, because no railroad train would reach Durango for another seven months. To the astonishment of her freighters she withstood the trip, established an office in a tent, and raced to publish the first daily paper, a race she won. Forty years old and a widow, the New York-born woman made her mark on Durango in the months ahead — gathering news, writing editorials, managing the paper, selling advertisements; nothing daunted her.

Caroline Romney was a hustler in the competitive newspaper

world. She had to be in Durango, where two other weeklies and four dailies competed for readers in a town of only 3,500. Issue after issue defended Durango's interests and approved or reproached actions and people, all the while recording local events.

Durango, the "new wonder in the Southwest," caught her fancy from the first. She assumed it would surpass her previous home of Leadville, itself a genuine mining wonder. "The King is Dead! Long live the King!" Caroline proclaimed on January 10. She championed her town when it went through a lawless period in March and April, 1881, and took out after one of the offending parties, the locally based Stockton gang. Their threats did not intimidate her; some members of the gang planned to "tree" the editor, until they discovered "he" was a woman. The only consolation was that a rival gang from Farmington, New Mexico, could be partly blamed for the trouble, a fact editor Romney did not overlook. During the turmoil of that April, she continued to encourage people to come to Durango. They had nothing to fear, she emphasized, now that the "baptism of blood" had faded into history.

She exhibited her editorial vehemence in the cause of women's rights. "Prove your fitness for men's pursuits, by doing successfully what men did," she advised. On February 19, 1881, editor Romney wrote: "The best way for women to pursue, in business enterprises at least, is not to wait for men to accord them their rights, but to go ahead and take them. Such women have so much practical work to do, that, as a rule, they haven't much time to talk women's rights. They do what is better—they act them." Caroline was a living example of her tenets. Three weeks later (March 12), she was encouraging girls to come: "We want girls who will go to church and to bible-class on Sundays," girls for buggy rides, girls to wait on tables, girls for sweethearts, "fat and funny girls," girls to civilize "their pioneer brothers."

Let her find something that offended her and she thrust quickly with her editorial pen. In September, 1881, the *Record* ran an expose of "opium dives," the ultimate degradation in Mrs. Romney's eyes. She continually worried about the proximity of the neighboring southern Utes, as did most of her contemporaries. The land could be better used by "hard working white men," she commented on January 21, 1882; at any moment the Utes might break into open hostilities, if something were not done. Nothing was done for the moment, so the stalemate remained.

There was wit and purpose in her writing style, best observed by letting her speak for herself. Two local items will illustrate:

> The football mania continues. Eugene Engley thought the ball yesterday was an issue of the evening paper and kicked it into the backyard of the First National Bank. Capt. Stanley set his dog at it. . . . Mr. Kellogg got it in his eye from the toes of Bruce Hunt. All had lots of fun and played until nearly dark. (March 28, 1882)

> The snow, which was some four inches deep yesterday forenoon, went away as if it had been sent for quick where the sun got full sweep at it. (April 22, 1882)

The first quote is a good example of her style. Editor Romney managed to make an ordinary event newsworthy, while mentioning several prominent men and taking a shot at a newspaper rival.

The *Record* feuded with Durango newspaper rivals over a multitude of slights and controversial issues, some of them political. In February and March of 1882 Caroline slashed at the Clipper Theatre and its "lewd girls." The temptations, bright lights, and music "easily seduced" the young, she warned, and "the stage itself panders to the lowest instincts of human nature . . . (Feb. 18, 1882)." This aroused the *Southwest*, which attacked the *Record* for its attack on the Clipper, and on they went.

The end came swiftly in early May, 1882, when Mrs. Romney sold out to the *Herald* without so much as a comment in her paper. She was not the first, already two other weeklies and two dailies had folded. Durango simply could not support them all. Precarious, indeed, was the life of a pioneering newspaper.

Caroline Romney was a fascinating woman. Her biases and opinions reflected much about the women of her generation. Durango was a better town for Caroline's having worked and lived there.

The "bright, cheery little woman" left Durango. She never remarried, despite having fluttered several male hearts, according to reports. Later she would work on Trinidad, Colorado, and El Paso, Texas, newspapers and live in Chicago. When she died in Denver in September, 1916, her long ago rival, the *Herald*, hailed her as a pioneer newspaper publisher and editor. By then she was just a memory of a fast fading pioneer past.

Partial map of the Western Slope as it appeared in 1879.

6.
For the Losers—Tragedy

For the Ute Indians on the Western Slope of Colorado, the last quarter of the nineteenth century produced a crisis in their civilization. A tragedy was about to unfold, although none of the participants foresaw it. Little seemed to have changed for the Utes as the nineteenth century opened. Trade between the Indians and the Spaniards reached a stable plateau, both relying on the other for needed services and trade goods. The Ute economy revolved around hides, slave/horse trade, and the buffalo. Perhaps 5,000 Utes controlled the rugged center of the Rocky Mountains. Warlike, they held their land against all comers. Changes, swift and subtle, had molded their culture over the past two centuries. Whether they realized it or not, the Utes were irrevocably tied to the more industrialized Spanish, from the iron pot to glass beads. The horse symbolized it all; it measured individual wealth, reflected tribal power, and supported existence. Gone was the stone age culture of the pre-1600 existence. The Utes combined three cultures: the old Ute, Plains (Buffalo), and Spanish.

If the past two hundred years had beheld remarkable change, the next eighty accelerated that pace. The Utes were about to be trapped in a cultural whirlpool of a power unknown to their ancestors. If the horse and the iron knife had revolutionized their life, what would happen when an aggressive, materialistic, even more industrialized people appeared to challenge the Utes for their very homeland?

The first changes passed almost unnoticed, or at least painlessly, from the Utes' point of view. Part of their land was sold to the United States in the Louisiana Purchase; neither seller nor buyer bothered to consult them about their wishes. That first American explorer (better described as a tourist), Zebulon Pike, and his party journeyed to see the land, passing through so fast in 1806–07 that the winter-camped Utes took little notice. Then Mexico revolted, threw out Spain (1821), and emerged overlord, in name, of the Utes. In 1848 the Ute land and people were assigned to the United States in the treaty that concluded the Mexican-American War. For the Utes, these changes were meaningless; life went on much as it had before.

The most noticeable consequence came with the trappers out of Taos, tramping up and down the mountain streams, seeking the beaver, whose ill fate it was to be in fashion in the 1820s and 1830s for hats and other apparel. The Utes made contact with Americans and their products. The trappers also brought whiskey, built a couple of wretched fort/fur-trading posts in Western Colorado, and intermarried with the Utes. The Utes traded buffalo robes and beaver pelts for commodities they now deemed essential. The trappers came, and then left when the fur market was gone and the beaver population depleted. The land and the people returned to their final quiet era.

As soon as the Americans occupied Santa Fe in 1846, negotiations began with the Utes, leading in December, 1849, to the first treaty between the two. For the Utes this agreement seemed harmless enough; they recognized the sovereignty of the United States and agreed not to leave their accustomed territory without permission. Perpetual peace and friendship were perfunctorily promised, and agencies and military posts were to be allowed on Ute land. Unbeknownst to either party, the days of Ute freedom were numbered. Although no definite reservation boundaries had been established, once the concept of specific land was discussed there existed the potential for signing away one part or another. Once land was "officially" given to Indians, a suspicion arose in the minds of some Americans that it must be valuable, obviously too good for "savages."

Early hints of trouble surfaced in the 1850s. Settlers moved into the San Luis Valley, leading to Ute raids and finally the so-called Ute War of 1854–56. The United States responded with force, and into the valley marched the army, building Fort Massachusetts and then Fort Garland.

Beyond the San Luis Valley the Western Slope still remained unchallenged Ute domain. Uneasiness penetrated even these mountains when the 1849 gold rush and its aftermath sent settlers swirling past on both sides. Here rested the crux of the matter—settlement.

The Spanish traders and the American trappers had not been settlers, only transients who offered goods and departed.

The final chapter of Ute independence opened in 1858 with the discovery of gold in Cherry Creek, where Denver would soon be located. This set in motion the 1859 Pike's Peak gold rush and a series of events, which, in less than a generation, stripped the Utes of nearly all their land and left them huddling miserably on small reservations, wards of the United States, a broken people.

What transpired was foreordained, despite some events which seemed to suggest there might be a different outcome for the Utes. Wherever Anglo-Americans contended with the Indians for land, conflicting interests led to disputes and the triumph of the former's overwhelming numbers, resources, and superior technology. A cultural clash and an economic rivalry, complicated by misunderstanding and fear, precipitated civil war between the Indian and the Anglo. Neither side was totally at fault nor could either find a solution short of capitulation by the other. What one had, the other wanted, and half a loaf simply would not do.

The first sign of transition appeared with the designation of three agency headquarters for the widely scattered Ute bands. The prospectors came within a year after the fifty-nine rush. They crossed the Continental Divide, hardly stopping to admire the scenery before panning the streams. They were edgy, and the Utes were concerned; both had reason to fear the other by reputation or rumor. Instantly the Utes' future became entangled with mining and could not be separated. Though Ute war parties rode through Denver in 1859 and 1860, even staging a "scalp dance" for the locals, the far distant Utes represented no threat to the tiny settlements nestled along the foothills. The same could not be said of the neighboring Plains Indians, a problem Governor John Evans tried fitfully to resolve in 1863. An outgrowth of his efforts was a conference with the Utes, in which the Capote agreed to cede the San Luis Valley and relocate on the Western Slope, a move dictated by increased white settlement in the valley.

Five years later, expanding pressure by Coloradans, both miners and farmers, saw the Utes at the conference table once more, this time in Washington, where a host of pleasantries not found in the West enhanced the atmosphere. Out of these negotiations came a treaty that defined a single Ute reservation, comprising roughly the western one-third of Colorado. In return the Utes were promised clothing, rations, and other annuities and told that the land would be theirs forever, protected from trespassers by the United States. "Forever" proved short.

The "Ute Problem," as the Coloradans derisively referred to it, was not resolved. Since the days of the Spanish, the San Juan Mountains in southwestern Colorado had been rumored to contain the "mother lode," where gold and silver could be scooped at the grass roots. Waves of prospectors and miners had tried to tap it, without lasting success, the last in 1860–61. Now, in the early 1870s, they came back.

This time they came to stay, at first for only the warmer months, then year around. The Utes rightfully objected, and the prospectors/miners argued that the Indians should not have the land when it could be put to "better" (more profitable) use by themselves. Caught in the middle, the Federal government found no remedy, only a storm of Colorado protests when it announced that permission to mine on the reservation would be refused. A tense situation in 1870 worsened in 1871. Pressure mounted from within Colorado to force the Utes to cede the mining region, or better yet, to remove them from the entire area. Both sides feared war; hotheads seemed to relish the thought. Charles Adams, Ute agent at Los Pinos, believed in 1872 that the excitement and distrust arose not so much from Ute desire to plunder, as generally supposed, but from their fear of being attacked and driven from the reservation. To defuse the situation Washington tried to negotiate for the mining land, getting nowhere, because, as Adams observed:

> the fear that should they [Utes] dispose of one part, prospectors and adventurers would immediately push farther on and use the same argument which they are using now, that as long as the boundaries of the reservation are not surveyed, every man has the right to go where he pleases on it unless it is proved that he is on an Indian reservation.[1]

This non-result inflamed Colorado newspapers and failed to stem the tide of immigration seeping onto Ute land. Continued agitation produced another Washington attempt the next year, which proved more successful; the Utes signed the Brunot agreement, giving up their claim to the San Juan Mountains.

Misunderstanding and discontent were the fruits. Miners and settlers assumed they had a *carte blanche* to move into the San Juans. The Utes disagreed. Their federally appointed spokesman, Ouray, expressed their sentiments during the 1873 conference. "We are perfectly willing to sell our mountain land, and hope the miners will find heaps of gold and silver. . . . We do not want they should go down into our valleys, however, and kill or scare away our game."[2] The wise and talented Ouray, much respected by Coloradans, and the best known Ute of his generation, was fighting a losing battle, as he knew. Reared for a time in Taos and a witness to the 1859–60 gold rush, he understood what was happening.

The San Juans were settled in the years that followed; as long as Ute land lay just to the south and north, however, there could be no peace. Even in the county and town named Ouray, residents jumped to the forefront of the fray — the "Utes Must Go." Every neighboring mining community echoed the cry. Were not those Indians wasting rich agricultural land, which "intelligent and industrious" farmers could turn to production? There was still the ever-present threat of an Indian War, and nobody really wanted the "savages" next door to them. When the final trouble came, it did not start here, however, but at the White River Agency farther north, near the present town of Meeker.

In one of the real tragedies of this drama, the misguided intentions of a good-hearted agent misfired, leading to the final resolution. Visionary ex-New York newspaperman and Union Colony organizer Nathan Meeker took it upon himself to mold the Utes zealously along utopian lines he had promoted in his writing. Within a year after his 1878 appointment, Meeker's ambitions entrapped him. He was determined to terminate the nomadic habits of his wards and turn them toward agricultural pursuits. The Utes looked upon fences, farm equipment, and classrooms as hated symbols that threatened their way of life, not the paths to Utopia Meeker envisioned. Nothing daunted Meeker as he railed against the Utes' large horse herds and ordered the race track plowed under; late summer of 1879 found the reservation in turmoil. Straying Utes were blamed for "depredations," as the newspapers called them, and some traveled as far as Denver to protest to the governor about "Father Meeker's" actions.

By September Meeker openly questioned the safety of his family and the other agency employees. "I have no confidence in any of them [the Indians] and I feel that none of the white people are safe." He requested troops for aid and protection in what had become a civilizing process gone astray. The troops rode out of Fort Steele, Wyoming, on September 21. Angry Utes tensely watched them come into Colorado.

Futile negotiations, some shots, and the battle was on, the Utes pinning the soldiers down thirty miles short of their reservation headquarters destination. Not until October 11 did they reach the agency, where they discovered Meeker and eleven other men dead and the women abducted. Charles Adams, working with Chief Ouray, finally secured their release. Persuasive Ouray convinced the agency Utes to surrender in what had become a cruelly uneven contest against an enraged Colorado, the Army, and a national uproar over the "massacre."

Events moved swiftly as most Coloradans joined San Juaners in demanding that the "Utes Must Go." Previous negotiations in 1878 to remove them had resulted in the southern band's accepting a smaller reservation along the New Mexico border. They had adamantly refused to join northern bands, a wise decision considering the Meeker troubles. After the "Meeker Massacre," the only question remaining was where the Utes could be shipped. Coloradans might have considered it a great idea to dump them into Utah, but that territory objected and the West presented few alternatives.

In January, 1880, a delegation of Utes, headed by Ouray, traveled despondently to Washington. A new agreement emerged from these talks. The Southern Utes (Capotes, Mouaches, and Weeminuches) would stay put, but the Tabeguache and White River bands were to be moved to Utah to settle on the already established Uintah reservation. In return for this land concession, the government promised to pay long overdue annuities and $50,000 in new annuities once the resettlement was completed. Although some difficulty arose in trying to get three-fourths of the adult Ute males to sign the document, it was accomplished and the Utes relocated in 1881.

Ouray, who tried so hard to achieve and maintain peace, did not live to see this last tragic episode; he died in August, 1880, while working for ratification with the Southern Utes. Nor did he see the Ute lands declared open in June, 1882, and settlers moving into the area north of Ouray, his namesake town.

No peace came to the battered Utes. They continued to hunt in the White River area, which gained population slowly. This habit, along with begging, annoyed area ranchers, who failed to find the Utes either fascinating or colorful, despite easterners' attempts to picture them that way. A small fight between a hunting party of Utes and settlers in August, 1887, was fanned by the press and local hysteria into the "Colorow War," named after the leader of the band. This melodramatic fake resulted in the national guard's rushing in to join a local posse in pursuit of the hostiles. Before reason could be reestablished, Colorado taxpayers had spent over $80,000 and solved nothing; the Utes continued to hunt until the area was settled.

The Southern Utes found no peace either since Durango emerged right on their doorstep. Its residents proved every bit as determined to remove the Utes as those of Ouray had been a decade before. Once more the Utes were caught. As early as 1886 and 1887, bills were introduced into Congress for Ute removal, with no results, primarily because of resistance from Utah and the Indian Rights Association. Finally, in 1895, a bill won approval, which gave the individual Ute families allotments of land and opened the rest of the reservation to settlement. Not all the Utes agreed with this idea, and the Weeminuche band, under the strong leadership of Ignacio, moved to the western end of the reservation, becoming today's Ute Mountain Utes. The Mouache and Capote bands settled on the eastern end of the reservation, in spite of stubborn pressure by locals to move them west as well. The remaining Ute reservation was opened to settlement in May, 1899, with predictions of another Oklahoma land rush. No second Oklahoma materialized.

Even with the Ute hold on Western Colorado dwindling to two small reservations, the cry for their land refused to die. As late as the World War I years, articles and letters agitating removal occasionally appeared in the Durango newspapers, but no further action was taken.

Nor were the homes of the Anasazi, now part of the Ute reservation, allowed to remain "lost." Ignacio and his band found local Colorado women desirous of gaining control over the ruins to save them from rising vandalism. After fruitless negotiations with the Utes and Washington bureaucrats, the ladies brought the matter to the attention of Congress. Finally, Mesa Verde National Park emerged, carved partly out of and on the edge of the Ute reservation. The Anasazi and Utes had at last found a home.

Give me health
O Manitou
For all my tribe.

Give me strength
To be with thee
And be as one

Now do I breathe
the scent of cedar
sage and pine
In thy great land.[3]

Rotary snowplow at Cresco on Cumbres Pass around 1910. *Courtesy Colorado State Historical Society.*

7.
The Iron Horse Cometh

All winter had been filled with heavy snows, numbing cold, and blizzards. The weather had been so bad at times that the clothes the workers wore froze. The wind was particularly vicious, blowing snow through cracks in the rough-hewn cabins, choking one by day and piling up enormous drifts by night. The snow became synonymous with cold. Warmth dominated every thought — morning, noon, and night; if only the wind would stop blowing and springtime would come to the Rockies! Yet, there was a railroad to be built, and in spite of the elements, men of the Denver, South Park and Pacific Railroad labored mightily in the bracing air of the Alpine Tunnel, 11,523 feet high on the Continental Divide of the Colorado Rockies.

Throughout the decade of the 1880s, narrow and broad gauge railroads wound their way across or through the Continental Divide to the previously isolated Western Slope. Building them was no easy task; sometimes, it seemed as if even the gods were against them. Canyons, roaring rivers, and high mountain ranges had to be conquered; violent winter weather wreaked havoc on both men and steel, and the nearly impossible task of financing the mountain railroads had to be worked out. No matter. Despite all these problems the railroads, like giant worms or snakes, moved methodically over the rugged Rockies and into Colorado's Western Slope. Today their names are chiseled into the annals of railroad history: Denver & Rio Grande, Colorado Midland, Rio Grande Southern, Denver, South Park and Pacific, Moffat Railroad, the Short Lines of Otto Mears,

Crystal River and San Juan, and many others.

Most of the railroads did not last long, but they had a profound impact on the Western Slope, that promising but still dormant mountain paradise across the Continental Divide. Perhaps a stanza from one of Edna St. Vincent Millay's commentaries on the 1920s best describes the railroads in Western Colorado.

My candle burns at both ends;
It will not last the night:
But, ah, my foes, and, oh, my friends,
It gives a lovely light.[1]

The coming of the railroad to the Western Slope was similar to a key unlocking a previously unopened door. Who knew what riches would now be unearthed? The mining, cattle, and farming industries owe their beginnings to the railroad. Previously, all three had been struggling infant enterprises, fighting desperately to get off the ground. Weather, isolation, and distance had defeated every attempt. The railroad meant that supplies could be brought more safely and at less expense than by burro train or mule wagon. More important, ore, cattle, and farm produce could be shipped out in bulk and with much greater speed than on the backs of burros or by mule wagon. For the great freighters like David Wood, Otto Mears, and J. C. McClure and their courageous burros and mules, an era was ending; for the iron horse, snorting steam as it wove up, down, and through the mountains, a great new era was just beginning.

When one discusses railroads on the Western Slope, he speaks in hushed tones of William Jackson Palmer's Denver & Rio Grande, "the biggest little railroad in the world." William Jackson Palmer was from Philadelphia. He distinguished himself in the Civil War and was instrumental in getting the Kansas Pacific and Denver Pacific Railroads into Denver in 1870. He also had a dream. While other railroad men envisioned making money through an east-west transcontinental route, Palmer's eyes swung south. He wanted to tie up the Colorado Rockies with the ancient Spanish trade routes through New Mexico and even into Old Mexico.

Palmer called his new narrow gauge railroad the Denver & Rio Grande and started building south from Denver in July, 1871. The fledgling Rio Grande was revolutionary and unique for the time. Palmer dreamed of running his narrow gauge track to Pueblo, up the Arkansas River through the Royal Gorge, over Poncha Pass to the San Luis Valley and the headwaters of the Rio Grande, and then down that stream to El Paso, Texas. En route, feeder lines would run west to newly opened mining camps on the Western Slope and elsewhere, and east to recently settled agricultural regions. The Rio Grande was also unique because of the narrow gauge track it used. Breaking away from the conventional four-foot eight and one-half inch broad gauge previously used on most railroads in the United States, Palmer's gauge was three feet wide.

There was much logic behind the use of narrow gauge track on the Rio Grande and nearly all other railroads that operated in the mountainous country of the Western Slope. A paper read by Robert Fairlie of England before the annual meeting of the British Railway Association in 1870 caught William Palmer's attention and tipped him off to the utility of using narrow gauge railroads in the mountains. Entitled "The Gauge of the Railways of the Future," Fairlie's paper argued that a narrow gauge track would be cheaper to build, equip, and maintain and would be more adaptable to mountain regions where traffic would often be light. Less ballast, thirty-pound rails, navigation of sharper curves, the ability to handle grades nearly twice as steep as standard gauge engines, and less tunneling, excavation, and rock work were all testimony to the utility and fiscal soundness of the narrow gauge.

The narrow gauge offered other advantages. Financing, always critical and hard to come by in the high risk mining camps, was easier to get for narrow gauge lines in the mountains. In addition, in the competition to build into a new and promising mining region on the Western Slope, speed was important, and narrow gauge track could be laid down much faster than broad gauge steel.

Palmer's Rio Grande did not enter the Western Slope for a decade. Then, in 1880, a great new mining region, the Gunnison country, began to boom. The opportunistic Palmer did not dally. He purchased Otto Mears' Marshall Pass Toll Road for $13,000, and in September, 1880, had his workmen grading and laying tracks up the east side of the pass with incredible speed. Speed was necessary, for the Rio Grande was racing John Evans' Denver, South Park and Pacific Railroad, building through the Alpine Tunnel to the north, into the Gunnison country. Like an advancing army, 1,500 men, operating out of numerous grading camps, worked their way up the east side of the 10,846-foot-high pass, and down the west side. In their wake they left a ribbon of narrow gauge track and a mile of snowsheds en route to the Gunnison country.

Down the Tomichi Valley came the Rio Grande crews. August 8, 1881, was a red letter day in Western Slope history. At 9:30 in the morning, one of the first passenger trains ever in Western Colorado steamed into Gunnison, having easily outdistanced the still-struggling South Park. Palmer did not celebrate long; his men were already laying tracks to the north to tap the Crested Butte coal mines, twenty-eight miles away near the Elk Mountains. West out of Gunnison work proceeded without interruption on the mainline until the head of the Black Canyon was reached. Only then was Palmer forced to slow down. In the bottom of the yawning gorge, the Gunnison River pounded its way fifty-five miles—one of the steepest falling rivers in North America—before it left the canyon not far from present-day Delta. Palmer was not awed. His surveyors had determined that the railroad could be built down in the canyon for approximately fifteen miles to Cimarron. There, the canyon was impassable and the railroad would have to leave the chasm. In the dark depths of the Black Canyon, Rio Grande crews, with dogged determination, blasted a grade out of the rock walls. The work was tough, dangerous, and cold. During the bitter winter days, the rays of the sun hardly ever reached the bottom of the canyon. The cold was brutal and rarely did the temperature get above zero. The last mile of the Black Canyon cost more than the entire construction through the Royal Gorge. But the work went on, and finally on August 9, 1882, a year after arriving in Gunnison, the Rio Grande extended its tracks to Cimarron. The Black Canyon had been breached!

Beyond the Black Canyon, Rio Grande crews crossed Cerro Summit to the west and then had clear sailing as they headed northwest through the Uncompahgre Valley and the recently settled agricultural towns of Montrose, Delta, and Grand Junction. From Grand Junction, only thirty miles of track remained to be built before the Rio Grande passed out of the Western Slope and headed into Utah in December of 1882. The narrow gauge line constructed by the Rio Grande from 1880 to 1882 was part of its mainline and was responsible for opening the Western Slope to the rest of the world. Psychologically, its impact was enormous; thousands of people flocked into the beautiful mountain region and men with money opened up their pocketbooks.

Palmer's band of steel through the Gunnison country and Uncompahgre Valley in 1881 and 1882 was only the opening gun in a network of railroad lines he had planned for the Western Slope. Another narrow gauge line was laid down at almost exactly the same time as the first, and under similar circumstances. Deep in southwestern Colorado lay a rugged, foreboding mountain region known as the San Juan country. Laden with silver and gold, the San Juan excited William Jackson Palmer's imagination even more than the Gunnison country. Here, there were real riches to be had!

From Antonito in the southern reaches of the San Luis Valley in 1880, Rio Grande crews headed for the San Juan. Their route took them over 10,015-foot-high Cumbres Pass and through the titanic Toltec Gorge sixty-four miles to Chama, New Mexico. From Cumbres Pass to Chama, Palmer's men struggled desperately to hold the grade to four percent, but the indomitable Philadelphian continued on. "The railway heard the tales of the prospectors and miners and looked westward . . . toward the land of promise." And there were the mountains in the distance like a beacon, "canopied with perpetual clouds; in front were castellated crags, art-like monuments and stupendous precipices. Having allured the railway into their awful fastness, the mountains seemed determined to baffle its further progress." Where was the railroad going, and where would it end? "It is, apparently, a railway hopelessly gone astray, a sort of knight-errant railway in quest of adventures, a New Columbus, with cars instead of ships, in search of undiscovered realms."[2]

Worry not. William Jackson Palmer knew exactly where he was going. His Rio Grande Railroad was one with a master prospector at the helm, one that followed the miner and burro, headed for riches and adventure. With the coming of spring in 1881, the Rio Grande pushed on, bound for a new town on the Animas River called Durango. The new community, with important help from the Rio Grande, had beaten out Animas City, two miles to the north, as the major town in southwestern Colorado. Palmer's line arrived in Durango in August, but that town was destined only to become a supply, smelter, and railroad center. The silver mines lay to the north, deep in the San Juan Mountains. Following a brief celebration in Durango, during which huge quantities of beer were consumed, the tireless tracklayers of the Rio Grande headed north into the mountains toward Baker's Park, a broad 2,000-acre expanse with towering peaks on every side. There, at the mining camp of Silverton, were the riches that Palmer coveted.

Laying track between Durango and Silverton forty-five miles apart, along the banks of the Animas River, was not easy. Heavy snows in mid-December shut down work until January, 1882. When work was resumed, intense cold, heavy snow, driving winds, and the Animas River Canyon slowed progress. Finally on July 10, 1882, Denver & Rio Grande tracks were completed to Silverton, marking the end of Palmer's San Juan division and the extension of the road nearly 500 miles from Denver. Silverton, which had lived near the edge of disaster since its founding in 1875 because of isolation and high freight costs, was given a new lease on life. The population of the town increased and the sound of pick and shovel and blasting was heard more frequently in the surrounding mountains.

The tremendous building program of the Denver & Rio Grande was temporarily halted in late 1881 and early 1882. Money was running short and Palmer was facing tough competition from the infamous Eastern financial shyster, Jay Gould, who had taken control of the Denver, South Park and Pacific. Following a power struggle over new building programs which he wanted for the Rio Grande, William Jackson Palmer resigned as president of the railroad on August 9, 1882. An era had ended.

Financial problems continued on the Rio Grande and the railroad went into receivership. With the appointment of William Jackson as president in 1886, the Rio Grande again went on the offensive, this time against a new rival, James J. Hagerman and his broadgauge Colorado Midland Railroad. Hagerman had made a fortune developing iron deposits in Michigan's Upper Peninsula but broke his health doing it. To recover from tuberculosis, he was sent to Colorado where he regained his health and became the owner of several silver mines in Aspen and a small number of coal mines near Glenwood Springs. Hagerman planned to build a railroad into both Leadville and Aspen to tap the rich mines of both towns. This "rich, ambitious, and restless invalid" threw a mighty scare into the Rio Grande which was already in Leadville and which had always regarded Aspen as its own territory.

Despite its financial difficulties, the Denver & Rio Grande considered Aspen and the Grand Valley on the Western Slope so important, it decided to build anyway. In September of 1886, the Colorado Midland steamed into Leadville via Ute Pass and was preparing to invade the booming silver town of Aspen. The Rio Grande was shocked into action. In late October, far behind the Midland, the Rio Grande decided that Aspen was a "pressing necessity." The company's annual report of 1886 cited the significance of the Roaring Fork camp:

> Aspen is recognized as second only to Leadville as a mining camp, but its development has been seriously retarded on account of its practical remoteness, due to its separation from the railroad system of Colorado by high ranges of mountains. The heavy cost of wagon transportation has been enough to consume the profit on all except the high grade ore, and, as the wealth of the camp is largely in low grade ores, it is not surprising that the work in most of the mines has been almost suspended, except for the purpose of development, until the advent of the railroad.[3]

The race was on! Under David Moffat, who had replaced the tired and ailing William Jackson as president of the Rio Grande, the Rio Grande laid track at a frantic pace in an effort to catch up with the Midland, itself hurrying over Hagerman Pass toward the Fryingpan River and Roaring Fork Valley. Starting north of Leadville on the Eagle River at Red Cliff where the Rio Grande halted building in 1881, construction crews laid narrow gauge track during early 1887. Following the fast-moving Eagle River, the workmen put down steel rails through the present sites of Minturn and Eagle and arrived in Glenwood Springs in October. However, there was not a moment to be lost; the Colorado Midland was rapidly approaching Aspen. While crews finished the Glenwood Springs extension, the forty-one-mile route to Aspen on the Roaring Fork was the scene of frenzied activity as Rio Grande crews raced for the silver town. On the night of November 1, the race with the Midland ended as the Rio Grande rolled into Aspen amidst a wild and jubilant celebration.

The mayor of Aspen recognized the significance of the Rio Grande when he exclaimed: "Before the arrival of the railroad Aspen was . . . inaccessible to or from the outside world. . . . Our mines have been practically idle, waiting for the coming of the iron horse."[4] Echoing the mayor's sentiments, perhaps with a tear in his eye, a local poet proclaimed:

Then here's to our Aspen, her youth and her age,
We welcome the railroad, say farewell to the stage;
And whatever our lot and wherever we be,
Here's God Bless forever the D. and R. G.[5]

Three months later, the Colorado Midland steamed into Aspen with the first standard gauge railroad across the Continental Divide in Colorado. In 1889, the Rio Grande built down the Colorado River from Glenwood Springs to Rifle, a distance of twenty-seven miles. Then suddenly and dramatically, after the Rio Grande and Midland had battled tooth and nail to be first into Aspen, they buried the hatchet and agreed to work together. In 1890, a broad gauge track was constructed from Rifle to Grand Junction where it made connection with the Rio Grande Western Railway into Salt Lake City. Both the Midland and Rio Grande had the right to use the track. This turn of events forced the Denver & Rio Grande to add a third rail on its line from Pueblo to Leadville, over Tennessee Pass, and down into Rifle. This new broad gauge line, completed in 1890, became the mainline of the Rio Grande and gave additional broad gauge service to the Western Slope.

The major lines of the Rio Grande had now been built on the Western Slope; all that remained were spurs or feeders. A standing joke about the Rio Grande shortly after its arrival in Leadville was that if a man on the cast side of Mosquito Pass had a wagon load of pumpkins for sale, the railroad would build a branch line across the mountains to reach him.[6] In 1880, the Rio Grande built a spur from Leadville over Fremont Pass to the mining town of Robinson, not far from the headwaters of the Arkansas River. In 1887, a thirty-seven-mile branch connected the great silver mining town of Ouray with Montrose. After prematurely building a grade from near Sapinero to Lake City in 1881, the Rio Grande finally completed a narrow gauge line to the Hinsdale County seat in 1889. Other short spurs ran to Gunnison country coal towns like Floresta and Anthracite, to Pagosa Springs, and to the coal and fruit lands along the North Fork of the Gunnison River east of Delta.

The silver panic of 1893 had a disastrous effect on the Denver & Rio Grande. The closing of the silver mines, collapse of mining communities, and general downturn in the economy kept the road on the brink of financial disaster. But the Rio Grande had resiliency and staying power. As the years passed, much of the Rio Grande line was abandoned, with tracks torn up. The fact that the Rio Grande still runs on the Western Slope today is a tribute to the "biggest little railroad in the world."

During the early and exciting years of Western Slope railroad history, the Denver & Rio Grande had one serious rival, the Denver, South Park and Pacific Railroad of John Evans. The legendary South Park! Many narrow gauge railroads were larger and almost all were more successful, but the South Park today has become somewhat of a folk hero in Western Slope history. Its place in the sun was fleeting, but while its star shone, it shone ever so brightly. The South Park was:

> poorly surveyed, poorly located, poorly engineered, poorly financed, and in financial trouble during most of its history. It lost every serious competition in which it engaged with its various rivals. As one among Colorado's many narrow gauge lines, it succumbed thirty years before the last of them passed from the scene, excepting those not strictly carriers of tourists.[7]

No matter. The South Park's heroic, if naive, struggles against overwhelming odds, the famous Alpine Tunnel, and the spectacular scenery it passed through gave it an enduring place in railroad lore. The South Park truly was a railroad with charisma—a railroad named desire.

John Evans' famous railroad was originally incorporated as the Denver, Georgetown and Utah Railway Company in 1872. Evans hoped to build a railroad up Clear Creek west of Denver to tap the rich Gilpin County mines of Central City, Georgetown, Silver Plume, and Black Hawk. Then the road would swing north and west across the Continental Divide at Berthoud Pass and into the promising coal and cattle country of northwestern Colorado en route to Utah. Unfortunately, William Loveland of Golden had other ideas. His Colorado Central Railroad was built to the Clear Creek mines in 1872 and he controlled Berthoud Pass, the only good pass across the Divide into northwestern Colorado. Stymied in his efforts to build the Denver, Georgetown and Utah, Evans organized a new railroad in 1873 — the Denver South Park and Pacific. This narrow gauge railroad would run from Denver into South Park, through the San Luis Valley, and into the San Juan mining country. From that point, it would eventually be extended to the Pacific Ocean. Ambitious plans indeed!

Because of financial problems, Evans' South Park did not cross 10,000-foot Kenosha Pass into massive South Park until 1879. By 1880, tracks had been laid into Buena Vista, only thirty-five miles from the booming town of Leadville. From Buena Vista, the South Park used Rio Grande tracks to get into Leadville following an agreement between William Jackson Palmer and John Evans. The agreement also stipulated that the South Park would be given the right to build into the Gunnison country. Though nothing forbade the Rio Grande from building into the Gunnison country via some other route, it was assumed that Palmer's line would not.

All of this transpired before Jay Gould of the Union Pacific purchased the South Park as a feeder line in 1880. Palmer was staggered by this sudden turn of events. John Evans he could trust; Jay Gould he could not. The Rio Grande head immediately ordered his engineers to begin grading from South Arkansas City (Salida) over Marshall Pass and into the Gunnison country. The race was on for the Gunnison country and, in the beginning, it appeared the South Park would win it. As early as 1879, John Evans' surveyors had carefully studied Chalk Creek, eight miles south of Buena Vista, as a possible route toward the Gunnison country. Grading and track-laying followed during 1880; by December of 1880, tracks reached St. Elmo, in the shadows of the towering Sawatch Mountains.

The big question confronting the South Park en route to Gunnison was how to cross the Continental Divide. Major James A. Evans, chief engineer for the South Park, considered Marshall Pass and the

Chalk Creek-Quartz Creek routes and chose the latter. It was a tragic mistake. As we have seen, the Rio Grande crossed Marshall Pass a year later with little difficulty and maximum four percent grades. Evans, however, chose the Chalk Creek route as shorter and more direct. The decision not to use Marshall Pass cost the South Park the Gunnison country market and contributed to the ultimate failure of the railroad.

Building up Chalk Creek from Nathrop past Hortense, Alpine, St. Elmo, and Romley was relatively easy, but, oh, the Alpine Tunnel. South Park engineers concluded that 12,000-foot-high Altman Pass separating the Chalk Creek drainage on the east side of the Divide from the Quartz Creek drainage on the west, was too tough to build over. Ignorant of the tremendous obstacles facing them, South Park officials decided to tunnel underneath the pass at 11,523 feet in elevation. Another tragic mistake had been made. On the Divide, the South Park faced one of the most inhospitable regions in Colorado, "where the titanic battle of the winter elements becomes a treacherous demon, ready at any moment to engulf the puny efforts of men who would dare bring their steel rails into that forbidden domain."[8]

Initial estimates indicated that the Alpine Tunnel could be bored through in six months. The estimates were optimistic; it took a year and a half. Instead of tunneling through the expected solid granite, South Park construction crews hit slide rock and decomposed granite, all of it veined by streams of water. Work began on the Alpine Tunnel in January, 1880, and South Park officials soon became aware of the ferocity of winter at high elevation. Terrific blizzards battered the region, piling up enormous drifts thirty and forty feet high. Working at high elevation, buffeted by fifty-mile-an-hour winds and freezing temperatures which fell to forty below zero, South Park workers walked off the job in droves. Most never lasted more than three days. The severe working conditions forced the South Park to recruit men from the Midwest by offering good pay and free transportation to Colorado. Although only 400 to 500 worked at one time to bore the tunnel, over 10,000 men worked for varying periods of time.

Despite the savage weather conditions, work went on from both the east and west portals of the Alpine Tunnel. Finally, at 8:30 in the morning on July 26, 1881, the crew working from the west end broke through to the east. So precise was the engineering that the width of the eastern and western bores was only off 11/100 of an inch. Alas, the Rio Grande arrived in Gunnison just less than two weeks later, and the discouraged South Park abandoned work on the line from

November, 1881, to April, 1882. Work did continue on the tunnel during the winter, however, with the first engine passing through in December.

The Alpine Tunnel was a wonder to behold, a remarkable piece of railroad engineering. Some railroad men, in hushed tones, declared that the tunnel was handmade of courage, determination, and fortitude. The tunnel was 11,523 feet high and was constructed with a slight apex in the middle to allow drainage out either portal. Half a million feet of California redwood timber and an additional 1,500,000 feet of timbering were used inside the tunnel. The tunnel was 1,771 feet long and, with the timbered approaches at each portal, measured 2,500 feet. Long snowsheds were built on either end of the tunnel to prevent snow from drifting in and blocking traffic. "These were closed by mammoth swinging doors attached to supporting timbers by great strapiron hinges. . . . Maintenance men tended the tunnel and operated the doors on signal from the engineers of approaching trains."[9] The total cost of the tunnel was a staggering $300,000.

From the West Portal, the South Park began its final drive to Gunnison as spring began to thaw the icy mountains in 1882. Below the portal, a thousand feet down, was the beautiful Quartz Creek Valley. The three-mile section of narrow gauge track built by the South Park from near West Portal to past the Sherrod Loop was one of the unique pieces of railroad construction in the United States. A sheer rock wall had to be conquered before the South Park could get to the valley floor below. Engineers and construction crews used prodigious amounts of dynamite to blast through a route. Sixteen times, cribbing, in the form of fitted rock, was built to form a shelf for the rails. The rock walls were two feet thick and ranged from 29 to 550 feet in length. Heights ranged from eleven to thirty-three feet.[10] The most spectacular piece of rock work was the gigantic rock wall at the Palisades. The wall of hand-cut, fitted stones, placed and held without the use of mortar, was 452 feet long, 33 feet wide, and two feet thick. It still stands in all its majesty today.

When the South Park reached the Sherrod Curve, the grade lessened and the construction, at long last, became easier. The railroad was then continued into the mining camp of Pitkin and ultimately down the Tomichi Valley, and into Gunnison, thirteen months after the Rio Grande, on September 2, 1883. The South Park permitted itself a day to celebrate the arrival in Gunnison, paid for by the sweat and blood of its construction crews, and then was off and winging again. This time the objective was the rich coal fields up the

Ohio Creek Valley to the north, and perhaps the silver camp of Irwin farther north over Ohio Pass.

South Park tracks ran into the coal town of Baldwin, seventeen miles from Gunnison, during the summer of '83. That was as far as the Denver South Park and Pacific ever laid tracks. South Park crews had graded a road from Baldwin over Ohio Pass into Irwin, but no tracks were ever laid on the grade. Why should they be? The Rio Grande was only ten miles from Irwin, and besides, the once-promising silver camp was nearly deserted by 1884.

The South Park Railroad had one more act to play—one more trump card to show on the Western Slope and then its day was done. In 1884, disgusted over high tolls charged by the Rio Grande to use its track into Leadville, the South Park built its own line into the "Cloud City." Beginning at Como in South Park, the struggling railroad, showing its usual flair for disaster, built a thirty-four-mile extension into Leadville. Incredibly, the South Park crossed the Continental Divide, not once but twice to get there. The road ran from Como on the east side of the Divide over Boreas Pass to Breckenridge on the west side, and then over Fremont Pass to Leadville on the east side again.

The South Park Railroad, like the leading character in a Greek tragedy, was destined to fail in Western Colorado. An economic recession which hit the Gunnison country in 1883 cost the line much of its carrying trade. In addition, the Rio Grande proved to be a fierce and tenacious competitor. What the recession and Rio Grande did not do to the South Park, the rugged geography and weather did. The expense of keeping the Alpine Tunnel open proved to be prohibitive in the face of heavy snow, drifts, and avalanches which periodically closed the road. The most severe of the snowslides was triggered in March, 1884, by the vibration of a South Park train above the luckless camp of Woodstock. The slide roared down the barren hill above the town and smashed into it, killing fourteen people. Woodstock was never rebuilt. In 1888, the Alpine Tunnel was closed by a rock slide 250 feet from the east portal. Because of the cave-in and tremendous expense in keeping the tunnel open, it remained closed for the next seven years. The tunnel reopened in 1895, but not before four men were asphyxiated helping to siphon the water and clear the rockslide inside. In October of 1910, the last train passed through the Alpine Tunnel before it was closed to traffic forever.

The remaining years of the Denver South Park and Pacific on the Western Slope were years of reorganization, financial problems, and abandonments. And so the South Park passed into history, a legend in its time and ours. Perhaps Mac Poor, author of *Denver South Park & Pacific*, best eulogized the famous narrow gauge of the Rockies:

> The old South Park road is not really gone, for it lives in the hearts and memories of many of us. In the great tradition of American railroading it will always live. It will live on in thousands of photographic albums, in thrice times thrice told tales of courage and defeat and in that aura of romance woven in the very name itself—The Denver South Park and Pacific.[11]

One can only add, "Amen."

Deep in the isolated San Juan country of the Western Slope, four railroads controlled by one man had their place in the sun during the years just before and after the turn of the century. The man's name was Otto Mears and the railroads were his famous short lines: the Silverton Railroad, Silverton Northern, and Silverton, Gladstone & Northerly, along with his famed Rio Grande Southern.

Just over five feet tall and weighing 110 pounds, diminutive Otto Mears was a giant of a man in Western Slope history. Mears was the Russian-born offspring of an English father and Slavic mother. Born in 1840, he was orphaned early in life and came to San Francisco to live with an uncle in 1851. When Mears arrived he found that his uncle had left for Australia. At the age of eleven, in a strange country, Otto Mears was on his own. No wonder David Lavender, writing about Mears much later, declared: "Life had honed him down, both physically and mentally, until he was as sharp and as resilient as the stub end of a piece of baling wire."[12] Mears worked at odd jobs before joining the northern army during the Civil War. Following his discharge, he made his way into the San Luis Valley where he opened a general store and homesteaded a wheat ranch. In 1867, Mears began selling supplies to the miners of California Gulch and soon realized that what was needed in the mountains of Colorado were good roads. Before he was finished, Mears constructed twelve major toll roads and three railroads, all but one on the Western Slope. He was called "the pathfinder of the San Juan," and was of major importance in the opening of the Western Slope. He died at the age of ninety-one in 1931, and following his request, his body was cremated with the ashes scattered over the San Juan Mountains he loved so well.

The San Juan country is a geographer's nightmare. Rugged 14,000-foot mountains, many steep canyons, countless waterfalls, avalanche country par excellence, and spectacular geographic formations make up the region. One more geologic fact stands out: the San Juan is one of the richest mineral sections in the entire Rocky Mountains. That was the lure which brought thousands of prospectors streaming into Lake City, Ouray, Silverton, and Telluride in the 1870s and 1880s. The scent of silver and gold filled their nostrils. By the mid-1880s, only the high grade mines were operating around Ouray and Telluride because of the transportation nightmare. Otto Mears' toll roads simply could not profitably handle the ore; the cost of shipping ore by jack train was prohibitive.

The situation changed in 1887. From Montrose, the Rio Grande extended a thirty-seven-mile branch into Ouray, the "Switzerland of America." To the north, out of Silverton, visionary Otto Mears had begun building one of his short lines, the Silverton Railroad, toward Ouray. The new railroad, sometimes referred to as "the road which ran from nowhere to nowhere," followed Mineral Creek out of Silverton toward the top of Red Mountain Pass, 11,018 feet in the clouds. By mid-1888, en route to the top of the pass, the Chatanooga Loop had been constructed. Now it was off to the rich mines at Red Mountain, Guston, Ironton, and Albany. By the autumn of 1889, the Silverton Railroad had crossed Red Mountain Pass and reached the town of Albany near the north end of Albany Park, seventeen and a half miles from Silverton. The road to that point had climbed five percent grades and traversed thirty degree curves, more drastic than any railroad in Colorado had yet attempted.

As Otto Mears looked longingly to the north from Albany, he knew that Ouray, temptingly, was only five miles away. If only the railroad could be extended down into that town, the transportation problem would be solved. Alas, the five miles might as well have been a thousand. Even the legendary Mears could not devise a way to get the Silverton Railroad from Albany down fearsome Uncompahgre Canyon to Ouray. The difference in elevation was a stunning 2,100 feet over the five-mile distance. That would require an average grade of eight percent and no space was available in the narrow chasm for switchbacks or loops. Sadly, Mears turned away.

Otto Mears was no quitter. If Silverton and Ouray could not be linked up by the Silverton Railroad, perhaps another road could do the job. Thus the Rio Grande Southern came into being. The new railroad was put on paper in 1889 and construction began in 1890. Mears' narrow gauge Rio Grande Southern was a masterful piece of evasion which linked Ouray with Silverton by building 168 miles of track from Ridgway to Durango. From Durango, Mears would use Rio Grande track to Silverton and, from there, his own Silverton Railroad to Albany. The entire scheme was incredible, but Mears had an ace up his sleeve. He knew that the region he was building through, one as large as Connecticut, possessed great mineral deposits near Rico, Telluride, and Ophir, and in addition, had great farming, cattle, and coal possibilities. Furthermore, Mears knew the entire region had no dependable transportation. He meant to provide it.

The Rio Grande Southern connected the middle and southern Denver & Rio Grande lines across the state by joining Durango with Ridgway. The unique railroad cut through the western flank of the San Juan Mountains as it wound its way south and then east to Durango. Out of Ridgway on the Rio Grande line, tracks were laid over Dallas Divide and into Placerville on the San Miguel River. From there, it was only sixteen miles to the potentially rich mining town of Telluride where beautiful Bridal Veil Falls dropped 365 feet to the valley. Mears' tracklayers hardly stopped; south they came, building the famed Ophir Loop and crossing Lizard Head Pass in the shadows of the San Miguel Mountains. By late 1891, the mining towns of Rico and Dolores had tracks. Near Dolores in December of 1891, Rio Grande construction crews building from Durango and Ridgway met. The road was finished. The first train made its way from Durango to Ridgway on January 2, 1892. The silvery San Juan, at long last, had its railroad.

The silver panic of 1893, overexpansion, and the tremendous expense of operating a railroad in the San Juan country shattered Otto Mears' dream. The Southern never paid a dividend on its stock and, in 1895, was taken over by the Denver & Rio Grande. The railroad served the mines of the region, but also carried sheep, cattle, lumber, and passenger traffic.

With the coming of the Great Depression in 1929, the Rio Grande Southern again came face to face with extinction. In 1931, seven automobile rail buses, called "galloping gooses" because of the way they waddled down the track, replaced regular train service. Pierce Arrow, Ford, and Buick engines were used to power the "galloping gooses." The last rail bus was retired in 1950 and Rio Grande Southern tracks were pulled two years later. A romantic, fascinating, and unique chapter of Western Slope railroad history had come to an end.

Otto Mears was hurt badly by the panic of 1893 and so were the mining camps of the San Juan. However, when the dreadful effects of the panic showed signs of easing in 1895, Mears incorporated the second of his famous short lines, the Silverton Northern Railroad. Construction of the railroad began in 1895, two miles out of Silverton, and proceeded northeast along the Animas River. By June, 1896, it had been built past Howardsville and Cunningham Gulch, and into Eureka, home of the Sunnyside Mine. Because of low silver prices and tough financial problems, the Silverton Northern line was not constructed the last four miles from Eureka to Animas Forks until 1903. Amazingly, the road was projected past Animas Forks into Mineral Point to the north, over a 12,000-foot pass near present-day Engineer Pass, and down Henson Creek into Lake City. Looking at the projected northern stretch of the line today, one is aware that only the gods could have built it.

From Eureka to Animas Forks at the 11,200-foot level, only one coal car and one empty could be taken up the staggering seven percent grade. On the way down, if an engineer valued his life, he never took more than three ore cars. Many were the hair-raising tales told about trips from Animas Forks to Eureka. Talk about a wing and a prayer! The Northern served the mines near the Animas River for many years, including the Gold Prince, Sunnyside, Silver Lake, and Highland Mary, but when the Depression hit in 1929, the railroad's years were numbered. In the spring of 1917, the Northern made its last trip from Eureka to Animas Forks. Following the closing of the Sunnyside Mine in 1939, the Silverton Northern passed into history; its tracks were pulled up shortly thereafter.

The third and last short line railroad in the San Juan was constructed in 1899, and for once Otto Mears was not involved, at least at the start. The new railroad was the Silverton, Gladstone and Northerly, and it was started by a group of Silverton, Maine, and New Brunswick stockholders who owned the rich Gold King Mine at Gladstone, nine miles due north of Silverton up Cement Creek. Like the Northern, the new railroad also hoped to build to Lake City where it would connect with a Rio Grande spur line built in 1889. After a history of financial difficulties, Northerly owners lost the road through foreclosure in 1915. The opportunistic Otto Mears, seeing a good opportunity, purchased the track and equipment for only $14,600. Another railroad bit the dust in Western Colorado.

Far away from the San Juan country, another railroad drama began unfolding from 1886–1888, as James J. Hagerman attempted to build a standard gauge railroad over the Continental Divide to the Western Slope, something that had never been done. To many railroad men it was considered an impossible task. Tuberculosis had wasted Hagerman to a frail 120 pounds, but the bracing Colorado air had put him on the road to recovery. Hagerman's newly purchased mines in Aspen and Glenwood Springs were also healthy; a railroad would make them healthier.

Hagerman raised $7,000,000 from his Eastern friends, organized the Colorado Midland Railway, and began building. His road ran from Colorado Springs up tough four percent grades over Ute Pass to South Park and then crossed Trout Creek Pass to Leadville. Now the fun began. The Midland pierced the Continental Divide west of the "Cloud City" and north of majestic Mount Massive with the Hagerman Tunnel, 2,164 feet long and 11,528 feet high. On the Western Slope now, the Midland laid tracks past the spectacular Hell Gate and then followed the Fryingpan River into Basalt. From Basalt, the Midland built a branch line to Aspen and continued on to Glenwood Springs.

The Colorado Midland was one of the most remarkable railroads in Colorado history. It was the first standard gauge to cross the Divide in Colorado and ran at a higher altitude than any standard gauge in the United States. The most spectacular section of the Midland was on either side of the Hagerman Tunnel. The grades and curves on the east and west approaches were astounding. In clearing a shelf for the tracks on the west side, it was necessary to lower men in bosun chairs from the top of the cliff at Hell Gate. After drilling holes and placing in sticks of dynamite, the men lit the fuses and signaled frantically to be hauled away. John Lipsey recalled the difficulties of the Midland:

> Of course it was beautiful to see and to hear three or four locomotives pulling one train, snorting up the four "levels" of this Midland Loop and around the three horseshoe curves. But profits flew out of the stacks of the big engines, along with the steam, smoke, sparks and cinders. And the screaming flanges on the marvelous curves bit into upkeep money as well as into the curving rails. The towering, latticed horseshoe bridge was a lovely thing, but it required constant guarding to prevent its burning. Snow makes high hills handsome, but it blinds the trainmen's eyes, blocks tracks, and slides across the right-of-way and sweeps away rails and ties and roadbed. Frothy mountain streams may be trout-havens, but they can soften an embankment and in flood rip out culverts and bridges. Brake shoes wore thin, and wheel tires had to be replaced early.[13]

The tremendous problems faced by the Midland on either side of the Hagerman Tunnel forced the construction of another, lower tunnel just to the north. The Busk-Ivanhoe Tunnel, located at 10,930 feet, was built from 1890 to 1893. By December of the latter year, trains began running through the new structure. The tunnel was 1.78 miles long and saved $70,000 a year in maintenance costs. Severe financial problems, caused by stiff competition from the Rio Grande, the panic of 1893, and the weather kept the Colorado Midland in financial distress during most of its existence. The railroad was purchased by Albert Carlton, a Colorado Springs millionaire, in 1917 for $1,450,000. The following year, the Midland shut down operations for good; the tracks were pulled in 1922. Adieu, Colorado Midland.

Another broad gauge made its appearance shortly after Hagerman's Midland. The Denver, Northwestern & Pacific Railroad, more popularly known as the Moffat Road, was the dream of David Moffat, one of the truly remarkable men of Colorado history. Born in New York in 1839, Moffat worked his way west to Denver in 1860. Before the turn of the century, Moffat, rich from his banks and mining ventures, proposed that the Denver & Rio Grande, of which he was briefly president, build a railroad through northwestern Colorado and into Salt Lake City, tapping the coal, petroleum, and oil deposits along the way. Railroad men in the East, afraid of a new transcontinental line, torpedoed the plan. The angry Moffat left the Rio Grande, incorporated the Denver, Northwestern & Pacific broad gauge in 1902, and, alone, began pushing west toward Salt Lake City. It was not easy.

Just west of Denver, Moffat construction crews were forced to declare war on South Boulder Canyon, often called "the tunnelingest piece of road in the Rockies." Twenty-eight tunnels were bored in the canyon and the expense was a shocking $78,000 a mile. South Boulder Canyon was bad but ahead lay Rollins Pass which was worse. Unable then to finance a tunnel under James Peak, Moffat built a substitute temporary crossing over Rollins Pass (also called Corona), 11,680 feet in elevation. Safely across the pass and onto the Western Slope, the Moffat Road ran down the Fraser River, then down the Colorado River to Kremmling. Beyond Kremmling lay Gore Canyon, a rugged passage through the mountains of the same name. It slowed but did not stop the trenchermen of David Moffat. On through the canyon they came to State Bridge. At that point the Moffat line swung north into the Egeria Park country and along the banks of the Yampa River. The building was easier now and the Moffat Railroad reached Steamboat Springs in early 1909.

David Moffat was broke by the time his railroad reached Steamboat Springs; he had exhausted a $10,000,000 fortune. Once one of the richest men in Colorado, Moffat was now in desperate financial straits. While in New York City in early 1911, attempting to raise money to build a tunnel under James Peak and extend his railroad west of Steamboat Springs, the aging and weary Moffat, broken from his labors, collapsed and died. Moffat had been a man alone in building the Denver, Northwestern & Pacific. He received little financial assistance from former friends in Denver; E. H. Harriman of the Union Pacific, fearing a transcontinental rival, saw to it that Moffat got no money from New York. Attempts to raise capital in Europe also failed. In addition, the wild and rugged terrain and the fierce elements on Rollins Pass added to Moffat's burden.

Though Moffat was dead, his spirit lived on. In 1913, the old Denver, Northwestern & Pacific was reorganized as the Denver & Salt Lake Railroad and the Moffat Line was extended forty-one miles west to Craig. The Moffat Road was now 232 miles from Denver. That was the end of the line; the road never ran past Craig.

There was more to the saga of the Moffat Railroad. Denver desperately wanted to be the major transportation hub of the Rockies, but to get that status, it would have to be on a viable transcontinental route. The Denver & Rio Grande provided a transcontinental connection, but in crossing the state, the railroad traveled far out of its way. First, its tracks dropped 112 miles south to Pueblo. After veering west from there through the deep Royal Gorge of the Arkansas River to Salida, the railroad wheeled back to the north for 100 miles before meeting the Colorado River on almost the same latitude as Denver. This roundabout way over poorly maintained tracks would never let Denver manufacturers compete with other transcontinental shippers. The solution was a tunnel underneath James Peak and a link with a transcontinental line. Although a Moffat Tunnel was proposed many times by Denver, it was always beaten back by Southern Colorado interests, led by Pueblo, which did not want to lose its gateway into the southern Rockies.

A devastating flood which hit Pueblo in June of 1921, killing over 100 people, finally forced a solution. Denver and northern Colorado agreed to vote in favor of flood control projects for Pueblo if a Moffat Tunnel were authorized. Pueblo had no choice. The Moffat Tunnel was authorized and work on a 6.2-mile tunnel under James Peak began in 1923. In 1928, at a cost of twenty-nine lives and $45,000,000, the tunnel was completed at 9,200 feet in elevation, the sixth longest in the world.

The completion of the tunnel was not the end of the Moffat Road story. The railroad still deadended at Craig, 232 miles northwest of Denver. A transcontinental connection was needed. The Denver & Rio Grande, opportunistic as usual, stepped into the breach. The Rio Grande bought a majority interest in the Moffat Railroad in 1932, with its eyes on a thirty-eight-mile stretch from near Bond on the Moffat Road to a point on the Colorado River east of Glenwood

Springs on its own line. Only thirty-eight miles of track separated the Rio Grande from giving Denver its first good transcontinental route. On June 16, 1934, the last spike was driven on the thirty-eight-mile cutoff from Bond to appropriately named Dotsero, and the last chapter of the Moffat Road was finally written.

There were other railroads that ran on the Western Slope. The narrow gauge Aspen & Western ran thirteen miles from Carbondale at the juncture of the Crystal River and Roaring Fork to the Thompson Creek coal mines. The road operated from 1886 to 1892. In the same region, the Crystal River & San Juan, "affectionately known as the 'Can't Run and Seldom Jumps,'" a standard gauge, ran from Marble to Carbondale shortly after the turn of the century. The railroad carried the finest quality marble in the world from the great quarries on Whitehouse Mountain above Marble. North of Grand Junction, the Book Cliff Railway ran eleven miles to the Book Cliff Coal Mine in the shadows of the spectacular Book Cliffs. One of the most fantastic railroads ever to run on the Western Slope was the Uintah Railway, which carried gilsonite, a black hydrocarbon used in paints, asphalt, and lining beer kegs, from the Uintah Basin in eastern Utah to a processing plant west of Grand Junction. The amazing narrow gauge operated from 1905 to 1939 and ran along grades of 7.5 percent and curves which bent 66 degrees. "It is the most difficult proposition we have ever seen," said one ICC member after viewing the railroad. In 1923, a design engineer for the Baldwin Locomotive Works in Philadelphia viewed the modifications for a Uintah engine and proclaimed: "This must be an April Fool's joke, there can't possibly be a real railroad like this."[14]

The main engineering problem on the Uintah was crossing the Book Cliffs, the divide between the Colorado River and Utah's Uintah Basin via 8,437-foot-high Baxter Pass. This thirteen-mile stretch was one of the great railroad building feats in history. In those few miles, the tracks rose 2,012 feet between Atchie and Baxter Pass and then fell 1,437 feet from the pass to Wendella on the Uintah Basin side. The grades were 7.5 percent and 5.9 percent respectively. The road resembled a can of worms dumped indiscriminately on the mountain pass.

For every railroad that made it on the Western Slope, there were ten that did not. They were the famous "paper or ghost railroads" which were incorporated but never laid tracks. Some were fantastic ventures. Failure was due to geography, lack of money or, more important, to the collapse of a mining region the road had hoped to serve. Many dreams were shattered by ghost railroads that never ran.

The railroads—what value were they to the Western Slope of Colorado? Perhaps the greatest value was psychological. Before the railroads crossed the Continental Divide, the Western Slope was inaccessible, save by mule or burro train, its great mines and promising cattle and farming industry stunted by a lack of easy transportation. Pessimism filled the air. Then came the snorting narrow gauges steaming onto the Western Slope, exuding optimism and confidence with every chug of the locomotive. Spirits picked up, a new day had dawned. The mining, cattle, and farming industries on the Western Slope owe their lives to the railroad.

The railroads of the Western Slope also pioneered a new science of railroading. Running at high elevation, in heavy snow and numbing cold, the railroads were forced to find practical techniques that would work in the mountains. Mountain tunnels, long snowsheds, rotary snowplows, helper engines, loops, unbelievably sharp curves, flanges, and stunningly steep ascents and descents made many Western Slope railroads legends in their time.

Railroads and proposed railroads greatly affected the Western Slope. Economically, they could make or break a town; politically, they dominated communities; socially, they provided excitement and optimism. We can see them now—men of legend and steel running the snorting, straining mountain locomotives against the ice, cold, snow, and anything else nature could throw at them. Against all odds, they fought the elements and terrain of the Western Slope to a standstill; this, after all, has been their story.

Placer miners in Enterprise Mine, 1909. *Courtesy Martha Carr.*

8.
Bully for Mining

Amid the excitement of a railroad boom and good days for mining, came the catastrophic crash of 1893. Colorado has passed through few crises equal to the crash of '93; it engulfed east sloper, West Sloper, farmer, miner, urbanite, and ruralite. There was no harbor in the economic maelstrom. Banks closed overnight, businesses failed, jobs evaporated, savings vanished, silver mining prosperity withered, and the jobless drifted; the physical impact was overwhelming. Harder to describe is the psychological impact on Coloradans. It appeared that the state had been chosen as a sacrificial lamb for Wall Street and eastern and European monied interests.

The 'men of the hour' will do well to chance their future with the silver problem. It must triumph in the end. August 12, 1893. — 'Silver is Still King.' *Grand Junction News*, October 14, 1893.

So far there has been no suffering among the poor people in town. The town trustees at their last meeting instructed the marshal to give employment to men with families only, and let the single men rustle somewhere else. — *Silverton Standard*, July 22, 1893.

Those who remain in the town must take courage, there is a better time coming, and when they do come those here will reap a rich reward. — *Silverton Standard*, July 22, 1893.

There are many desperate people in all parts of the state at this time, and if you have valuables take good care that they are not stolen. — *Pagosa Springs News*, August 11, 1893.

A ray of humor brightened even those dark days. The August 18,

1893, issue of the *Pagosa Springs News* quipped: "Numerous Durango husbands are advertising that they will not be responsible for debts contracted by their wives. Rather tough on the wives during these hard times."

"War, conspiracy, betrayal"—emotional terms designed to tie the long festering silver issue with the crash and incite the battle. The number one silver state took offense at anything that adversely affected its livelihood. Tension that had been building for twenty years, whipped by skilled orators and impassioned editors, exploded that summer, and for the next three years monopolized America's attention and, for a decade, Colorado's. One's stand on the question measured his future in the state. Woe to the "gold bug," Republican, or those tainted with anti-silver heresy.

To sketch quickly what happened: in 1873 the United States stopped coining silver dollars, an action brought about because the world price of silver was higher than the government's established figure. Ever-alert Americans hoarded their silver dollars, and the coin virtually stopped circulating. Few noticed Washington's action, fewer cared, because silver miners were not selling to Washington; they obviously stayed with the world market. In the next four years, however, the world market price slipped, a result of increased silver mining and a decreased market. Suddenly the mine owners turned to the government, only to find that Uncle Sam was not buying at his once supported price. Thus the "crime of 1873" was perpetrated.

Western cries for relief resulted in the Bland-Allison Act of 1878, authorizing the Secretary of the Treasury to purchase between $2 and $4 million of silver bullion monthly and coin it into dollars. The Sherman Silver Purchase Act (1890) provided for the purchase of 4.5 million ounces of silver per month at the market price. The solution was fine up to a point—Washington purchased silver. What galled Coloradans was the lack of a guaranteed price; the bullion price eroded from $1.29 to 73¢, and the miner with his ore got less than that. What they wanted was a return to the once maintained 16-to-1 ratio between the price of silver and gold. The fact that gold sold at $20 per ounce would then have stabilized silver at $1.25.

To broaden their base, silver spokesmen appealed to the hard-pressed, debt-ridden farmers. Farmers had no real interest in a higher silver price, but the plea was sweetened with such words as "the money of the people" and "unlimited coinage will restore prosperity." In contrast, gold was pictured as the money of the rich, a cruel tyrant who depressed prices. These were emotional, transparent arguments, yet convincingly delivered and unquestionably effective. By the 1890s support grew. Then came the crash and in the scramble for a scapegoat, the eastern establishment and the Republican party seized upon the Sherman Silver Purchase Act. The purchase of silver, eastern Republicans claimed, drained the treasury, and undermined faith in the Federal government. A special session of Congress repealed the act over vigorous protests by the silver/agrarian spokesmen, led by Colorado's Senator Henry Teller.

With the stage set, the drama moved toward the 1896 presidential election. The Republicans, loyal to their interests, backed gold; the Democrats wavered, then, swayed by the generation's greatest orator, William Jennings Bryan, nominated him and espoused silver. "You city clerks and farming folks, you miners and cow-pokes," vote for Bryan.

> The silver sentiment is rolling over the country like the veritable tidal wave which it is. Everybody is joining the procession and the goldbugs are going crazy with grief and amazement. — *Silverite-Plaindealer* (Ouray), August 7, 1896.

> Our Religion! Silver First, Politics Last. — *Mancos Times*, September 11, 1896.

> In our next issue we expect to congratulate *President* Bryan. The tale will soon be told. — *Silverton Weekly Miner*, October 30, 1896.

The tale was told that November, but alas, Silverton never congratulated President Bryan. Colorado kept the faith, and the Western Slope voted overwhelmingly for Bryan. No presidential candidate before or since has equaled Bryan's percentages. His vote cut across all economic, political, and county lines. A sampling of county returns shows this:

Delta	1,565 Bryan	130 McKinley
Routt	1,300 Bryan	100 McKinley
Pitkin	3,020 Bryan	16 McKinley
La Plata	2,764 Bryan	85 McKinley

Silver, dead as a national issue, was alive in Colorado for years to come. The Western Slope's cry went unheeded in its first real show of regional unity.

Three years before, on another emotion-charged issue, women's suffrage, West Slope males had joined with their eastern Colorado brethren to grant the ladies the vote. The majorities had been far less overwhelming than Bryan's, and San Miguel County even marched off on its own, voting no; Garfield County approved by a mere eight votes.

All the fanfare and fervor clouded the fact that Western Slope mining continued to prosper. The San Juans easily shifted to mining gold, with silver as a by-product. Those districts unable to make the transition were faced with a shattered silver market, lower grade ore, and mounting expenses. Even within the San Juans, smaller camps collapsed, their mines unable to make the adjustment. Tragedy and despair stalked this land, but so did opportunity—with some limitations. Opportunity called from already-established districts and camps, opportunity circumscribed by rising corporate control and emerging industrial mining. No new Central Cities, Leadvilles, or Aspens, however, acted as safety valves for the disenchanted, the unemployed, the footloose.

The San Juans, meanwhile, became the Western Slope's greatest pre-World War I mining district, and San Miguel County was on its way to forging past Pitkin as the top ranked. Though arguable in terms of mining significance, Telluride surpassed Aspen as *the* mining town.

Second-ranked for a long time in Colorado mining, the San Juans rated only behind dependable Lake County and amazing Cripple Creek in the years 1893–1915. With superb railroad connections, well developed regional smelting, a matured supportive economy of agriculture and commerce, and abundant financing, the San Juans were also ready with plenty of ore. This would not, however, be a rush/boom phenomenon, the district was two decades too old for that. Nor would the entire district benefit equally; it narrowed down to the three major towns—Ouray, Silverton, and Telluride.

There were no more famous or productive mines on the Western Slope, nor, for that matter, in Colorado, than Ouray's Camp Bird, which averaged $1.3 million annually for the decade following 1901. Telluride's Tomboy is also notable, averaging just under a million for twenty years. Their new distinction gave rise to a host of other Camp Birds, Smuggler Unions, and Tomboys, whose developers were convinced that the name would bestow bounty on a hole and a hope. Naive investors fell victim to a reputation, a common speculator's plight. This custom had been prevalent for decades with every bonanza mine in Colorado and elsewhere; an "abominable, stupid practice,"[1] muttered the New York *Mining Record*.

Working for day wages, for absentee owners, and as only one member of a large crew was not the dream that motivated the Pike's Peak gold rusher or kept Colorado mining moving for the next thirty years. It did, however, prove the new reality of corporate-controlled, industrial mining. The poor man, the average miner, found himself frozen out of the market. He became a hired hand, no different from his counterpart in the steel mill or the eastern factory, only a tiny voice in the roar of an impersonal, profit-oriented business.

All the necessary components came together: technology in the form of machine drills and more powerful engines; electricity; college-trained mining engineers and geologists; physical plants worth hundreds of thousands of dollars; and investors who knew nothing more of mining than they had read in the paper or the promotional brochures. By the turn of the century, even a new miner was appearing from eastern Europe, confirming the United States' immigration pattern of the past decade.

James D. Hague, a noted mining engineer, examined the Tomboy property in 1896 on behalf of some prospective purchasers. The investigation included visits to the mine, sampling of ore, an examination of the books (smelter returns, etc.), and all property. What he found reveals the changed times. A 1,900-foot wire tramway connected mine and mill; the tram buckets were able to deliver twenty tons per hour. The mill, powered by electricity and backed by steam power for emergencies, crushed and amalgamated the ore, then treated it further. Obtaining water for the operation was a problem, so the company dammed a lake and built a pumping station and 1 ½ miles of pipeline to insure a steady supply.

Hague huffed and puffed through the mine, not an easy task for a 60-year-old New Yorker at the Tomboy's 11,500-foot elevation. He walked the 2,500-foot main tunnel, climbed up winzes, examined stopes, and came away convinced that if the price were right, his clients should buy. When they accepted his recommendation, Hague was paid $5,000 plus all expenses for his examination. They promptly (and wisely) hired him, and he became president of the Tomboy Gold Mines Company, an English-owned corporation.[2]

The individual miner's position was weakened in these circumstances. Where he had once worked with the owner, and then only to earn a stake to go out on his own, now he labored a 10- to 12-hour day for the company and its stockholders. The pay scale varied, depending upon one's specialization. The Silver Lake Mine near Silverton paid the following wages:

Superintendent	$8 per day
Foreman	$6 & 4.50
Carpenter	$4
Timberman	$3.50
Machine man (drills)	$3.50
Miner	$3.50 & 3.00
Trammer	$3.00 & 2.75
Shovelers	$2.75

Cooks at the boarding house received $3.50 and waiters $2. The wages might seem high for the United States of the day, but the cost of living was much higher in these mountainous regions.

Mining is a dangerous occupation in any era; the miners of the 1890s and 1900s were especially abandoned to the whims of fate and foible. Life insurance companies refused to provide coverage; some fraternal organizations at least offered burial policies, one reason for the surge in their membership in mining communities. The Caroline Mining Company inaugurated a company insurance program as early as 1895. The catch was a stipulation that all who joined released the company from blame in case of accident.

Other company-applied rules bedeviled the men. To insure a full boarding house, the Golden Fleece Mining Company near Lake City ordered all unmarried employees to patronize theirs. Even at this date the majority of the miners remained single; either their life style or occupational hazards discouraged marriage. Stockholders liked to have the boarding house turn a profit, an idea that sat uneasy with the miners.

Worker morale suffered under the long hours, trying conditions, and danger. Some resorted to the ages-old tradition of highgrading rich ore to supplement their income. Companies and stockholders preferred to call it stealing and adopted stringent rules and regulations to prevent such misappropriations of future profits. They even went so far as to fire whole crews if one member were caught stealing.

Management did not approve of unions, the only way for the miner to counterbalance the owner's domination. Local unions could not compete with the national organizations, though they attempted a few disjointed strikes. When the Western Federation of Miners organized in 1893, San Juaners helped launch it. This union for hard-rock miners quickly gained acceptance throughout the San Juans and much of the West. Locals were started at Telluride, Ouray, Silverton, Red Mountain, Henson, Ophir, Rico, and Durango, all of which combined in 1898 to form the San Juan District Union of the WFM. The miners' reasons for organizing were obvious: they wanted pay commensurate with employment dangers; safety and health laws; employment for union members; and, among other things, a home for disabled members. Hoping to maintain friendly relations with management, the WFM, nevertheless, proclaimed the right to strike. "Socialistic," "unAmerican," screamed the owners, having difficulty understanding why anyone with a job was unhappy. Battle lines hardened by 1900, closing a decade of increased labor/management tension and strikes.

When violence came, it was to the largest and most powerfully entrenched union and corporate-controlled district, Telluride. The "16-to-1" local there had even founded a hospital, but management remained unimpressed. Two stubborn groups, each determined to have its own way, clashed over wages, rules, personalities, and which was going to dominate. From 1901 to 1904 a series of violent strikes, centered in Telluride, rocked the San Juans. Men lost their lives, civil rights were trampled into the muck, court decrees were flouted, mines shut down, neighbor turned against neighbor, and militancy became a way of life. In the end management won, but at tremendous cost. Conservatively estimated, it cost three-quarters of a million dollars just to station the National Guard in the strike-torn district. The price in human lives, injuries, bitterness, and violated civil rights cannot be measured.

The reputation of the San Juans and all of Colorado, as the conflict hit Cripple Creek and other districts, was tarnished. Anarchy bred a climate unlikely to attract investors. That camaraderie which characterized earlier years was also lost along with that frontier faith and optimism. They vanished with yesterday's dream of making a fortune out of every little claim.

Lost in the shuffle had been the effort to achieve the eight-hour day; some companies were willing, provided wages were reduced proportionately. In the Dunton district in 1902, for example, miners and timbermen received $2.50 and board for the eight-hour day. The larger mines paid a little more, Silver Lake, $3 for miners in 1907. Long established custom required surface workers to put in a nine- or ten-hour day, still down from the earlier twelve hours. A six-day week was not uncommon.

Living conditions at the mines could be poor or quite plush, particularly at some of the large operations above Telluride. The steam-heated Smuggler Union's boarding house furnished electric lighting and a "cozy and homelike lounging room with a large open fire place." The food, Thomas Rickard observed, was surprisingly good as a rule. He knew from experience, having been a mining engineer and consultant for years in the San Juans. The companies usually charged $1 per day for board and lodging. Mealtime was a sight to behold. Miners "attacked the food with no restraint or manners," commented a startled viewer, shoveling it onto plates in huge quantities. "Ravenous" was the only word to describe their appetites, and they did not linger over conversation.[3]

Thomas Walsh, whom the Camp Bird made several times a millionaire, addressed the Colorado School of Mines graduates in 1908.

Summarizing the changed conditions in a speech that might sound patronizing today, he presented an enlightened approach. He advised his listeners, as future employers, to treat their men with humanity and justice. Employers, he said, should provide clean, comfortable quarters, wholesome food, and have medicines on hand. Money spent for their comfort, Walsh concluded, was well spent in producing good work results and the miners' appreciation and loyalty.

More idealistically, Walsh recommended having a "heart to heart talk" with the men and "fairly and squarely" presenting one's own case and theirs to avoid strikes. He advised trying to get on the best side of their nature, "To use a mining phrase, you will be prospecting in human hearts, and may discover beauties of character little suspected."[4] How Victorian this approach to labor/management relations. One can imagine how the veteran of local "16-to-1" and the labor wars might have reacted in 1903, if Walsh had tried his theory. One might also honestly wonder how the engineering graduates fared with such advice, yet it pointed in the right direction. The miner had to be treated as a man, not simply as another mule in the mine.

The San Juan was not the only Western Slope mining district prospering, just the most spectacular. In these closing years of the dominance of precious metal mining, other districts managed a brief last fling, but they proved evanescent and the era faded rapidly.

By the 1890s Summit County was old, at least for a mining region. A generation had passed since the Blue River discoveries. In those intervening decades, placer mining gave way to quartz, and several production years of over a million dollars were recorded. Throughout it all, men poked and dug in those familiar gulches and stream beds, convinced that gold, overlooked earlier, still lay hidden there. To the non-miner such faith appeared to be misplaced and nonproductive, except for those who managed to eke out a bare existence. Appearances aside, gold actually did remain in low-grade deposits. The question of the 1890s was how to move enough gravel cheaply to make profits greater than the effort and the cost. The problem was nothing new; miners of 1860–61 had wrestled with it, too.

No practical solution was advanced until Englishman Ben Revett arrived in the mid-nineties. A mining engineer, and an even better natural promoter, Revett studied the gold-bearing gravels buried forty or more feet below the valley floor; he found them of such low grade quality that huge quantities would have to be worked. Experienced in placer mining, he decided that dredging offered the answer and organized the first dredging company in 1897–98, backed by Boston capital. A new day dawned for Breckenridge.

Floating in its own pond, the dredge inched slowly ahead. A mechanical marvel of buckets, chains, pulleys, and gears, it could dig far into the gravel bank, work tons of gravel, separate the gold from the waste, and stow the rocks in a sterile ridge that marked its wake. For the next forty years, those clanking, groaning dredges shattered the mountain stillness. In the once beautiful valley of the Blue, they left behind a ravaged land. "Industry is always to be preferred to scenic beauty," one dredge superintendent reportedly commented. Today's Breckenridge resident might take exception to that remark.

Revett's early dredges proved too small and too light for the deep, coarse gravel they tackled. Neither he nor the others who started companies gave up, though; eventually they devised dredges that worked. Breckenridge became Colorado's dredging center, although its best production paled in comparison to California's. Dredging was not cheap, either in initial outlay or running expenses, and the season was limited by water availability and winter freeze. Some dredges did not last a year; others labored for a couple of years before giving up, swamped by too low returns and too high costs. There were never a great many operating in any case—four, for example, in 1909.

Breckenridge enjoyed a mild boom in the twentieth century's first decade. A special mining issue of the *Summit County Journal*, November 3, 1906, called it "faith rewarded" and dwelt on the fortunes being made. The years 1908 through 1915 were good ones, and those into the twenties were not bad. Thereafter, with the exhaustion of the available sites, that period clanked to a close.

Revett's dream succeeded, but monetarily, it returned him little. His success came more from his role as a promoter than as an operator—he did create interest and find capital. Revett pioneered in the use of electricity, all-winter operation, and is given credit for the introduction of bucketline dredging in Colorado. The monument to his idea, however, is not a sight the tourist, Coloradan, or environmentalist enjoys seeing now. Such criticism comes easily today; at that time, though, environmental concern took a far back seat to industrialism. Dredging meant jobs, investment, prospering economy, and promotion. When the Blue and Swan mining districts and Breckenridge seemed to be slipping into that fatal coma before demise, dredging promised a revival. More than that, it offered a more permanent future. Can anyone say that as a local resident in 1900 he would have rejected such prospects?

Without dredging, Summit County's mining would have languished after the turn of the century. Government geologist Frederick

Ransome reported in 1909 that neither known reserves nor potential new deposits offered promise of a permanent revival for lode mining of gold or silver. No dredges or anything else came forward to save Gunnison County, whose production continued the downward trend noticed in the 1890s. Aspen had similar problems and, if lead had not saved the day, its production total would have fallen alarmingly. In 1910–11, Aspen imported two deep-sea divers to help pump out the Free Silver shaft, in hopes of allowing the Smuggler, Mollie Gibson, and others to continue operating. The procedure worked, and for several years Aspen climbed back over the million dollar level. No one was helped by the silver price slump, which bottomed in the 50¢ per ounce range by the early 1900s.

The Aspen district had one more exciting moment, different from most of the rest of Colorado mining. Twenty-three miles from Aspen as the crow flies was the community of Marble. Nearby, the Colorado-Yule Marble Company quarried marble, which was used in the Colorado State Capitol, the Field Building (Chicago), and the Lincoln Memorial (Washington, D. C.), among other buildings. The operation and town peaked just prior to the first World War, then rapidly declined.

Mining in these declining districts was a far cry from what it had been in a booming Telluride or once prosperous Aspen. Starting in 1906 Carroll Coberly lived and worked at Ashcroft, long on the shady side of its life. Two daily papers, passed from one reader to another, served the whole camp. With no jack train at hand, Coberly had to go to Aspen to rent animals when he needed them. Any old-timer would have sympathized with his complaint that no amount of mauling would speed one stubborn burro which would not keep up. Also familiar was the domineering, know-it-all mining engineer (this one from Michigan), who arrived in the summer of 1907 to show the boys how to run the mine. He foolishly spent investors' money on mill machinery, selected a poor mill site, and then left when winter came, scared off by the snow piling up on his site. The company went broke after such extravagances. That company went broke, but Coberly and others went on; mining was in their blood.

Miners' attire changed little over the years; they still wore "long handled" underwear all the time, with overalls, "brilliantly designed" suspenders, a flannel shirt, and hobnail boots to complete their outfit. Winter and summer, their one consuming interest was "centered on mines, veins, and ores."[5] Reflecting back, Coberly concluded that, after all, it had not been such a hard life.

Carroll Coberly and his friends had few places to go, now that the hardrock mining era, as they knew it, was dying. Ghost towns already dotted the Western Slope landscape, tombstones of a generation—epitaphs of what might have been or what used to be.

A hard day's journey from Ashcroft, in Eagle County's Gilman district, provided a view of both the past and the future. Prospecting parties reached there as early as 1860, but not until 1879, in the aftermath of Leadville, were profitable silver-lead veins discovered near future Red Cliff and Gilman. Great promise that was never fulfilled marked the 1880s and 1890s for Eagle County; one reason was that bane of local mines—zinc. Smelters, unable to work it profitably, actually penalized miners for a too high percentage in ores shipped to be smelted.

Refined means of separating zinc and an increased demand for the metal at last led to its profitable mining. Production topped $200,000 in 1910 and hit a million dollars five years later. Eagle County had finally arrived; only neighboring Lake County, repolishing lost splendor with a zinc boom, surpassed it. Not to be outdone, San Juan, Summit, and San Miguel counties upped their zinc production. Primarily this was large-scale, corporate mining, increasingly based upon technical knowledge and victim to the whims of the world market. The old-time prospector and blast-and-pray type of mining had vanished, a relic of an earlier age.

Also newly profitable in Western Colorado's mineral treasure trove was uranium. In one of the most isolated spots in Colorado in the 1890s, west of the San Miguel River, prospectors kept finding a lemon-colored ore which mystified them. Tom McKee, Montrose photographer and part-time prospector, never forgot the hot, dusty, dry trips to prospect in Paradox Valley. Generations of prospectors who followed him came to know what he went through. The ore, finally identified by a French chemist as uranium, was called carnotite, after mining engineer and chemist Marie-Adolphe Carnot. This upset McKee, who wanted to name it after Colorado or Montrose. All this transpired about the same time the Curies discovered and successfully experimented with radium, which created interest and a market.

McKee, his friends, and others busily staked claims all over the landscape, and the *Montrose Enterprise* hailed the new "Uranium County."[6] Alas, it would not be, production exceeded the market. For the first, but not the last, time a uranium boom had busted.

Interest revived in 1910–11. The construction of a mill at the head of Paradox Valley helped, as did Federal participation, shown by Washington's involvement in the National Radium Institute.

Formed as a joint venture by government and physicians to obtain radium for medical purposes, the corporation operated mines and a plant for production and investigation of new processes. Private companies and individuals busily dug away too, hoping to reap a fortune in a market that relied on European purchasers.

Carnotite also contained vanadium, a drawback at the moment because the separation from radium proved troublesome and costly. Prospectors struggled with handicaps beyond the limited market and reduction expenses. Transportation reminded one of 1859—over steep, narrow, curving trails called roads—and the railroad came no nearer than sixty miles. Horses and mules tugged as they had for generations and were joined by a mechanical rival, the truck, which found the going tough under the adverse conditions. Freight expenses could bankrupt a mine before it got started. Water was scarce, sometimes a mile or more from camp, ruling out even the Saturday night bath. Generally, small ore pockets offered little lasting security, and the only profitable market existed for the finished product, not raw ore. Find and sell was the motto.

The end came abruptly; war broke out in Europe and as the trenches and barbed wire were extended, radium purchases receded. Eventually they stopped and nearly all uranium mining operations ceased. Prospecting followed suit and until the "boys" returned from over there, uranium mining was a war casualty.

Carnotite was not the only ore that captured attention in the Paradox Valley. Copper created a mini-rush that resulted in one famous mine, the Cashin. The little village of Bedrock got its start as an amusement and supply center for the miners. By 1910 the excitement had died away; local ranchers and freighters probably profited most from this unexpected market. Montrose, in fact, was considered an agricultural county despite the carnotite and copper activity and small gold placers on the San Miguel and farther east in the Cimarron area. Neighboring Mesa and Delta counties produced even fewer results in precious metals. Mesa County's Unaweep copper district, the best known, shipped some ore prior to 1913, when an examination by the U. S. Geological Survey found most of the properties idle. The two counties' total production of $17,500 through 1915 would hardly have been a week's worth of bragging for the Camp Bird or the Tomboy.

The San Juan activity and zinc mining kept the industry from retreating to a secondary position on the Western Slope by 1915. Mining, which had created, nourished, and broadened settlement, stimulated investment, and promoted the region, could no longer sustain that role. Exploitative as it was, mining had run a fast pace since the 1870s. Around the now decaying core stood the foundations of permanency — agriculture, urbanism, tourism, light industry, and transportation — a heritage to which the mining industry could point with pride. The prospector, his burro, and the old-time miner were gone; the dominance of the mining industry was also gone. Never again would its impact be as total or as significant to Western Colorado. While mining has continued to be a major economic and regional factor to the present day, the old ways, the old spirit, were mined out.

Throughout most of its first five decades, Western Slope mining took second place to the fame of east slope mining districts. Competition for investors' money and promotional advantage, initially unintentional, grew intense.

No Western Slope mining district or community could surpass or equal the wealth and glamour associated with Central City, Leadville, or Cripple Creek. Aspen came close; Telluride was too late and scarred by the labor wars. To attract money and investors took patience, as the San Juaners discovered when competing against Leadville; they had to prove themselves before the investors took them seriously. Railroads obviously reached the east slope districts earlier, since they came from the east. Better transportation and finances helped the east slope districts develop faster and thereby attract more interest and profits, which created a spiral that deprived the less fortunate Western Slope of money that might have come its way. Promotion, regional and national, favored a Leadville or Cripple Creek, not a Gothic or Hahn's Peak. Only Aspen bucked this trend successfully for any length of time.

Although the great days of eastern slope hardrock mining were also gone by 1915, its silver and gold mines had proved wealthier, its mining towns more influential, and its statewide influence the most significant. The Western Slope, too long a bridesmaid, developed symptoms of exploitativeness, an infectious case of second-class Colorado citizenship. Nothing fatal, it was symptomatic of a problem that would be repeatedly, and sometimes bitterly, confronted in the twentieth century. Western Slopers developed a phobia; they received the crumbs while the eastern slope, mostly Denver, took the cake. Some of the attitude was natural, particularly against larger, wealthier, and politically powerful Denver. Durango was not even a year old when it was hissing at that "selfish, greedy" town. Denver's location, though incidental to the problem, sharpened the reaction. During the 1893 panic, Denver banks stopped accepting "country" checks, which in-

117

furiated Silverton, among others. The *Standard* advocated not accepting Denver checks, "In time Denver may learn that she is not the state."[7]

A love-hate, need-repulse, praise-criticize relationship evolved between east and West slopes, typical of what occurred in several other western states and regionally between the federal government and the West. Time would tell what this portended for the still growing, still maturing Western Slope of Colorado.

9.
The Age of Coal

Coal. The name is not as romantic and exciting as silver and gold, and coal towns have not exhibited the charisma of their precious metal neighbors. Yet, throughout the history of the Western Slope, coal has been at least as important as gold and silver, and today it has taken on even greater significance.

Millions of years ago, a black, solid and combustible carbon was formed by the partial decomposition of vegetable matter without free access of air, under the influence of moisture, great pressure and temperature. The result was coal, billions and billions of tons of it, in Western Colorado. Suddenly, after many years of declining production, coal was back again.

From the beginning, coal had always been an integral part of Western Slope history. Hardy miners, many of them from southeastern Europe, worked in coal mines in such diverse locations as Durango, Crested Butte, Somerset, Cardiff, Coal Basin, Oak Creek, Redstone, Floresta, Marion, and many others. Coal production reached its peak in Colorado at the end of World War I, and then steadily declined, except for a brief revival during World War II. The reasons for declining coal production were many. Oil and natural gas made inroads into coal consumption; labor unrest, culminating in long strikes and violence, caused problems; and coal proved to be a major polluter of the environment. Many of the coal mines on the Western Slope went the way of the Colorado Fuel and Iron Company's "Big Mine" at Crested Butte, which shut down in 1952.

119

The revival of coal in Colorado and Western Colorado began as a barely perceptible movement in 1960. During the 1960s, coal production inched upward every year except 1963 and 1969. The energy crisis, vividly demonstrated by the oil embargo of 1973, dramatically accelerated coal production. For years scientists had warned of an impending energy crisis, but politicians and the American public were oblivious to it all. Shortly after the Arab embargo, the United States had its first energy crisis. Oil and gas prices shot up, long lines of automobiles waited to get what gasoline was available, the fifty-five mile an hour speed limit was imposed, and the cost of home heating suddenly skyrocketed.

The American people were stunned; in a nation of affluence not accustomed to doing without, the truth came hard. One thing was sure — with a dollar and twenty-five cent gasoline and $250 a month heating bills, the good life was in trouble. The only way to revive the American dream was to find new sources of energy. And that involved the Western Slope.

The coal mines of the nation have been described as the "Red Cross" of the energy industry. They help out in emergencies such as world wars and energy crises, and then step back in a standby condition until needed again. Well-planned growth has never been predictable or possible. The boom and bust cycles native to the coal industry fluctuated with the price and availability of other energy sources.

Since 1973, after a long eclipse, the age of coal has dominated not only Western Colorado, but also the Rocky Mountain West and the nation. What has happened since that time is reminiscent of the mining boom in Western Colorado a hundred years ago. This time, however, coal and not precious metal is the source of the boom. Major eastern corporations like Exxon, Atlantic Richfield, and Peabody have surveyed every inch of the Western Slope, invested millions of dollars, and have competed for the right to mine on federal lands. The ensuing coal boom has led to a population explosion in Western Colorado, the creation of boom towns like Craig, and a myriad of economic, social, and political problems for that region.

The United States looks to coal as a solution to its energy needs of today and the future. Because a great deal of the nation's coal is located in Western Colorado, that section has become more significant than ever before. But coal has always been an important product west of the Continental Divide, even if the nation has only recently recognized that fact. What is the history of coal in Western Colorado? What role has it played in the development of that mountain land west of the Rockies? As Al Smith used to say, "Let's take a look at the record."

Early travelers were aware of the existence of coal in Western Colorado nearly a decade before it opened. Coal was known to exist in the Animas Valley in Southwestern Colorado as early as 1872. Ferdinand V. Hayden became aware of extensive coal deposits during his geological expeditions in the mid 1870s. Sylvester Richardson, founder of Gunnison, discovered large coal fields in the Gunnison country in 1873 while on a 600-mile exploring expedition. Coal was discovered in the Grand Valley east of Grand Junction and in Coal Basin and Spring Gulch south of Glenwood Springs in the early 1880s. The extensive coal deposits of northwestern Colorado were discovered later because the region did not really develop until the arrival of the Denver, Northwestern and Pacific Railroad in 1908. However, as early as 1889, and probably before, men working for the Colorado Coal and Iron Company prospected for coal in the Yampa and White River country.

Most of the coal discovered was bituminous, but some fine anthracite deposits existed near Crested Butte. In the beginning, coal was used to power the railroads as they laid down their bands of steel on the Western Slope. Without coal, the early railroads would not have run, and the Western Slope would not have developed.

One of the earliest and greatest coal towns in Western Colorado was Crested Butte, gateway to the spectacular Elk Mountains, twenty-eight miles north of Gunnison. Located at nearly 9,000 feet in elevation and annually buffeted by heavy snows and cold temperatures, Crested Butte initially was the major supply town for the many silver camps nearby. But as early as 1878, coke was produced in small pits using pine wood as fuel. William Jackson Palmer, head of the Denver & Rio Grande Railroad, perked up his ears. With high quality coke available for future Colorado steel mills, Palmer and other money men began to think of Crested Butte as a coal town.

The future of Crested Butte as a coal town was secured on November 21, 1881, when the Denver & Rio Grande Railroad completed a twenty-eight-mile narrow gauge extension from Gunnison. By the summer of 1882, Crested Butte boasted a population of 1,000, almost all of whom were Irish, Scot, or English, along with a dozen saloons, five hotels, and a bank.

The Colorado Coal and Iron Company, dominated by Palmer, bought up 320 acres of prime coal land from early pioneer Howard Smith and opened up the Jokerville Mine just west of town in 1882. One year later, the mine was shipping twenty-two cars of coal daily, including four cars of coke. One ominous feature of the mine was a high gas content.

Like all coal towns, Crested Butte was dirty, foul smelling, and represented a picture of desperation to its miners. Yet, coal was king and the Jokerville was the major mine. Below the Jokerville were Crested Butte's prized beehive coke ovens. By 1884, the early coking pits were gone, replaced by 154 coke ovens made of brick and encased with stone. The ovens were connected by a large track which ran next to the openings, allowing the coal to be drawn to them by mule. The ovens were heated red hot before the coal was dumped in. After baking for forty-eight hours, the coke was allowed to cool and was then loaded by fork onto waiting railroad cars next to the ovens. By 1884, the Colorado Coal and Iron Company was producing 175 tons of coke per day.

It was bitter cold in Crested Butte on the morning of January 24, 1884, and the shifts had just changed at 7:00 A.M., at the Jokerville Mine. The miners of Crested Butte were about to experience the fearful cost of coal mining. At 7:30, a gas explosion in the Jokerville shattered the calm as well as the families of many miners. Fifty-nine men were killed in a mine that had never been safe because of gas seepage. That the Colorado Coal and Iron Company was guilty of gross negligence in the explosion was obvious. The mine was so dangerous that foreman John Gibson entered it only six times during the previous year. One miner referred to the Jokerville as "the slaughter-pen of the C.C. and I. Co. . . ."[1] *Harper's Weekly*, after interviewing many of the miners, concluded: "The mine is said to have always been considered dangerous. Experienced men declared it to be the worst they ever saw, the amount of gas generated being unusually large and very deadly."[2]

The Crested Butte coal disaster was the worst in Colorado to that date and shocked the people of the state. Yet, the disaster was all too typical of coal mines in Western Colorado and elsewhere. Ruthless exploitation of miners was common. A mule was worth more to coal companies than a man. After all, a mule cost $200, but a miner cost nothing. No group of men ever worked harder for less money under intolerable working conditions than coal miners. Many of the miners in Western Colorado were immigrants from Austria, Italy, and countries which came into being after World War I, like Yugoslavia and Czechoslovakia. With little money, no knowledge of the English language, and families to support, the miners did what they were told. Most were brutally exploited by mining companies. Living in company towns, paid with company scrip, the miners lived a marginal existence and often worked with the strength of desperation. They worked in gaseous, unsafe mines, developed black lung disease, were cheated in their pay, and died or were crippled in terrible accidents.

Whatever their background, the coal miners became hardened and disciplined by generation after generation of adversity. They became as hard and solid as the mountains they worked in. We owe them a debt of gratitude that can never be repaid. From the fading ferment of the past can still be heard the coal miner's refrain: "Sixteen tons and what do I get, another day older and deeper in debt; St. Peter don't you call me 'cause I can't go, I owe my soul to the company store."

The Jokerville Mine never reopened after the disaster. Instead, ten years later, the famed Big Mine was opened by the newly formed Colorado Fuel and Iron Company. During its first fifteen years of operation, the Big Mine produced 2,000,000 tons of coal and 500,000 tons of coke.

Crested Butte's Big Mine was only one of nine coal mines which dotted the surrounding mountains turning out bituminous, anthracite, and coking coal. Denver & Rio Grande engineer Lewis Lathrop remembered:

> Half a dozen coal mines worked full blast. Both anthracite and soft coal poured in never-ending streams from the surrounding mountains. . . . Long banks of coke ovens made the night sky lurid with leaping red flames and the sickening-sweet odor of coal being baked into coke hung heavily over the snow-covered town.[3]

Between 800 and 900 miners doggedly turned out many millions of tons of coal in and around Crested Butte. It was a common sight to see 100-car Denver & Rio Grande coal trains steaming through the East River Valley heading for the tough pull over Marshall Pass and thence to the Colorado Fuel and Iron steel mills at Pueblo. At the anthracite mine at Floresta, eleven miles west of Crested Butte, the largest coal breaker west of Pennsylvania was constructed in 1898 at a cost of $98,000.

By 1952, when the Big Mine shut down, all of the Crested Butte coal mines were history and the age of coal seemed at an end. High transportation costs and competition from gas and oil marked the end of an era — or did it?

Eight miles southwest of Crested Butte, along the banks of Carbon Creek, the little coal town of Kubler came into being in the midst of bituminous coal deposits in 1881. The Kubler mine operated almost continuously until 1913 when it shut down. It reopened many years later but only for a short time. Kubler was a small town with a small coal mine and was rather insignificant except for the fact that it was owned by the Rocky Mountain Fuel Company. And therein lies the significance. From 1927 to 1951, the president of the Rocky

Mountain Fuel Company was one of the great figures in all of Colorado history. Josephine Roche was a Vassar and Columbia University graduate who became a progressive reformer after the turn of the century, serving as Denver's first female police officer, working in the famed Denver Juvenile Court under Judge Ben Lindsey, and finally, taking over for her father as president of Rocky Mountain Fuel.

Josephine Roche's task was a large one; she was now the head of the second largest coal company in Colorado. Following the killing of seven strikers by company guards at the Columbine Mine near Lafayette on November 8, 1927, Miss Roche went to the mine and ordered all company guards disarmed. Thus started a new and unheard of relationship between the company she now headed and her workers. In 1928, Rocky Mountain Fuel became the first coal company to recognize the United Mine Workers. Josephine Roche dedicated herself to fight the Rockefeller millions in the coal mines and to recognize decency and humanity within labor. Her motto was: "to substitute reason for violence, confidence for misunderstanding, integrity and good faith for dishonesty."[4] She paid her workers seven dollars a day, an unheard of sum then and they responded with the highest per miner coal production in Colorado. She insisted on decent housing for her miners, built schools, and insisted on tough safety standards in her mines. In an industry that heretofore had been barbaric and vicious in its treatment of miners, Josephine Roche was a breath of fresh air. When she died at the age of ninety-one in 1976, she was mourned by the common man — the miners who worked for her at Kubler and other coal mines throughout the state.

Near Durango in southwestern Colorado exists a coal field approximately seventy-five by one hundred miles. Initially used by local residents, the coal became very important when the Denver & Rio Grande Railroad arrived and a thriving smelting industry was created. Railroad and smelting operations needed coal, and a promising new industry seemed to be on the horizon. Coke ovens were soon constructed and more coal mines were opened south and southwest of Durango. Early coal production was used locally because of Durango's isolated location and high transportation costs.

During the 1890s, despite the Panic of '93, coal mining expanded in the San Juan country. The completion of Otto Mears' Rio Grande Southern Railroad to Rico, Telluride, and Ridgway opened new markets near some fine coal deposits. The small hamlet of Porter became Durango's first satellite coal camp and the leading coal producer of the region for years. This claim was only of local significance, however, since Durango's peak coal production in 1907 — 189,000 tons —

was only two percent of the state total. The Porter coal mine employed seventy miners at its peak; the coal deposits were limited there, and the mine shut down in 1908. Luckily, the Perins coal mine, west of Durango, and a thousand feet higher, picked up the slack and saved the local industry. The town of Perins, 200 strong, grew up around the mine. A declining demand for coal, exhausted deposits, and antiquated methods of mining led to the demise of Perins in 1926.

Hesperus, twelve miles west of Durango, began as a coal mining community in the 1890s and came into its own with the arrival of the Rio Grande Southern. Southwest of Durango in nearby Hay Gulch there existed (until recently) living proof that the free enterprise system could still work in the coal industry unencumbered by federal red tape. Violet Smith is seventy-three years old, six feet tall, weighs 185 pounds, and operated her King Coal Mine with a few hired hands without federal advice from 1936 until 1977–78. At that time she sold out and gave up active management.

She is a folk hero in La Plata County and is well known to federal coal inspectors in the West. Violet Smith did not like the federal government telling her how to run her business. She chased a series of federal inspectors off her land in the last decade, armed with a pick handle and butcher knife. They stopped coming back. Believing that mine safety rules were written by faceless bureaucrats who never saw a small coal mine, Violet refused to follow unreasonable and non-applicable regulations. "They wanted me to do things like build a bathhouse next to the mine for God's sake. My house is next to the mine. What the hell would I need with a bathhouse?"[5]

Violet Smith's King Coal Mine never experienced a major accident or injury, the best proof of all that her mine was safe. A sign on her property warned: "No inspectors allowed on this property. This is our property. We are capable of minding our own business. King Coal Mine." Several years ago, Secretary of the Interior Rogers Morton threatened to come personally to Hay Gulch to force Violet Smith to obey federal coal regulations. Violet "told him to get his rear end on out here if he thought he was big enough."[6] Morton did not show up and neither did any other federal officials who perhaps decided that discretion was the better part of valor. Violet Smith has been and still is a testimonial to the power of the individual against the vast bureaucracy of the federal government. She personifies the popular phrase from the movie "Network": "I'm mad as hell and I'm not going to take it anymore."

The coal mines of southwestern Colorado were never more than a regional operation. Small deposits and isolation handicapped any efforts at expansion. The situation is still true today. The sites of Perins and Porter are marked only by mine dumps and foundations, ghosts of another era.

Many years before Crested Butte and Floresta were settled, Ute Indians found their way into the Elk Mountains by way of a trail up the North Fork of the Gunnison River and over 10,007-foot high Kebler Pass. The North Fork country, pioneered by Enos Hotchkiss, Sam Wade, and others in the early 1880s, consisted of cattle ranches and fruit farms by the turn of the century. Coal had been discovered in the region in the early 1880s, and during the next decade a few blacksmiths packed the black fuel out on horseback and sleds. Because of the isolation and lack of a market, coal had been all but forgotten along the North Fork by 1900.

When the Denver & Rio Grande Railroad constructed a narrow gauge line from Delta up the North Fork of the Gunnison River to Somerset in 1902, coal suddenly became an important product. Now for the first time, easy transportation was available. Soon the coal towns of Bowie, Somerset, Oliver, and Bardine sprang to life within a stretch of ten miles near the head of the North Fork. Somerset, named for a coal camp in Pennsylvania, was the largest of the camps. The Colorado Fuel and Iron Company quickly bought up the coal in the area and turned Somerset into a company town following the pattern of Crested Butte. Somerset was almost completely isolated from Gunnison County of which it was a part. Not until the Kebler Pass road was completed to Crested Butte in 1919 did Somerset and its satellite coal camps have good access to Gunnison County.

From a small town consisting of eighty tents and a work force of seventy-five men in 1903, Somerset grew rapidly during the first decade of the twentieth century. The boom years of the North Fork coal town came during World War I when the demand for coal was high. More than 300 miners dug coal from the underground caverns. From the Somerset mine alone, 1,000 to 1,200 tons of coal were produced daily. Today, the Somerset mine is owned by United States Steel and turns out 2,000 tons of coal a day. Underground fires still burn in mines near Somerset. Steam and smoke spurt from the hills during all seasons of the year, justifying the Utes' name for the region—"Fire Mountain." Geologists tell us that Fire Mountain may continue to burn for a thousand years. Today, Somerset has slipped toward oblivion, with many residents moving to new homes in the lower end of the North Fork Valley. Only recently were the remaining residents assured they would not be forced out of their homes by the construction of a new highway.

Dozens of small coal mines from Delta to Bardine operated along the North Fork before and after the turn of the century, providing fuel for an increased local population. However, many of the mines only operated sporadically and production was low. Today, the situation has changed dramatically. Along a fifteen-mile stretch from Paonia past Somerset, thousands of tons of coal are being dug every day. This is an amazing revival of an industry that almost became extinct in the North Fork Valley in the 1950s. Some of the coal mined stays in the area to provide heat; a larger volume is shipped to Utah steel mills; but the greatest amount of coal makes its way in long unit trains to generate electrical power in other states.

In the North Fork Valley five huge coal mines are engaged in mining large seams of black rock formed by compressed vegetative matter from the days of the dinosaurs. More mines are expected as the demand and cost of energy soar. Two of the mines, Colorado Westmoreland's Orchard Valley mine at Paonia and Sunflower Energy's Blue Ribbon mine along Hubbard Creek, northeast of Bowie, stand in stark contrast to the famous fruit orchards of the North Fork which surround them. Nearby, operating from old mines which have existed for decades are three mining ventures in Gunnison County; U. S. Steel's Somerset mine at Somerset, the Bear Coal mine to the east, and farther east the Hawk's Nest mine operated by Western Slope Carbon Inc. Expected to join the group in 1980 is ARCO (Atlantic Richfield), which will mine the ridge between the North Fork and Minnesota Creek near Paonia. ARCO also has plans for its own housing community near Paonia for a work force of 500 miners. ARCO's operation will produce 2,500,000 tons of coal per year, eclipsing the combined current production of an estimated 1,700,000 tons of coal in the valley by the other five mines.

Dramatic changes have taken place in the North Fork Valley during the 1970s and more are sure to come. The tremendous increase in coal production is but a harbinger of more mines and more coal in the future. Many more millions of tons of coal, many on federal lands, exist in the North Fork country and have coal companies green with envy. Accompanying the increase in coal production is an increase in population. Nearly 700 miners are presently employed in the North Fork coal mines and another 500 to 600 will soon be employed by ARCO. Because of the recent boom in North Fork coal mining, Delta County's population is projected to increase by 3,800 people by 1980; 11,950 by 1985; and 16,800 by 1990. This means more schools, improved roads, additional water and sewage facilities, and all the other services which come with increased population. In addition, coal silo conveyors, storage silos, rail loadout facilities, power plants, improved and expanded rail facilities, and unit trains will irrevocably alter the landscape and style of life in the North Fork Valley. One thing is certain, things will never be the same again.

North of the North Fork Valley, past the muddy country and over surprisingly low McClure Pass, one enters the stunningly beautiful Crystal River Valley. Long noted for its world-famous marble deposits and picturesque landscape, the valley also has had a history of coal production. That history takes us to John Cleveland Osgood, a legendary titan of corporate enterprise, who was responsible for the development of coal in and near the Crystal River Valley.

Osgood was born in Brooklyn, New York, in 1851. At the age of nineteen, trained as a bookkeeper, he left New York for Iowa. There he soon became involved with the White Breast Coal Company and Chicago, Burlington & Quincy Railroad and was sent to Colorado to investigate the coal resources of the state. Osgood liked what he saw and quickly moved to Colorado. In 1892, he was instrumental in establishing the Pueblo-based Colorado Fuel and Iron Company. As president of the C.F.&I., which owned extensive coal lands across the state, Osgood made up his mind to create an ideal, clean mining community. He had seen the run-down, filthy, and squalid camps of coal miners in the East and had observed the quiet desperation of men who died before their time. He wanted a better way of life for his miners in Colorado.

Midway between Carbondale on the Roaring Fork River and Marble on the Crystal, Osgood built his ideal mining community — Redstone. But first things first. North and west from Redstone, near the headwaters of Coal Creek, lay Coal Basin, site of extensive coal deposits and superior coking coal at 9,500 feet in elevation. In 1898 Osgood began developing Coal Basin, the source of coal that was to be coked at Redstone. Osgood's C.F.&I. employed 265 miners, who produced just over 1,000,000 tons of coal from 1898 to 1909. Coal Basin[7] became a model coal mining community with over seventy large cottages to house the men, a fine clubhouse for entertainment, a library, school, good medical facilities, and a fine safety record among the miners.

The major problem confronting Coal Basin was transportation; how could one navigate the steep grades and winding canyon up Coal Creek to the coal deposits? Osgood was equal to the task. From 1899 to 1900, a twelve-mile narrow gauge, highline railroad was built from

Redstone into Coal Basin. At Redstone, the line connected with the broad gauge Crystal River Railroad which, in turn, ran into the Denver & Rio Grande at Carbondale. Osgood's great desire to reach Coalbasin is borne out by his construction of the highline. A train of thirteen cars was able to straighten out only once between Coal Basin and Redstone and then only for a short distance. The average grade on the highline was 3.6 percent with a maximum grade of 4.4 percent. Maximum curvature was forty degrees. The railroad ascended 2,242 feet in twelve miles.

The coal from Coal Basin was brought to Redstone where it was washed, screened, and transformed into coke in Redstone's 249 coke ovens and then shipped to the C.F.&I. steel mills in Pueblo. After the railroad reached Redstone, Osgood began developing "The Ruby of the Rockies." Three hundred people lived in Redstone, mostly the men who worked the beehive coke ovens. They lived in luxury compared to other miners. Eighty-seven company houses resembled Swiss chalets. The Redstone Inn housed bachelor employees and included a barber shop, electric lights, hot and cold water, a laundry, telephones, a reading room, and steam heat. A clubhouse was also built, complete with showers and lockers. Two miles from Redstone, Osgood built his own home, Cleveholm, a massive and luxurious forty-two-room castle. Completed in 1903, Cleveholm was lush with baronial opulence. The floors of the huge rooms were covered with priceless oriental rugs. Woodwork was of solid mahogany, ceilings boasted gold leaf, and crystal chandeliers hung with stunning elegance.

The entire cost of Redstone was $3,000,000, an expensive social experiment. Cleveholm alone cost approximately $700,000. The completion of Osgood's manor was the pinnacle of his career. Everything went downhill from there. In 1903 he lost control of the C.F.&I. to John D. Rockefeller and George Gould. Two years after the severe panic of 1907, the Coal Basin mine and Redstone coke ovens shut down because of economic difficulties. The heartbroken Osgood left Redstone in 1913 with the village deserted. Still a rich man, he traveled widely for the next twelve years but could not forget his beautiful home in the Crystal River Valley. In 1925, stricken with cancer, he returned home to die. The end came on January 4, 1926, at Cleveholm. An idealist of sorts, Osgood was ahead of his time in labor-management relations. His ashes were scattered in the valley he loved so much.

The growth of a Western steel industry during World War II and the extensive high quality coal deposits which remained led to renewed interest in Coal Basin in the 1950s. The Mid-Continent Coal and Coke Company bought up the coal deposits, constructed a new road to replace the old highline railroad, and began mining in 1953. Today, Mid-Continent operates five mines around Coal Basin; the combined coal production per year is nearly 1,000,000 tons or nearly as much as the C.F.&I. was able to scratch out of the region in its near-decade there. Instead of railroad cars carrying the coal, huge trucks transport the black diamonds to the railroad at Carbondale.

North of Coal Basin, en route to Glenwood Springs, another Western Slope coal region sprang into prominence during the 1880s when the Roaring Fork and Crystal River regions were in their infancy. In 1883, Walter Devereux was a young Princeton- and Columbia-trained mining engineer working in Aspen. Devereux had been brought to Aspen by Jerome Wheeler to manage some silver mines and to construct a smelter. To smelt the silver ore adequately, Devereux needed coal, and in 1883 he set out on an exploring expedition. He did not need to travel far. Just west of Aspen, near Glenwood Springs, he found extensive coal deposits along Thompson Creek, Four Mile Creek, South Canyon Creek, and Jerome Park. Devereux quickly formed the Grand River Coal and Coke Company and soon six- and eight-horse teams were freighting coal to Aspen. When the Denver & Rio Grande and Colorado Midland railroads arrived in Aspen in 1887 and 1888, the transportation of coal became easier and cheaper, leading to further development. If silver was queen in the Roaring Fork Valley, coal certainly would be the royal escort.

As trainloads of coal rolled into Aspen to provide power for smelters, steel mills also got into the act. The Colorado Fuel and Iron Company needed coke for its blast furnaces. The great demand for coal led to the creation of several small coal towns south of Glenwood Springs. Cardiff, Sunlight, Marion, and Spring Gulch all began as Grand River coal and coke towns in 1887. Cardiff, two miles south of Glenwood Springs along the banks of the Roaring Fork, was chosen as the location of a coal-coking industry following the arrival of the Colorado Midland Railroad in 1887. Eventually, 240 coke ovens were constructed and Cardiff, usually shrouded by a haze of smoke from the ovens, became an important coal town.

Sunshine (now called Sunlight), located approximately seven miles south of Cardiff near the head of Fourmile Creek, also began in 1887 as a coal town. The Grand River Coal and Coke Company sold its mines and coke ovens at Cardiff to the C.F.&I. in 1892, so Sunshine became a company town in that year. The mine operated sporadically through 1917; the Rocky Mountain Fuel Company leased the mine in 1907 and continued to dig coal for several more years. Farther south near Jerome Park, the little coal camp of Marion began, also in 1887. Marion employed 100 miners at its peak and survived until just before World War I. For a short time, the little camp had fifty coke ovens, but soon gave way to Cardiff. Spring Gulch was the last coal town of the region and, aside from Cardiff, was the largest. Over 100 Austrian and Italian miners worked there in 1890. Like the other nearby coal camps, Spring Gulch closed its doors about the time of World War I.

The Colorado Fuel and Iron Company produced 142,000 tons of coal from the Union Mine between Marion and Spring Gulch and 3,371,000 tons of coal from the Spring Gulch mine from 1887 to 1912. Today, the Anschutz Coal Company owns the coal lands from Spring Gulch to Thompson Creek to the south and is mining coal. The company hopes to reach full production of 1,000,000 tons of coal per year in the very near future. Just west of Glenwood Springs, along South Canyon Creek, there is talk of another major coal development. Plans are afoot to develop the steeply-pitched, smoldering coal seams of the Grand Hogback. The development would be a multimillion dollar operation capable of mining 1,000,000 tons of coal per year. Coal development seems destined to continue in the beauty of the Roaring Fork country.

North and east of Grand Junction, spread out in a wide arc from Loma in the west to Cameo in the east, is a massive deposit of coal—the Book Cliffs field. Forty miles long and highlighted by the famed Book Cliffs rock formation, this coal field has been a traditional producer in the past. Today, however, mining activities and proposed mining activities dwarf the operations of the past. The largest past producer of the area was the Cameo mine which produced over 4,000,000 tons of coal from 1899 to 1969. In addition, the Mount Lincoln, Gearhart, Garfield, Palisade, and Riverside coal mines produced nearly 1,000,000 tons of coal through 1969. Near Cottonwood Creek, south of Cameo, three coal mines produced 400,000 tons of coal through 1968. During the early days of coal mining in this region, two coal towns were born—Cameo in 1907 just east of Palisade, and Carpenter in 1890 north of Grand Junction. The latter even had its own railroad, a quaint little twelve-mile line called the Book Cliff Railway.

Today, as the decade of the 80s unfolds, the situation has changed remarkably. Small coal operations are a thing of the past. The Book Cliffs region has hit the big time. By 1985, 1,500 to 2,000 miners will be working in coal mines. Those mines which are currently producing or are on the brink of beginning operations represent 230,000,000 tons of recoverable coal. Five major mining operations are or will be in full production by 1985. They include:

1. *Cameo Mines 1 and 2* on both sides of the Colorado River near the town of Cameo. General Exploration Colorado Company will employ 400 miners to mine 30,000,000 tons of coal over a forty-seven-year period.

2. *Loma Mining Project*, thirty-five miles northwest of Grand Junction in the Douglas Pass area of western Garfield County. Sheridan Enterprises plans to develop six underground bituminous coal mines with 900 miners producing 100,000,000 tons of coal over a twenty-five-year life span. The coal will be sent by rail to utility markets in the Midwest and Southwest.

3. *Cottonwood Creek Mines 1 and 2* located on the south side of the Colorado River at the mouth of DeBeque Canyon, fourteen miles northeast of Grand Junction. Mid-Continent Coal and Coke Company hopes to mine 62,000,000 tons of bituminous coal over twenty-five years. Four hundred miners will be employed and the coal will be shipped to electric generating companies outside Colorado.

4. *Farmers Mine*, twelve miles northwest of Fruita. This mine is owned by Coal Fuels Corporation and has 7,000,000 tons of recoverable coal. Two hundred men will work the mine.

5. *Roadside Mine near Cameo*. General Exploration owns this mine which has 20,000,000 tons of recoverable coal. The mine will employ 120 men.

In the not-too-distant future, hundreds of unit trains (100 cars, each carrying 100 tons of coal or an estimated 100,000 tons of coal per train) will be carrying their cargoes heading east for use in generating plants, utilities, and industry. By 1985, 600 unit trains, or nearly two per day, will be moving along rails, bringing back memories of a bygone era on the Western Slope.

And now we have finally come to northwestern Colorado—the big boy or superstar of the coal industry in Colorado. Here is where the action is and will continue to be—here is where much of the strip mining in Colorado takes place. Of the eight major coal producing regions of the state, the greatest resources and highest current rate of production are located in northwestern Colorado. Over fifty percent of all coal produced in Colorado comes from Routt and Moffat counties.

Strangely enough, unlike the other coal regions of the Western Slope, northwestern Colorado does not have a coal tradition. Aside from Oak Creek, Phippsburg, and Yampa, no major coal towns existed in the region. The great, sprawling section drained by the Yampa and White rivers was primarily cattle country, with some farming and some great oil fields near Rangely. Sparsely settled, far from convenient coal markets and without a railroad until the arrival of the Moffat line in 1908, northwestern Colorado had little need or desire for a coal industry, even though the existence of huge coal deposits were known as early as the 1870s when the surveyor F. V. Hayden mapped the region.

Nearly all the coal mined in northwestern Colorado is strip-mined. Doing the stripping for Energy Fuels, one of the major coal companies, are draglines with seven, fourteen, and twenty-one cubic yard capacities — and "Effie." "Effie" is a $10,000,000 dragline of staggering proportions. It boasts a boom 325 yards long (longer than a football field) and operates a bucket which lifts out fifty-five yards of coal per bite, equal to that carried by four average sized dump trucks. The coal is then trucked to a nearby tipple for crushing, screening, and loading into railroad cars.

In 1977, of the approximately 12,000,000 tons of coal mined in Colorado, 7,422,188 tons came from the Green River coal field in northwestern Colorado. Thirteen mines, nine of them surface, in Routt and Moffat counties, thus turned out sixty-two percent of all the coal in Colorado. However, two mines, the Edna north of Oak Creek and the Energy Fuels mine twenty-five miles south of Steamboat Springs, combined to produce 5,000,000 tons of coal. By 1980, northwestern Colorado's coal mines will produce 11,500,000 tons of coal per year. During the next fifteen years, it is believed that 226,000,000 tons of coal will be mined in northwestern Colorado, most of it high-grade coal with low sulphur and ash content taken from strip mines.

The growth of northwestern Colorado, caused primarily by coal in the 1970s, has been fast and hectic — perhaps too hectic. Major coal companies such as Energy Fuels, Peabody, Colowyo, American Fuels, Empire Energy, Midland Coal, Pittsburg, Midway, and many others have changed the entire character of the region. Ten years ago, northwestern Colorado was a quiet, rural ranching country, sparsely populated, with important oil fields, a few small coal mines, and a great winter sports area at Steamboat Springs. No more. Today the region has been transformed into a booming section of the state with great and continuing coal development, a large increase in population, an influx of big money, and tremendous social, economic, and environmental problems. And the boom is just beginning. Soon more people, more money, more development, and more problems will plague the once-peaceful land of the White and Yampa rivers.

In 1977, a West Coast writer looked at Craig, the biggest boom town of northwestern Colorado and predicted: "As Craig goes, so perhaps, goes the rest of the American West."[8] Located in the middle of 38,000,000,000 tons of coal, Craig truly has been a boom town since the early 1970s. The population of the town has rocketed from 4,000 in 1970 to 10,850 in 1978 en route to a projected 15,400 in 1990. The latter figure may even be conservative. Growth has brought prosperity, but has also brought trailer houses, higher taxes, more alcoholism and prostitution, more pollution, and a change from the high quality of life Craig residents once knew. Nearby Hayden's population has jumped from 763 in 1970 to 1,500 in 1978 and it is still growing. Other towns such as Steamboat Springs, Oak Creek, Yampa, Meeker, Dinosaur, and Rangely have also seen population increases and extensive changes caused by coal development.

The combined population of Routt, Moffat, and Rio Blanco counties in northwestern Colorado in 1974 was 21,700. By 1978, the population had nearly doubled. Certainly the development of the many coal mines has been the major cause for the population increase, but there have been other causes as well. The building of two coal-fired power plants, one at Hayden with a capacity of 450 megawatts, and another near Craig, built at a cost of $700,000,000 with a 760-megawatt capacity, has also led to growth. Two more coal-fired generating plants are planned in the area with a total capacity of 1,760 megawatts. The cost could easily exceed a billion dollars and consume 6,600,000 tons of coal annually to the detriment of clean air in the region. Growth has and will continue to come from extensive railroad development. Already 1,200-unit trains are leaving the region annually via the Denver & Rio Grande Western Railroad. By 1990, that number will almost quadruple. A twenty-three-mile railroad spur has been built by W. R. Grace and Company from just south of Craig to its Colowyo mine near Axial, and another sixty-three miles of track are projected to be built by 1990. With the additional trackage, spurs, siding, and loading tipples, a new railroad era is at hand. Coal mines, power plants, and railroads caused the boom in northwestern Colorado, but the spinoff businesses which cater to miners and construction workers are having their day too. Service stations, liquor stores, trailer parks, restaurants, and, as always, the lecherous land speculators have become prosperous.

If one lets his mind wander today, he can recall the glory years of the Western Slope — the age of mining before the turn of the century.

134

The great mining towns pass in review—Silverton, Aspen, Telluride, Ouray, and many others. But those were mines of gold and silver. A historian once declared: "The more things change the more they become the same." That is certainly true on the Western Slope today. It should not surprise people that mining has made a stunning comeback in Western Colorado. That region was always a great country for mining and, in a way, it never left. It just took a rest. Only what is taken from the soil has changed today. Instead of mining gold and silver, we are mining coal, uranium, molybdenum, and oil. And oil shale looms on the horizon.

The Western Slope has become one of the major boiler rooms of the West. Its potential for great energy development has made industrialists and developers drool with envy. Energy sources with great potential include thermal, solar, nuclear, oil shale, and coal. With the exception of coal, all other sources of energy are in their infancy, perhaps many years from total development. Not so coal. Coal exists in great reserves, has adequate transportation, has been a traditional source of energy, and has the technology needed for mining. There is little doubt that Western Colorado will be a major supplier of coal to help meet the expanding energy needs of the nation. This will lead to great changes in Western Colorado—some good and some bad.

The good changes are obvious. Coal development has led to a higher standard of living for people in Western Colorado. The technology being developed by the coal industry may also have a spinoff effect on other fledgling industries such as oil shale and uranium. Railroads are being upgraded and expanded. In fact, this industry may be making its own comeback because of coal. Finally, Western Colorado is contributing its share toward solving America's energy problems.

Now for the bad news. Not too long ago, a leading environmentalist surveyed the changes occurring in the American West and, with a bit of irony and sarcasm in his voice, declared: "The first time around we took care of the easy stuff—Indians, buffalo, hills filled with gold—but this time we're getting serious."[9] He was, of course, speaking of the ravaging and raping of the West by coal companies, land speculators, major utilities, the Water & Power Resources Service, Chambers of Commerce, and others to whom money is everything and the environment is nothing.

Coal already has brought, and will continue, directly and indirectly, to bring thousands of people to Western Colorado, an arid land not capable of supporting large numbers. The increased population will put additional pressure on already scarce water resources. This alone may be the most devastating blow the Western Slope will suffer. Coal is already responsible for two coal-fired generating plants near Craig and Hayden. Forty more are planned for Colorado, with over half ticketed for the Western Slope. The coal-fired plants would have a total output exceeding 50,000 megawatts and would spew filthy clouds of fly ash, sulphur dioxide, and nitrogen oxide into the previously clear blue skies of Western Colorado. The most intense concentration of plants would occur between Durango and Montrose where six generating plants are on the drawing boards, with a total planned capacity of 13,250 megawatts.

Because half of Colorado's coal production comes from surface mines and that means the Western Slope, reclaiming the land ravaged by strip mines becomes very important. One is aware of the "hit and run" tactics employed by coal companies which devastated West Virginia and Kentucky. Although there has been some limited success in reclaiming coal lands, one is haunted by the 1973 National Academy of Sciences report on the subject which declared: "In the Western coal areas, complete restoration is rarely, if ever, possible." Even simple revegetation "will require centuries."[10]

Aside from the fact that coal development in Western Colorado will tear up the land, use very scarce water, pollute the air, destroy much of the aesthetic and pristine beauty of the region, and bring about all kinds of social, economic, and population problems, we have not yet touched upon the worst evil. That evil is the possibility, in fact the probability, that Western Colorado may become a major energy colony for the rest of the nation, at the expense of its quality of life. That is exactly what is happening as major corpo rations, not Colorado-based, make decisions in eastern and midwestern board rooms which will change Western Colorado forever. Local residents have little or nothing to say about what will be done to their land and their lives. Though a good portion of the energy produced now and in the future on the Western Slope will be consumed in Las Vegas, Phoenix, and southern California, the mining and burning of the coal will take place in northern Arizona, southern Utah, and Western Colorado, "where a small . . . population is being cajoled into giving up its birthright of fresh air, clear skies, and open space in exchange for a few temporary jobs."[11] The coal could be mined and shipped by rail and truck to southern California and the big cities and burned there, where it is needed. However, the public utilities and the oil, coal, and power companies want mine-site burning of the coal, so they can escape air-quality standards imposed on the cities.

The last days of the 1970s are over. Once again, as 100 years ago in Western Colorado, the roads are swarming with miners—coal miners this time. They call it progress, but we all know what it is again—the boom before the bust. The land, the water—in fact, Western Colorado's quality of life—are in danger. Not so long ago, the countryside was peaceful and tranquil, with clear blue skies and clean water. Now the land is threatened and in danger. The post-war era was wonderful and it lasted thirty years. But now everything has changed. Western Colorado is adrift on the high and turbulent sea of change, and cannot foresee what lies ahead.

David Wood. *Courtesy Colorado Historical Society.*

He Matched the Mountains
David Wood

Today the name David Wood does not awaken vivid memories in the minds of Western Slopers, but it did in the last two decades of the nineteenth century. The David Wood transportation lines, the largest and most active in the region, hauled freight to nearly every nook and cranny of the Slope. Dave Wood was *the* freighter in a day and time when people depended on this individual for their livelihood.

Without freighters, settlement would not have taken root on the Western Slope before the coming of the railroad. They transported goods by mule and burro to the highest mountain mine, and by wagon wherever the trail and grade allowed. Even after the arrival of the railroad, freighters transported cargo from the depot to distant customers. The automobile and truck finally forced them out of business.

Nothing daunted them, neither mud, snow, dust, nor storm. They hauled everything from needles to bulky mine equipment and even joked about hauling the mountains, if necessary. A sampling of Wood's correspondence shows that he carried corn, oats, beer, cheese, hardware supplies, powder, wine, cabinets, stamp mill machinery, clothes, and on and on. Customers could become irate if goods did not arrive on time. Annie Carter of Telluride berated Wood in 1887 for not shipping her case of wine soon enough and told him to ship it by stage, as she was in a great hurry for it. Customers defaulted, leaving Wood with bills due for freighting and little chance

139

of collecting. Wood extended credit as a necessity of business life and was sometimes left holding the bag. He took as much risk as any of the other pioneers, although newspaper comments could make it appear that freighters reaped all the rewards by charging exhorbitant rates.

By the time Dave Wood reached Western Colorado, his career was nearly as varied as the frontier itself. A Civil War veteran before reaching his teens, Wood traveled west with his family to Kansas to farm, when the guns fell silent. The cattle business beckoned, and the Wood family, father and sons, drove cattle northward out of Texas to the railroad. Beyond Kansas another frontier called, Colorado, and in 1876 Dave Wood took horses there to sell and decided to stay. Restless, searching, Dave moved on to the San Juans. There, in 1877, he started a passenger and express line between Lake City and Ouray. From this beginning he became the freighting king of the Western Slope.

In the years that followed, Wood freighted to mine and camp in the far flung San Juan mining district and its neighbor, the Gunnison country, then nearly all of the settled area. With optimism and confidence, he expanded. To succeed, Western Slopers had to dare and plunge. Wood was no exception. He operated stages, purchased land and ranches, sold grain and other goods on the side, and built a road in Ouray and Montrose counties so he could carry freight into Telluride. A natural horse trader, he bargained shrewdly. Occasionally a deal fell through, as it did with "Shoestring." The new owner wrote Dave, "I cannot manage him quite enough in harness, . . . he is hell in the stable trying to get over into the next stall." He decided he did not want "Shoestring," but would buy "Frank" instead.

The railroad's smoky coming curtailed Wood's activity, especially when Otto Mears drove his Rio Grande Southern into Telluride and Rico. Being of an optimistic nature, Dave turned his attention to a staging venture into Cripple Creek, a project just launched when the crash of 1893 hit Colorado. Overextended and in debt to underwrite his latest venture, and confronted with immediate railroad competition, Dave Wood was one of many who lost heavily in this economic convulsion and clinging depression. In the end, he was left with little more than his ranch home at Dallas in Ouray County.

Dave Wood would never again know the prosperity and influence of his freighting days. He dabbled in mining and ranching and always kept an eye out for another investment boom, a boom that never materialized. The hearty old-timer lived until March 9, 1944, active almost to the last. By then he had become a legend in his own time.

To open the Western Slope, a person had to be like Dave Wood—optimistic, tough, determined, and willing to gamble now and then. That he lost much in the crash and 1890s depression does not dim the significance of what he accomplished. Many were like him, but few did so much to open the Western Slope for the generations that came after. In the end Dave Wood matched the mountains.

Stacking hay in the fall of 1908. *Courtesy North Fork Historical Society.*

10.
Land of the
Hard Way Eight

Sometimes in the late spring when the leaves again begin to bud on the trees and the smell of summer is in the air, or on one of those gorgeous fall days when the aspen turn the brightest yellow anywhere, one can imagine the Western Slope as it used to be, unpeopled except for the Indians and tranquil. Perhaps Robert Service, writing about Alaska in *The Spell of the Yukon*, described the feeling of the Ute Indians for their home and the primitive days of long ago.

> There's a land where the mountains are nameless,
> And the rivers all run God knows where;
> There are lives that are erring and aimless,
> And deaths that just hang by a hair;
> There are hardships that nobody reckons;
> There are valleys unpeopled and still;
> There's a land — oh, it beckons and beckons,
> And I want to go back — and I will.[1]

Long before the Indians of Mesa Verde came to Western Colorado, dinosaurs roamed the region which was then tropical. Large dinosaur bones found near Delta and Dinosaur National Monument bear witness to the presence of the huge mammals millions of years ago. The dinosaur was long extinct when the majestic buffalo appeared on the Western Slope. Called "mountain bison" by mountain men, the buffalo regularly wintered in valleys of the Rocky Mountains and then moved into mountain meadows or tundra as the snow melted. They were huge, with bulls weighing 2,500 pounds and cows

1,600 pounds. Many were the mountain passes they crossed to get to the Western Slope. One of the best known is Cochetopa Pass, or "pass of the buffalo."

Following the dinosaur and buffalo on the Western Slope came cattle, the bellwethers of the great range cattle industry which would soon dominate the thinking of the region west of the Continental Divide. Just behind the cattlemen came the farmer, or nester, as he was called. Initially, the Western Slope did not present an appealing picture to either the cattleman or farmer. The high mountains, biting cold, long winters, and arid land seemed to be insurmountable obstacles that not even the optimism of ranchers and farmers could overcome. But these were hardy people, used to adversity and hard times and they had a great yearning for their place in the sun.

When the first white men came to the Western Slope they saw some lush, green valleys and grasslands but all too often their gaze fell instead on sagebrush and water-starved earth. This was an arid land, despite the great snows of the mountains. Most of the water ran off in the spring without soaking into the ground, and the scant rainfall of summer and fall put the Western Slope into the desert category. But the first men and women of the Western Slope did not see the aridity, cold, and barrenness of the land; they saw instead, an unpeopled land of opportunity. Let the skeptics say what they would, the Western Slope looked awfully good to settlers used to hardship and privation.

The Ute Indians, natives of the Western Slope, prevented all but a few intrusions on their land prior to 1873. The Treaty of 1868 had "given" the Utes possession of all land west of the 107th meridian, or almost all of Western Colorado. However, in 1873, rich strikes of silver and gold were discovered in the San Juan in southwestern Colorado, and a virtual deluge of anxious miners threatened to descend upon the mountains like swarming locusts and cause an Indian war. A nervous United States government immediately sent one of its Indian Commissioners, Felix Brunot, to conclude a treaty with the Utes inducing them to give up the San Juan.

Despite Ute occupation of the rest of the Western Slope, it was a foregone conclusion that the days of the Utes were numbered west of the Continental Divide. The Western Slope was too good to leave to the "uncivilized barbarians." The Utes had to go! Increasingly throughout the 1870s, white cattlemen and farmers encroached on Ute land, sometimes with disastrous results. Farmers followed miners into the newly discovered mining regions of the Western Slope, hoping to reap enormous profits from the sale of badly needed food products to voracious miners.

Following the opening of the San Juan country in 1873–74, Robert McGrew and Jim Downey established a dairy farm outside of Silverton and sold milk in the mining camp for 50 cents a gallon. In 1876, the two men increased their herd to sixty-two and moved them to Antelope Park west of Silverton. Although milk was sold to miners and passing wagon trains for twenty-five cents a pan, butter was where the money was. That precious commodity sold for from sixty to seventy-five cents a pound from May 15 to late November. The butter was sold in five-pound balls and sold like hot cakes in the San Juan mining camps.

The beautiful Elk River Valley was the scene of some farming in 1867, following the discovery of gold at Hahn's Peak. Hay was grown for animals used in the mining camp. S. B. Reid even raised vegetables, considered very rare and at a premium in mining camps. In the Gunnison country, an idealist named Sylvester Richardson looked the region over in 1873 while a member of a geological expedition. He liked what he saw and organized an agricultural colony over the winter in Denver. The next May, Richardson established his agricultural colony near present-day Gunnison. Though he was optimistic that he could grow potatoes, vegetables, grains, and other foodstuffs, he soon became aware of the hostile environment he had entered. With a seventy-day growing season, lack of moisture, and unbelievably cold winter weather, Richardson sadly concluded that ranching might have to replace his hoped-for farming. Other small farms sprang up on Indian land in the 1870s in the Mancos Valley in southwestern Colorado.

A start had been made in Western Slope agriculture in the 1870s, but only a start. The Ute Indians, isolation, arid lands, and a short growing season were seemingly insurmountable obstacles for the early farmers. Typical of the view held by many regarding Western Slope agriculture was the one held by three men who explored a portion of the inhospitable land in June of 1880. Dr. N. Jennings of Gunnison, E. C. Smith, a well-known scout and a reporter for the *Denver Tribune* proclaimed the Western Slope unfit for civilized man. The three excepted only "some small valleys along the North Fork and the Grand," thereby saving at least some of their reputations for posterity. The men reported that the great majority of the Western Slope was too rugged and mountainous to have any value for agricultural and grazing purposes.

For civilized man it is apparently about as valuable as would be a representative section of the Desert of Sahara. To parties contemplating a

145

visit to this region, our advice would be, don't go. Except to the seeker of excitement in toilsome and dangerous mountain climbing, or the ardent sportsman, or the lover of the picturesque and grand in nature, there is absolutely nothing to tempt anyone to the northwestern section of the reservation.[2]

If farmers were interested in the Western Slope in the 1870s, cattlemen were more interested. They were aware of great profits made in cattle east of the Continental Divide, and looked longingly at the free and almost ideal grazing land to the west. Barring the path of settlement, however, were the ever-present Utes. Ute presence or not, early cattlemen filtered into the Western Slope in the 1870s. In the Paradox Valley in 1878, Fred Mayall brought in the first cattle. The following spring, en route to Lone Cone Mountain, the rancher was overtaken by Utes, whipped, forced to eat grass, and run out of the country. Some of the first cattle were trailed into Middle Park in 1876 and by 1879 the miniature park was sparsely settled. Despite threats by the Utes, ranchers and farmers quickly took up natural meadows along the Grand, Fraser, and Blue rivers, as well as on Troublesome and Muddy creeks.

To the south, the fledgling cattle industry got underway in the Gunnison country, led by Alonzo Hartman who had been in charge of the cow camp for the Los Pinos Indian Reservation since 1872. Mild winters from 1874 through 1879 lulled the early cattlemen into a false sense of security. Alas, the winter of 1879–80, with heavy snows and 40 below zero temperatures, killed ten percent of the cattle and brought home the hard reality of what the weather was really like. Around the rest of the Western Slope, cattlemen braved the Ute menace and stubbornly, in pockets, started the range cattle industry. They came to the Uncompahgre Plateau, Mancos Valley, and to the hot springs near the San Juan River.

In northwestern Colorado, amidst the plateaus, fast-flowing rivers, and canyons, a great cattle industry first reared its head in Brown's Park, early used by fur-traders. There in an area bounded on the north by the Wyoming border, on the south by the White River watershed, on the east by the Continental Divide, and on the west by the many canyons of the Green River system, cattle had grazed as early as 1849 when Cherokee Indians, heading for the California gold fields, wintered there. During the winter of 1871–72 in Brown's Park, George Baggs wintered 900 New Mexican steers he was trailing northward without losing one. From that time on, Brown's Park was used as both a summer and winter range. Not too far away, on the banks of the Yampa River, James Crawford and family from

Missouri put down roots in 1875 and Steamboat Springs soon came into being. The door of opportunity for ranchers and farmers on the Western Slope had opened just a crack.

Nathan Meeker, who had headed the very successful agricultural Union Colony on the eastern slope, also saw the possibilities of farming across the Continental Divide when he became agent of the White River Ute Reservation in 1878. The Meeker massacre of September, 1879, which followed Meeker's unsuccessful efforts to change the Indians, signaled the end for the Northern and Uncompahgre Utes on the Western Slope. Following the Treaty of 1880, they were forced out of Colorado and on to the Uintah Reservation in eastern Utah. The Meeker massacre was only the catalytic agent which forced the Ute removal; in truth, the fertile land and rich mineral deposits had made removal a foregone conclusion long before. It did not take long for ranchers and farmers to stream into Western Colorado.

The choicest of all the farming and ranching locations on the Western Slope lay at the junction of the Colorado and Gunnison rivers. Hardly had the Utes passed the junction of the rivers than settlers flocked in. Although the Ute lands were not officially opened for filing until June, 1882, all prime farm land near the rivers was taken by the end of September the following year. The first ranch appeared on September 10 and the town of Grand Junction, initially named Ute, was located on September 26. The Grand Valley was bestowed with many gifts; it had water for irrigation from two great rivers, the soil was fertile, and the weather, unlike other Western Slope regions, was warm and mild. As early as March, 1882, work on irrigation canals began and when the Denver and Rio Grande arrived in November of that year, farmers and ranchers around Grand Junction knew they lived in the promised land.

South of Grand Junction lay the Uncompahgre Valley, a wide-open dale of 175,000 acres with seemingly ample water available from the Gunnison and Uncompahgre rivers. The farmers and ranchers wasted no time and by the end of 1882, Uncompahgre (soon renamed Delta) was located near the junctures of the Gunnison, Uncompahgre, and North Fork rivers. Montrose, initially called Pomona, after the goddess of fruit, sprang up in the sagebrush flats twenty miles farther south. The anxious farmers and ranchers should have heeded John Gunnison, who referred to the Uncompahgre Valley as a desert unfit for cultivation as he passed through in 1853. Gunnison knew what he was talking about. Following the arrival of the Denver and Rio Grande in 1882, a rush of homesteaders streamed into the valley. Ditches of considerable size were dug for irrigation, but it was soon found that only water for 25,000 acres was available. Foreclosures were made on 20,000 acres of land and the future looked bleak for the Uncompahgre Valley.

The North Fork Valley was a different story. Just south of Grand Mesa, which supplies it with much of its water, the North Fork Valley is long and narrow. It extends for over twenty miles from the head of the North Fork to its juncture with the Gunnison River. The valley has immensely fertile soil caused by great deposits of silt which filtered down throughout the years; it also has a very mild climate which allowed a great fruit industry to develop almost from the beginning of settlement. In September of 1881, Sam Wade, Enos Hotchkiss, and a small party of men entered the North Fork Valley via Black Mesa and discovered thorn apple and buffalo berry growing in abundance. This fact, plus the warm climate and good soil, prompted Wade to bring in fruit trees the following spring. It was not easy; he had to shovel snow for three weeks over Black Mesa before he could enter the North Fork Valley. Nevertheless, the famed fruit industry of the North Fork had begun and the towns of Hotchkiss, Cedaredge, and Paonia were soon laid out.

Farming on the Western Slope has always been a risky business because of its unique topography and climate. The elevation is high, sometimes too high for crop production. Raising crops at elevations from 4,586 feet at Grand Junction to over 9,500 feet in some of the high mountain valleys demanded a lot of faith and luck. At high elevation, the period free from killing frosts is short. However, even a sixty- to seventy-day growing season can be sufficient on the Western Slope with certain adaptable crops. This is due to climate modification influenced by protective mountain ranges, readily available water during the growing season, ample snow cover during the bitter cold winter months, and the intensity of sunlight to speed up the maturation of plants.

Mining led to high altitude farming because of the great need for fresh produce. The miners paid high prices for fresh fruit, vegetables, or new potatoes. Hay was also in big demand for the mules and burros used in the mining industry. Taking a chance on the weather for an opportunity to make big money, farmers found to their surprise that they could raise potatoes, radishes, turnips, onions, cabbage, lettuce, rutabagas, and even fruit in the high country. If gardens and farms survived in one area, other farmers followed the example and moved in; if early high elevation agriculture was frozen out in another region, farmers stayed out. It was all a game of chance.

Despite some success at high elevation, most of the successful farming on the Western Slope took place at lower elevations in protected valleys with irrigation water available from nearby streams or rivers. Examples include the Grand, North Fork, and Uncompahgre valleys and some small pockets of land around Dove Creek and Nucla. Other regions such as the White River, Yampa, Gunnison, Paradox, and Eagle River valleys, and Middle Park were either too high, too cold, or too arid for much farming. Cattle and not farming made up the history of those areas.

Fruit became king of the farming industry on the Western Slope shortly after the removal of the Utes. There were many doubters when the fruit industry began. The U.S. Department of Agriculture, as late as 1888, declared Colorado unfit for fruit-raising because of high altitude, poor soil, and a lack of moisture. The Department could not have been more wrong. The North Fork led the way. Following Sam Wade's introduction of fruit into the region in 1882, the North Fork boomed. Apples, peaches, and pears predominated as one fruit orchard after another was planted. In 1893, the North Fork was recognized as a great fruit-raising area after Sam Wade and W. S. Coburn won six first places in competition at the Chicago World's Fair. Fruit soon rivaled cattle as the major industry of the North Fork. Orchards were planted on tablelands and mesas which were free of alkali, mild, and free of insect enemies. During the 1890s many fruit districts in Colorado and around the nation were hard hit by drought and freezes, but not the North Fork. Soon representatives from commercial houses in the midwest came to the sheltered valley to compete for the high quality fruit. Orchards increased, prices rose, and the price of land shot up. From 1899 to 1902, it was not uncommon to see 65 fruit-laden wagons in a row heading to the railhead at Delta. The dust kicked up by the horses could be seen miles away.

The rapidly developing fruit industry, along with a growing cattle industry and coal production at Somerset at the head of the North Fork Valley, induced the Denver and Rio Grande to build a branch line from Delta to Somerset in 1902. The arrival of the iron horse led to an even greater boom in the fruit industry, with farms selling for over $3,000 an acre. From 1904 to 1909, orchards could be seen everywhere in the North Fork Valley. Hotchkiss doubled its population and Paonia increased from 250 to 1,200 residents. The tremendous growth of the fruit industry could not last and in 1910, a depression hit. Competition from the northwest dropped prices, freezes came for the first time in memory, and fruit-destroying pests descended upon the orchards. Many orchards were pulled, with the land being used for general farming or grazing. The North Fork eventually pulled itself out of the depression, but even today only produces a quarter to a third of the fruit it did during the glory years from 1904 to 1909.

The North Fork fruit industry was challenged by another great agricultural section of Western Colorado, the Grand Valley. That fertile valley, still called Grand because the Colorado River which runs through it was named such prior to 1921, is long and narrow, stretching from Glenwood Springs in the east to Grand Junction in the west. Two men first saw the possibilities of the valley as a fruit-raising mecca. One was Elam Blain who planted peach seeds between Grand Junction and Palisade near the Grand River in 1882. The other was William Pabor who planted fruit trees near today's Fruita in 1883. Following a tour of the region two years before, Pabor's written articles on the region did much to arouse interest in that section of the Grand Valley. From this beginning, the west end of the Grand Valley became a fruitgrower's paradise. Palisade was laid out in 1893 east of Grand Junction and became the center of the peach industry in Colorado. During the 1890s spring frosts periodically destroyed much of the Grand Valley's fruit crop. But one area—Palisade—escaped damage. The farmers soon realized why. Ten-thousand-foot-high Grand Mesa towers south of Palisade and the cliffs called the Palisades border the town to the north. Their rocky walls soak up the sun's heat during the day, then slowly radiate the warmth over the orchards at night. In addition, a breeze called the "peach wind" blew down the canyon at night, protecting the upper valley from frost. In season more than two hundred refrigerated railroad cars of peaches per day were shipped from the Grand Valley with ninety percent coming from Palisade. Pears, apples, peaches, and cherries made up the great fruit orchards of the Grand Valley; they were responsible for the birth of both Palisade and Fruita, and aided greatly in the growth of Grand Junction.

There were other fruit regions on the Western Slope. Montrose County looked promising before the turn of the century but the high altitude made fruit-raising hazardous and the region diversified its agriculture after the turn of the century. Montezuma and La Plata counties in southwestern Colorado early produced apples, pears, peaches, plums, and cherries, but primarily for local production. The high cost of freight and distance from markets hurt further development there. Strawberries were raised prolifically in and around Glenwood Springs for some time after the turn of the century, but they no longer play a major part in Western Slope agriculture.

The Uncompahgre Valley, like the Grand and North Fork, had its fruit boom on the mesas west of the Uncompahgre River from 1885 to the early 1900s. However, by World War I, insects, freezes, and overproduction took their toll and many of the orchards were pulled out. Only a small percentage remain today. The agriculture of the valley has always been more diversified, primarily to supply early mining towns in the region like Ouray and Telluride. The entire future of the Uncompahgre Valley, however, was threatened before the turn of the century by a lack of available water. That, however, is a later story.

Though many said it could not be done, sugar beets made their appearance on the Western Slope in the 1890s. Charles Mitchell, a Grand Junction druggist, was responsible for the new industry. He became interested in the possibilities of sugar beet production following his wife's trip through a sugar factory in Grand Island, Nebraska, in 1892. The following year, sugar beets were planted and three carloads were shipped out. By the turn of the century, Charles Cox, John Campion, Charles Boettcher, Charles Mitchell, and others incorporated the Colorado Sugar Manufacturing Company and built the first sugar factory in Colorado in Grand Junction. The town of Grand Junction donated 1,500 acres of land as an incentive for building the factory, and sugar beet fields soon dotted the Grand Valley. The sugar factory led to the planting of more sugar beets around Olathe and Delta. The industry became so big in Delta that the Uncompahgre town got its own processing factory in 1920, when the Holly sugar beet factory was built. Mexican laborers were imported during harvest to work in the beet fields. Today, both factories in Grand Junction and Delta have shut down because of the glut of sugar on the world market which led to low prices. The sugar beet industry is but a memory on the Western Slope.

Potatoes were planted early on the Western Slope in the Uncompahgre Valley and at Carbondale on the Roaring Fork River and were sold to the nearby mining camps. Pioneer William Dinkel planted two acres of potatoes on the Roaring Fork in 1881 and harvested 200 sacks which he sold to the Aspen miners. The silver panic of 1893, which wiped out many mining camps, and high transportation costs temporarily ended potato production, but by World War I, production was up again on the Western Slope especially in the Uncompahgre Valley. Other potato growing regions included Fruita and Loma west of Grand Junction, known for early potatoes, and the Garfield-Eagle district.

Delta County began honey-production shortly after Ute lands

were opened in the Uncompahgre Valley in 1883. Twenty colonies of bees were shipped in during that year and honey grew along with fruit as a major industry there. The high and dry climate was perfect for providing honey a flavor unexcelled anywhere in the United States. During the 1920s, over half of the colonies of bees in Colorado came from the Western Slope. Delta County with 7,000 and Mesa County with 6,000 led the way. These two counties alone shipped forty carloads of honey a year.

The only true agricultural colony to survive on the Western Slope was Nucla, located near the mouth of the San Miguel River by the Colorado Cooperative Company in 1894. The exact location was Tabeguache Park, 20,000 acres of fertile but arid land. The first task of the colonizers was to bring water seventeen miles through a ditch and wooden flume from San Miguel Canyon to the park. By 1904, the world's highest and longest irrigation flume was completed; it had been a herculean task but water now flowed into Tabeguache Park. Land was cleared, canals were built, and fruit, grain, and vegetables soon were harvested from the virgin soil.

Another colony, albeit not utopian, was the creation of Voleny Hoggatt, a six-foot-two, two-hundred-twenty-pound dynamo, in 1916. Hoggatt, a writer for the *Denver Post* and champion of the common man, established the Great Divide Colony thirty miles northwest of Craig, and all but ruined the cattle industry of Moffat County. Literally hundreds of homesteaders arrived from all parts of the country and took up over 100,000 acres of choice cattle range. Some of Western Colorado's best grazing land was replaced by some of the worst wheat, vegetable, and alfalfa land. By the mid-1920s, the Great Divide Colony had lost its steam and most of the homesteaders left, victims of a lack of water.

Looking backward, farming on the Western Slope has always been a hazardous business. In the early days of the 1870s and 1880s, Ute Indians, a lack of transportation, and a lack of knowledge about rainfall, climate, and soil conditions led many a farmer into disaster. Following the turn of the century it was found that irrigation was absolutely indispensable if farmers were to succeed. Without irrigation water from the many rivers, the Western Slope was nothing more than a desert. With water, the rich soil made the region a farmer's paradise. The last fifty years of Western Slope agriculture have been as risky as the first fifty. Orchards have been pulled, the sugar beet industry has collapsed, the cattle and sheep kingdoms of the past have faded, and less land is being farmed. The problems have been many. Drought has all too often reared its ugly head.

Today we know that the Colorado River does not produce as much water as once thought. Early freezes have greatly hurt the fruit industry. Foreign sugar has glutted the market and driven prices so low that farmers have stopped planting sugar beets. Cattle prices have been consistently low. But most tragically for Western Slope farming, people and real estate developments have replaced farms. With a depressed economy, many Western Slope farmers and ranchers have sold their land to real estate developers for much more money than they could ever make farming. It has been the only way they could make money from their farms. Thus, land in the Grand Valley, Animas River Valley, and around Grand Junction has been taken out of agricultural production. In other parts of the Western Slope, such as northwestern Colorado, the White River Valley, and the North Fork, much farming and grazing land has been sold to coal companies for development. Sadly, farming on the Western Slope seems to be fading from the scene.

The day of the cattleman dawned on Colorado's Western Slope in the 1870s, a decade or so after the eastern slope. The Ute Indians still owned the land, but ranchers drooled when they thought of the open valleys with rivers running through, the lush high mountain parks, and the great market for cattle which was sure to mean big profits. One cattleman declared: "The Western Slope isn't a land area, it is a cattle range." Isolated early cattlemen made their way into the Gunnison, Uncompahgre, Paradox, White, and Mancos valleys as well as Middle Park and northwestern Colorado by the middle to late 1870s, usually at the risk of their lives. But it was not until the Meeker massacre in 1879 that the region really opened its doors to the bawling cattle. The massacre and the final Ute treaty in 1880 brought cattlemen trailing in across the Continental Divide.

Even after the Utes were moved to Utah, they remained a serious threat to the cattlemen of the Western Slope. In southwestern Colorado, pitched battles between Utes and cattlemen in the Montezuma Valley and along the Dolores River killed over twenty Indians and numerous whites during the 1880s. Along the Mancos and Dolores rivers cattlemen and their families slept in the sagebrush during Indian uprisings to avoid being massacred. In northwestern Colorado, in the Yampa and White River valleys, the Utes continued to be a constant source of trouble to beleaguered cattlemen.

The Western Slope cattle industry, after a belated and trouble-filled beginning in the 1870s, swung into high gear during the decade of the '80s. The Utes were gone, railroads had penetrated the mountains, and the land was free under the Homestead Act. The virgin land had hardly been touched; only a few buffalo, Ute Indians, and wild horses had sampled the freedom and serenity of the region.

Northwestern Colorado, with its wide-open range, was the home of the wild mustang. One pioneer of the region wrote of them:

> They are the wild horses of the Western plains and are known as mustangs or broncos. Their home is the wide open range, red desert and the dark hidden folds of the mountains. They are as wild as a tornado, galloping over prairies, zig-zagging through foothills, flying along canyon ledges, churning up dust until they are lost in clouds of it. Of all the things they love the best is liberty.[3]

Wild game such as deer, elk, and bear abounded on the Western Slope, especially in the northwest, which was the scene of many hunting expeditions in the late 1870s and early 1880s. In Egeria Park, the Preston King family recalled that a road which ran by their ranch was "just covered with wagons, four horse teams taking out game that had been killed."[4] Many of northwestern Colorado's early settlers first saw the region while on a hunting expedition there.

The stream of homesteaders and cattlemen never seemed to stop on the Western Slope in the 1880s. They filled up the Gunnison country, the Grand Valley, Middle Park, the Yampa, White River and Uncompahgre valleys, the Mancos and Animas River regions, and even clawed their way into the wild, arid, and cliff-ridden Paradox country. Soon, primitive ranching communities sprang up, including Mancos, Craig, Meeker, Yampa, Toponas, Rifle, Hayden, and Norwood. Each man had his dream — a ranch, plenty of water, and freedom. By the end of the 1880s, thousands of cattle had infiltrated every nook and cranny of the Western Slope. A new age had dawned.

During the 1880s land on the Western Slope was free for any man willing to risk his neck and a small amount of money. By gaining possession of the water holes and streams, a cattleman could control an immense amount of range. At first, there was plenty of land. The principle of "first in time, first in right" applied to the range just as it did to water under the doctrine of prior appropriation. Few contested this right even though it was not written into law, and the cattleman protected it. In the early years, the cattle business operated according to custom and tradition. A man's range was well defined by agreement with neighbors; a code of honor existed. Early homesteaders and cattlemen got along with each other.

Plenty of land was still available for both homesteaders who began to take up land on the Western Slope and the cattlemen who preceded them. As long as the nester did not fence in water or interfere with the free movement of cattle on the open range, he was welcome — in small numbers. There soon came the day in the late 1880s when too many homesteaders poured into the Western Slope, filing on the best lands and tying up water cattlemen had been using, but did not own. In northwestern Colorado, too many cattle were driven in too fast. They came from Texas, Arizona, the plains around Denver, Wyoming, and Utah. The cattle did well until the winters of 1885–86 and 1889–90. The summers had been dry and the winters were ferocious. Along the White River during the winter of 1889–90, ranchers lost 65 percent of their cattle.

By 1890, cattlemen were aware of serious problems west of the Divide. An immediate problem was weather. Throughout most of Western Colorado, cattlemen soon found that they could not feed their cattle in the winter by running them on the open range. Snows were too heavy and the weather too cold. Bitter and expensive lessons were taught to ranchers of the Gunnison, White River, Yampa, and Middle Park countries. Even so-called milder regions of Colorado were not immune to harsh weather; witness the terrible winters of 1886–87 which devastated the cattle industry of the eastern slope. Cattlemen on the Western Slope, with a sigh of resignation, realized they would have to harvest hay for their cows to bring them through the winter.

During the early 1880s, an unprecedented demand for beef sent cattle prices to the highest levels the industry had known and led to a critical problem on the Western Slope. The range was overstocked. Most of the grazing land on the Western Slope was public domain and open to anyone — homesteader, sheepman, or cattleman. The cattleman did not see it that way. He had been in the region first, had risked his life against Indians, and had invested all of his money in building up his herd. He did not like the startling increase of 160-acre homesteads with fences which increasingly dotted the open range. He also did not like the threatened intrusion of sheep, and he damn sure did not like the federal government telling him what to do on land he regarded as his own.

Despite John Wesley Powell's admonition in 1879 that a 160-acre homestead in the West was not nearly large enough to sustain a farmer and his family, farmers continued to settle the Western Slope. Cattlemen, used to grazing their cows on the open range, were outraged when the homesteader fenced off his spread. This practice disrupted normal grazing patterns, often cut cattle off from water, and with homesteaders' small herds, added to a big rancher's stock, badly overgrazed the range. The result was confusion, open violation of the law, broken dreams, and horrifying violence. The big cattlemen of the Western Slope fought back by illegally fencing the public domain, burning out homesteaders, and gaining control of large acreages of land. If a rancher controlled land along a stream, he also controlled the grazing on either side. By filing on a homestead himself, and by having his cowboys file on others that they immediately and illegally sold to him, a rancher could control an enormous amount of rangeland. And why not, he had been there first.[5]

The Western Slope range cattle industry was dealt a terrible blow by the savage winter of 1885–86 with its heavy snow and intense cold. Half the cattle of the White River Valley died and the rest of Western Colorado was hit hard. Still, the region recovered; from 1884 to 1890, Delta County's cattle industry boomed. Northwestern Colorado also supported immense herds along the Yampa and White rivers. The Gunnison country was another great cattle region, and the Paradox, Grand, Animas, and Mancos valleys were not far behind. Upwards of 100,000 cattle grazed on Western Slope ranges prior to 1890. The first Western Slope cows shipped to an eastern market were shipped on the Denver and Rio Grande Railroad over Marshall Pass to the Denver stockyards by William Boot of Montrose in 1882. The cattle filled two cars and marked a new era in the Western Slope cattle industry.

During the late 1880s, cattle prices dropped drastically, signaling the approach of the disastrous panic of 1893, which nearly destroyed the Western Slope and Colorado. Changes came quickly in Western Colorado. English and eastern investors, who had thought cattle raising was an easy route to fortune, cashed in their chips and quit the business entirely. Some ranchers cut their herds, improved the breeding, and sought out permanent hay lands on which they could raise winter feed. Others stunned their neighbors by turning to sheep.

These were bad days for the cattleman; he was fighting a war for survival and seemed to be losing. The open range days were over, killed by falling cattle prices, dangerous overstocking of the range which had turned once-lush pastures into dust, and by more and more homesteaders fencing in the open range. Then there was the matter of the federal government. Shocked by the raping of Western lands by competing cattlemen, sheepmen, and homesteaders, and finally aware of its haphazard land policies, the federal government realized that the supply of free land in the West was dwindling. The remaining public lands were picked over. It was badly abused—overgrazed and oversettled.

After years of neglect the federal government moved decisively in 1891 by withdrawing forest lands from the public domain. For the next decade, these lands were closed, their use forbidden. A Congressional resolution of 1894 specifically prohibited pasturing livestock on the forest reserves. The Western Slope, with much of its land owned by the federal government, was stunned. Coming when competition among cattlemen, homesteaders, and sheepmen was at its height, the government edict against grazing the reserves started feuds which led to violence and discontent that simmered for forty years.

On the Western Slope, much of the mountain forest land now closed had been sheep range. Nomadic sheepmen had moved their flocks from one public range to another and from state to state with the season. Traditionally, they moved into Colorado from Utah and Wyoming for grazing, depending on the area and type of range. Banned from the forest reserves, the sheep outfits, in desperation, invaded the territory of the cattleman, already harassed and angered by local sheepmen and homesteaders, along with range pirates from Oklahoma and Texas. The last shipped cattle into Delta and Montrose by train, trailed them across the public domain, and into the Uncompahgre Forest where they grazed without permits through the summer. There was no federal enforcement agency present and the invaders were too many and too well-armed for local ranchers to do anything. Local cattlemen lost both range and cows.

The years around the turn of the century were not years of reason. Fighting a war of survival and bitter over government land policies, the cattleman was goaded beyond endurance. Unable to comprehend that the old ways were gone, he failed to realize he was no longer master of the range. There was no open range anymore. The cattlemen fought back desperately by denouncing the government through stockgrower associations, feuding with homesteaders, and by an all-out war against sheep. The war was a long one, and it was bloody.

The trailing of sheep into the open range of the Western Slope brought the issue of cattle vs. sheep to a head. The war began in 1888 and continued past World War I. The cattlemen argued that they should control the range because of prior appropriation and because "everything in front of sheep is eaten and everything behind is killed." Cattlemen claimed that the sharp hooves of the sheep caused erosion and that a gland between the animals' toes exuded an odor over which cattle would not graze. On top of all that, two-thirds of the sheepmen in Colorado were carpetbaggers, not even residents of the state. Sheepmen countered that they had as much right to the public domain as the cattlemen, that sheep had been in Western Colorado as early as cattle and that if grazed properly, sheep did no more damage to the range than cattle. In reality, the problem was racial and economic. The cattleman was Anglo and sheepherders tended to be Mexican or Basque. In addition, whoever controlled the range and public domain would also survive and prosper economically.

Thus war came to the Western Slope. Cattlemen drew up boundaries beyond which they would not let sheep pass, gave sheepmen deadlines to get off of good range land, killed sheep, sheepherders and their dogs, and drove sheep outfits from the range under threat of death. As early as January, 1888, the *Meeker Herald* had warned that cowmen along the White River were in no mood to be "imposed upon." Cattlemen in their fury went on a rampage against sheep for the next three decades; it was not a pretty sight. Sheep were clubbed to death, forced through rings of fire, driven over cliffs, poisoned, and shattered with dynamite bombs. The widespread killing of sheep penetrated every section of the Western Slope.

Near Craig on the Yampa River in 1896, a masked band of cattlemen killed two Mexican sheepherders and clubbed 300 sheep to death. They warned the owner, Jack Edwards, a tough Welshman, to leave the Colorado range. Ten days after the deadline for leaving, Edwards still had 30,000 sheep in Moffat County. A masked band captured the sheep titan, put a rope around his neck, and lifted him into the air three or four times before he agreed to leave the country. Edwards proved to be a man of courage; despite the attack and his promises, his sheep ran along the Yampa River for many years to come.

Along the White River in 1894, the story had been the same. When sheep were trailed into the White River from Utah in increasing numbers, cattlemen acted quickly to save their range. They beat up sheepherders, slaughtered sheep by the hundreds, and forced sheepmen to agree to leave within a year. At Collbran, on the north side of beautiful Grand Mesa, sheep were driven from that part of the mesa with great ferocity in a war that raged from 1892 to 1894. They have not returned to this day.

Reason was also not prevalent in the Gunnison country. In 1902, two members of the Gunnison County Stock Growers' Association were temporarily expelled for keeping a few sheep for domestic use. When ex-president Alonzo Hartman supported expelling the two cattlemen, he was asked if he did not eat mutton. The shocked Hartman caused a roar of laughter from the gathering by admitting: "Yes, but I am ashamed of it."[6] Perhaps in no region of the Western Slope were sheep more hated and opposed than in the Gunnison country; in no region was the slaughter of sheep so great. In June, 1901, twenty

158

nightriders slaughtered 2,300 sheep near Iola on the Gunnison River. The sheep were part of a herd of 10,000 that had been brought in past the Cimarron dividing line established by the cattlemen. Three years later, sheepmen again tried moving into cattle range and again the Gunnison country erupted into violence. This time the trouble came in Taylor Park. Five thousand Utah sheep were moved from Castle Creek near Aspen over Taylor Pass. Nine days later 100 masked men tied up two sheepherders, ran 1,500 sheep into a large corral, and systematically shot and clubbed the animals to death.

The cattle-sheep war on the Western Slope continued unabated until after World War I. Sheep killings continued in the Uncompahgre and North Fork valleys, in northwestern Colorado, and in the Gunnison country. "With blazing rifles and sixguns the western Colorado Night Riders held back for awhile the menacing tide of migratory sheep, but this . . . group of cattlemen . . . were playing against a stacked deck—falling beef prices, depletion of their winter ranges by homesteaders, and opposition of the federal government. . . ."[7] Gradually, the cattle-sheep war faded into history. Federal regulations on the public domain, strict enforcement, and well defined, informal boundaries designating cattle and sheep range ended the killing and slaughter. As a matter of fact, many Western Slope cattlemen turned to sheep before World War I because of a severe drop in beef prices and a rise in the sheep market. Shades of Benedict Arnold! Today, sheep outnumber cattle on the ranges of Western Colorado.

The creation of national forest reserves by President Benjamin Harrison in 1891, which eliminated grazing, mining, homesteading, and timber cutting, shocked the Western Slope, but a lack of enforcement caused little outcry at first. The reserves were used as usual despite federal regulations. During the 1890s, more reserves were added but the government allowed prospecting, grazing, and selective timber cutting. Then Teddy Roosevelt, a man familiar with the West and Western Colorado, became president in 1901. Roosevelt was aware of the devastation and raping of the western range and resources and determined to do something about it. In 1905, the national forest reserves, controlled by the Interior Department, became national forests with supervision transferred to the Secretary of Agriculture. Roosevelt's chief forester, Gifford Pinchot, persuaded the president to establish twenty-one new forests, embracing 40 million acres, in 1907 and to charge grazing fees for cattle and sheep using the federal range. Western Slope cattlemen were infuriated and fought the measure, but because of internal conflicts among themselves, their protests came to naught. When Fred Light of Aspen tested the government by deliberately trespassing on national forest land, he was arrested. The cattlemen took the federal government to court, but in 1911, after many appeals, the United States Supreme Court upheld his conviction of trespass and ruled that the government did have the right to regulate federal lands by charging fees to users. The decision forced Western Slope cattlemen to obey the law, which now was being enforced vigorously.

Western Slope cattlemen soon accepted reality and worked with the Forest Service to regulate grazing, halt forest fires, and conserve the water of the high country. Today, the cattlemen agree that the establishment of the national forests saved the Western Slope range from overgrazing and impending disaster.

Shortly before leaving office in 1908, Teddy Roosevelt tried to put the entire public domain, and not just national forests, under direct federal control. Congress, under intense pressure from the cattle industry and western states, refused. However, events soon brought the issue to a head. Spurred by the great Depression and the depletion of millions of acres of the public domain because of overgrazing, Congress passed the Taylor Grazing Act of 1934. By now, even diehard Western Slope cattlemen realized the necessity of such an act; if something were not done, there would soon be no range to graze on.

Representative Edward T. Taylor of Glenwood Springs and Colorado's Fourth Congressional District was the man behind the Taylor Grazing Act and one of the great men of Western Slope history. Taylor had served in the House of Representatives since 1908, was one of the ranking Democrats in that body, and was the chairman of the powerful House Appropriations Committee. What Ed Taylor wanted he got, and what he wanted was a grazing act. The timing was perfect for such an act. The New Deal was riding high, Democrats controlled Congress, and livestock men themselves were clamoring for regulation of the rest of federal lands.

Although Ed Taylor was responsible for the 1934 grazing act, the man who was responsible for its success was its first director, Farrington Carpenter, an Eastern-educated, Western Slope bred cattleman from Hayden on the Yampa River. Carpenter, then in his forties, was a lawyer and a Republican, but was a close friend of Taylor. He was intelligent, fair-minded, and most important, was gifted with common sense. He, like Taylor, was one of the greatest men ever produced by the Western Slope. Working for Harold Ickes, the Secretary of the Interior and "one of the meanest and pettiest men I have ever known,"[8] Carpenter successfully fought attempts to create a

160

large bureaucracy to administer the act. Instead, he turned the job of apportioning the range over to the stockmen themselves. It was a stroke of genius. Stockmen might lie and take liberties with the federal government, but it was impossible to fool one's own neighbors on an advisory board deciding how the range would be used. With a $140,000 budget, $60,000 of which he did not use, and seventeen technicians borrowed from the United States Geological Survey, Carpenter made the Taylor Grazing Act a brilliant success.

Alas, as a conservative Republican working for a spiteful and jealous New Deal Democratic boss, Carpenter had a rough time personally and knew his days were numbered. After being fired by Secretary Ickes several times, only to be rehired immediately because of Ed Taylor's intervention, Carpenter finally resigned in November of 1938 and returned to his ranch at Hayden. The job of regulating the public domain was completed; it had been done well. Homesteading had been ended except on reclamation projects. The single most vital factor in the advance of the American frontier—free land—passed from the scene. From now on, men could use the nation's grass and timber only under the supervision of huge federal bureaus.

The Western Slope did not give in easily. A final episode, involving national forests and not the Taylor Grazing Act, occurred in 1939 in the Uncompahgre country. At issue was the Forest Service's right to change the number of animals a stockman was allowed to graze on public lands—his permit. Over the years permits had become vested rights and the worth of a man's ranch was based in part on his permit. Ranchers screamed that the new rules amounted to illegal confiscation of property rights; the Forest Service declared that the range belonged to all Americans and when it deteriorated, it was their duty to reduce the numbers of animals using it. The issue came to a head in 1939 when the Forest Service announced that fifteen ranchers running over 14,000 cattle in the Uncompahgre National Forest would have to accept a twenty percent cut. They refused and challenged the federal government in a test case watched by all stockmen. After fourteen years of meetings, argument, and appeals, Secretary of Agriculture Charles Brannan ordered the cuts made. From this decision dated the principle that no private individual could obtain a vested right in the public lands as to be beyond the rule of government agencies.

The years since 1950 have seen a decline in the number of sheep and cattle in Western Colorado, and an accompanying decline in farming. The stockmen and farmer pay outrageous prices for machinery, fertilizer, insecticides, and fuel; taxes have gone up. Yet, the prices they receive for their products has stayed about the same. Many farms and ranches have been sold to real estate developers for much more money than their owners could make working the land. One finds it hard to blame ranchers and farmers who have been fighting a losing battle for a quarter century for selling out.

They pay eight to one if you throw two fours on the crap tables of Las Vegas today—"the hard way eight"—and those are about the same odds of success a rancher or farmer had in the history of the Western Slope. Drought, frost, heavy snow, the federal government, predators, alkali, and vicious competition for the limited good land available often beat the farmer and rancher into submission, but the legacy of both live on. For the farmer and rancher had a dream and the dream was and still is dear to the hearts of all the people of the Western Slope—the right to be left alone—to be free.

11.
"When You and I Were Young, Maggie" Nineteenth Century

A dream, it is said, lives forever; so does a photograph, which momentarily freezes time and captures everything in front of the camera's lens. Photographers crossed the divide almost as early as the pioneers. They understandably concentrated much of their early attention on the mining communities and their mines; by the turn of the century, however, as settlement expanded so did the photographers' horizons.

Bruce Catton wrote that "America is equally a tale of might-have-beens and used-to-bes," as well as the more oft-told successes. The photographs which follow were selected to show not the famous, but the ordinary Western Slopers and their haunts. Examine them closely, for they are you and you are they a hundred years ago. The dreams, the joys, the griefs, and the failures cannot be captured by the camera, but they existed nevertheless. Use your imagination and come back to another time, so distant, yet so near. Study these photographs, for each has a story to tell and another story behind it.

The Green Grove is gone from the hill, Maggie
Where first the daisies sprung;
The creaking old mill is still, Maggie
Since you and I were young.[1]

[1] "When You and I Were Young, Maggie," Folksong.

163

164

Upper left. The Utes roamed over the Western Slope when Americans first penetrated the region. Their tragedy was that they stood in the way and held something a more powerful people wanted. Their most famous leader, Ouray, sits in the front row, third from the left; in the second row, far right, is Otto Mears, probably the most famous Western Sloper of his day. *Courtesy First Federal Savings.*

Lower left. From Red Cliff (Eagle County) to Rico (Dolores County), mining spread across the mountains, reaching nineteenth century heights at Aspen and in the San Juans. Red Cliff would eventually come into its own as a zinc producer, while Rico had a moment of glory with silver in the 1880s. Both of these districts were amazingly lengthy producers, each still active into the 1970s. Numerous small mining camps were scattered throughout the mountains, full of anticipation, short on production. *Courtesy C. M. Engel, Rico Colorado.*

Above. All prospectors hoped to discover a mine like the Tomboy in Savage Basin high above Telluride, which produced over $24,000,000 before major mining ceased in the 1920s. Quite a settlement grew around the mine, including cabins, boarding house, school, YMCA, and a tennis court. Owned for a long time by English investors, Tomboy operations showed what a big business mining had become. *Byers photo courtesy Harriet Backus.*

166

Upper left. Most Western Slope mining never reached the Tomboy pace. The thrill of the search and the expectation of development summarized the reward of most prospectors and miners. They left behind a hole in the mountain, a mine dump, and shattered dreams. This coal mine at Crested Butte was one of the more successful ones. *William Henry Jackson photo courtesy Colorado Historical Society.*

Lower left. While gold and silver captured headlines, copper, zinc, lead and coal were also mined in the nineteenth century. This turn-of-the-century photograph of one of the major coal camps, Crested Butte, shows the coke ovens in the foreground. Coal mines tended to attract primarily recent immigrants, because of their lower pay scales and more dangerous working conditions. *Courtesy Michele Veltri, Crested Butte.*

Above. These are the men who opened the Western Slope, the miners and surface workers, plus management, and the extremely important cook. Mining was more than just digging ore out of the ground. It took carpenters, blacksmiths, common laborers, hoist operators, and others to keep the miners going. This unidentified crew posed in Hinsdale County. *Courtesy Denver Public Library, Western History Department.*

167

Mining advertised and promoted the Western Slope more than anything else in the nineteenth century. Bonanzas in Aspen and Silverton and high hopes at Ruby, Pitkin, and Breckenridge whetted interest. None of these surpassed Telluride, however, which did much to promote the Slope, including sending a gold and silver exhibit to the World's Fair in Chicago in 1893 to rival "Little Egypt," cotton candy, and the famous Ferris wheel. *Courtesy Colorado Historical Society.*

168

The future of the Western Slope rested on its being able to solve the problems of isolation and transportation. The "stubborn" mule of legend kept many mines and camps supplied; so did the burros shown being loaded at Homes' Store in Ouray. Horses also pulled supplies, equipment, and people into the mountain canyons and river valleys, as they did here at Pitkin. Together they made settlement possible. *Courtesy Milly Moorhead, Ouray and Bob Williams, Gunnison.*

Upper left. Horses and mules might do for their time, but their days became numbered when the railroad appeared. The Denver and Rio Grande opened large segments of the Western Slope to settlement. Repair and maintenance at round houses such as this at Cimarron (August, 1885) kept those engines running. *Courtesy First Federal Savings.*

Lower left. One of the important industries that came with mining was logging. Unsung and often ignored by history, the logger was essential to mining and all settlement. These logs are being hauled into Crested Butte. *Courtesy Helen Watters, Gunnison.*

Above. Here at the Ames Power Station on the San Miguel River the first alternating electric current was generated to operate a mine. Electricity solved one of the pressing mining needs: cheap power that did not have to be freighted to the site. It also brightened town and home. Telluride and Aspen pioneered in the use of electricity. *Courtesy Western Colorado Power Company, Fort Lewis College.*

171

172

Upper left. Water was the key to unlocking the riches of agriculture (and mining, to a degree) on the Western Slope. Towns appeared along the rivers and so did early farms, but once settlement moved away, water had to be brought along. Flumes and canals were constructed throughout the region to transport water. This flume was used to get water to the U.S. Gold Placers on the San Miguel River. *Courtesy Denver Public Library, Western History Department.*

Lower left. Early farmers found the virgin soil rich and some amazing harvests resulted. Discovering the length of the growing season took time and resulted in many disappointments. These men are loading hay at Hinkle's Spur up the Ohio Creek Valley north of Gunnison in the 1880s. *Courtesy Bill Ender, Gunnison.*

Above. Nothing has been more overglamorized, nor caught the public's fancy longer, than the cowboy. Western Slope cowboys found the work hard, the hours long, and the pay meager. Some of the cattle watching the branding look placid enough, but they could turn into hellions when their turn came to be roped. *Photo courtesy First Federal Savings.*

173

Upper left. Culture came early to the Western Slope. What town, or mining camp for that matter, wanted to be without an "opera house." An opera never played in most, but they indicated that the people were striving for something more than red-light district entertainment. The actors, actresses, and orchestra are ready in Craig—curtain going up in the mid-1890s. *Photo courtesy First Federal Savings.*

Lower left. The most popular indoor sport for the masculine contingent, and they predominated, was the diversion of the red-light district. This title covered a multitude of "sins," from saloons to prostitutes. Despite an often-portrayed romantic image, the life of the "soiled dove" offered only a hard and degrading existence. Aspen's row sat by the railroad tracks. *Courtesy Denver Public Library, Western History Department.*

Above. Play ball! Baseball was the most popular sport in the late nineteenth century. Most towns and a few mines and smelters fielded their own nines. Fierce competition resulted, and it was not unknown for a team to import "ringers" for a crucial game, particularly a pitcher. Neither the fields nor the equipment would pass muster today, thus scores like 28-21 were not uncommon. Pitkin's team seems to be doing well this day. *Courtesy Bob Williams, Gunnison.*

Even in the nineteenth century, tourism started to take hold of the Western Slope. Ouray, almost from its birth, advertised itself as a tourist attraction, as did Hot Sulphur Springs for the invalids. Two of the most popular attractions over the years have been skiing and outdoor recreation. These skiers posed at Irwin in 1883, including one fellow who could not stand up. They would have said they were snowshoeing, not skiing. The bathers are dipping in Grand Lake, probably around the turn of the century. *Courtesy George Mellen, Gunnison, and Colorado Historical Society.*

III
Where Have All the Good Days Gone
1900-1945

Each community has its story about the first automobile to chug into town, sometimes with the aid of a horse. When they were a new toy, people tried to be the first to take a car here and there. This pioneer auto to reach the Tomboy got only part way, then needed horse help. *Courtesy Patty McCall.*

A generation before, it had been a wilderness; now the Western Slope had become part of the American scene. Like the rest of the country it suffered through two world wars, a devastating depression, and other assorted ills. The good times came and changes too. By 1945 it was not the region of forty-five years before.

12.
Water: The Achilles Heel

In the beginning there was sufficient water on the Western Slope of Colorado. It is not true today. A hundred and twenty-five years ago the rivers ran free, unimpeded by dams, ditches, and canals, and nature took care of its own. For the few Indians, and later, the few white men who trapped the beaver, water had been plentiful. When the miners descended on Western Colorado in the 1870s, water assumed a more important role. Only then did men learn the bitter truth: the Western Slope was a very arid land. "Impossible," cried the skeptics, pointing to the mountains and the heavy snows of winter. But it was true. The lack of trees, high plateaus with little vegetation, and sagebrush which covered even some of the valleys proved the aridity of the land.

The Indians and mountain men knew, and the miner soon found out, that during the summer and fall, precipitation was scanty on the Western Slope. To be sure, during the spring the rivers ran full, often flooding over their banks as the melting snows of the mountains cascaded down canyons and ravines to the valleys below. Alas, much of the water ran over frozen ground and did not saturate the soil; the rest flowed out of the Western Slope en route to the Pacific Ocean, because there were no dams or reservoirs to keep the precious liquid at home. Even the heavy snows in the high country were deceiving, dry and powdery, unlike the wetter snow of the rest of the country. All too often the dry snow only produced an inch of water for every thirty inches of snow.

181

The Indians and mountain men were aware of the lack of water on the Western Slope, but myths die hard. Placer miners who worked their way across the Continental Divide to the Blue River, San Juan, and Gunnison countries in the early 1860s were soon aware of nearly dried up streams during the late summer and early fall. But the lack of large numbers of people on the Western Slope hid the aridity of that section from most observers. Thousands of miners flocked into Western Colorado during the period from 1874 through the 1880s, but the silver panic of 1893 depopulated much of the region. From 1893 until the middle 1950s, the Western Slope languished, a sleeping giant, containing rich prizes of energy, precious metals, snow, and, most of all, water that it could not use.

The lack of growth in Western Colorado had some potentially dramatic consequences. If Western Colorado could not make use of the water it had, then under the western water law doctrine of prior appropriation, other sections and states could. They came like a thousand buzzards circling their prey. The eastern slope of Colorado needed and demanded water diversions under the Divide to sustain the majority of the state's population. The lower basin states of Arizona, Nevada, and California, through the Colorado River Compact of 1922, got their share; and even Mexico wanted its palm greased with water. If that were not enough, various special interests, including ranchers, farmers, industrialists, municipalities, conservationists, and the federal government fought each other to get the lion's share of Western Slope water. It was all incredible, but the war for water had begun.

The Western Slope is a mountainous land with some of the highest elevations of any state or major section of a state in the Union. Because of the mountains which drain a disproportionate share of the West's moisture from the passing clouds, the Western Slope is the source of many major rivers within Colorado. The Yampa, White, Dolores, San Juan, Gunnison, Eagle, Roaring Fork, Animas, and Uncompahgre are all rivers which head in Western Colorado. All are tributaries to the mighty Colorado River, "the most cussed and discussed stream in North America." This great river heads on the Western Slope near the town of Grand Lake in Middle Park and, on its way to the Pacific Ocean, drains much of the American Southwest. "It is not a particularly heavy-flowing stream [it ranks only about sixth among the nation's major rivers], but it is virtually the sole dependable water supply for an area of 244,000 square miles including parts of seven western states—Wyoming, Colorado, Utah, New Mexico, Nevada, Arizona, California—and Mexico."[1] The influence of the Colorado River has been felt far beyond its own watershed. Its waters have been diverted hundreds of miles to feed urban, industrial, and agricultural growth in regions like eastern Colorado, western Utah, and the faraway coastal plain of southern California.

Only twenty percent of the Colorado River Basin lies inside the Western Slope, but seventy-two percent of the water in the river originates in that section. So, quite unwillingly, the Western Slope is responsible for much of the water used by Arizona, Nevada, and California. And therein lies the rub. The heart of the Colorado River problem is the fact that the river does not carry a great deal of water, certainly not enough for all the demands made upon it. Only a handful of cities, farms, and industries exist in the Southwest because of the lack of water. Although chambers of commerce will not admit it, most of the West, including Colorado and the Western Slope, has been condemned to remain a desert, and nothing that mortal man can do will change that fact.

"Indians were the first inhabitants of the Western Slope to tackle the problem of distributing water according to man's desires rather than nature's imperatives."[2] The Mesa Verde Indians used rain water for irrigation, carrying the water from catch-ponds to fields, or digging diversion ditches for such purposes. But the desert proved unyielding. A prolonged drought between A.D. 1272 and 1299 was a major reason the Mesa Verde Indians were driven out of southwestern Colorado forever.

The few fur-trappers who plied their trade in Western Colorado took advantage of the many streams to trap the beaver, but some also diverted stream water to small gardens they had planted. The men of Fort Robidoux, near today's Delta, raised fine gardens made possible by irrigation water diverted from nearby streams. The fur-trading frontier ended in Western Colorado by 1845, and for the next decade and a half, no one gave much thought to water. There seemed to be and there was plenty of water for the few residents of the mountain region.

The first major users of water on the Western Slope were the miners who came in small numbers to pan streams in the 1860s, and then came by the thousands to mine silver in the 1870s and 1880s. They appropriated water greedily and with reckless abandon for all phases of their operations—for sluicing, for hydraulic mining, for dredging, and for stamp mills and smelters. "They also used water for flushing away their waste, a flour-fine substance called tailings, [turning] some of the most beautiful . . . Western [Slope] streams into repulsive flows of gray sludge."[3]

Mining companies resorted to fantastic and expensive means to obtain the water they so desperately needed. Ditches were dug, flumes constructed, and miles and miles of pipe were laid. One of the most fantastic projects was the six-mile-long hanging flume of Dolores and San Miguel canyons, fed by a ditch originating near present-day Uravan. Started in 1890 to provide water for a giant hydraulic project on a high gravel bench called Mesa Creek Flats, the snaking wooden structure was six feet wide and four feet deep. It was anchored by cables and braces to the side of smooth red sandstone cliffs far above the Dolores River. During seven years of work from 1890 to 1897, the promoters spent nearly $200,000 on the Rube Goldberg contraption and although they eventually got some water through it, the project proved to be a financial disaster.

The miners also recognized water as a valuable source of energy; it was used to generate hydroelectric power. Roaring off mountains and cascading through canyons and ravines, the water only needed to be harnessed to create cheap and clean power. Scores of mining mills utilized hydroelectric power, including one of the best known and most photographed—the Crystal Mill between Crystal and Marble in the Gunnison country, which provided power for the Sheep Mountain Mine.

Mining's great contribution to the Western Slope economy was not only the millions of dollars dug from the earth, but also the impetus it gave to agriculture. Thousands of mules, horses, and burros had to be fed locally grown grain and hay. Men in the mining towns had to be provided meat and vegetables. As a result, a solid farm and ranching economy was established, a development greatly aided by a transportation network originally built to serve the mines. Agriculture required water for irrigation, and lots of it. As mining slumped in the 1890s, agriculture became the region's top industry. It remained the major industry for some time only because, through yeoman efforts, it was able to get ample water for irrigation. Even before the turn of the century, as now, agriculture gulped down more than eighty percent of the water used on the Western Slope.

"Much Western Slope land is as fertile as a stray alley cat."[4] According to Felix Sparks, fiery Colorado water expert, much of Arizona and California have longer growing seasons than the Western Slope, but less water is needed in the latter region to bring comparable crops to maturity. The problem, albeit a staggering one, is to move stubborn streams out of their normal channels to the fertile land. Some irrigation took place in the 1870s, usually involving small diversion ditches from streams to adjoining bottom lands. The pace picked up in the 1880s with larger projects undertaken. By then, everyone recognized the aridity of the land and the critical importance of water. By the turn of the century, 226,000 acres of land on the Western Slope were irrigated, less than half the acreage which could realistically be watered.

The Western Slope, with only a fraction of the population of Colorado, makes up approximately thirty-three percent of the land area and is responsible for a staggering sixty-nine percent of the water. The fertile land, long growing season in much of the region, and plentiful water made irrigation projects feasible and likely to succeed. Thus, one of the first major irrigation projects in Colorado was constructed on the Western Slope.

The removal of the Uncompahgre Ute Indians to a reservation in Utah in 1881 opened the lush and beautiful Uncompahgre Valley to white settlement. Made up of the area drained by the Uncompahgre River which heads near Red Mountain Pass and empties into the Gunnison River at Delta, the region includes much of present-day Montrose and Ouray counties, the town of Delta, and the eastern half of San Miguel County. It was a beautiful valley in 1881, mostly unpeopled and still, and waiting for the white man to bring it to life. When the region was first settled, and the towns of Delta and Montrose sprang up, it was felt that the Uncompahgre River and its tributaries would provide enough water for all of the valley's tillable 175,000 acres. It was not to be. Farmers found that water was available for only 25,000 of the acres. During the next two decades, depression and despair came to the once-promising Uncompahgre Valley with large tracts of land, valueless without irrigation water, deserted. Yet, a mere twenty miles away, plenty of water was available as the mighty Gunnison River pounded its way through the 2,000-foot-deep Black Canyon.

Many men dreamed of diverting the Gunnison River through Vernal Mesa, which separated the Uncompahgre Valley from the Black Canyon, but the task seemed impossible. The state of Colorado even became interested, and with very little regard of where it was jumping, dipped deep into the muddy waters of reservoir and canal building. The result was State Canal Number Three, underwritten to the tune of $25,000 in 1901—a B-B gun for hunting elephants. State Canal Number Three was later called the Uncompahgre Project. The small amount of money for bringing water to the Uncompahgre Valley was soon exhausted and the project appeared dead.

But wait! A new federal agency, the United States Reclamation

185

Service, became interested in the project. However, before risking millions of dollars, the agency wanted a complete exploration of the Black Canyon to determine if a diversion tunnel was feasible. Prior to 1901, no one had ever traversed the awesome gorge. The Ute Indians considered it suicide to go into the canyon, referring to it as "big rocks, much water." Yet, on August 12, 1901, two men attempted to perform the impossible — conquer the Black Canyon.

Abraham Lincoln Fellows of the United States Geological Survey and his twenty-nine-year-old aide, William Torrence of Montrose, were the men upon whose shoulders the hopes of residents of the Uncompahgre Valley rested. Fellows and Torrence entered the Black Canyon at the mouth of the Cimarron River, carrying only a small rubber raft, two 600-foot-long silk lifelines, rubber bags to hold their food, and hunting knives. What followed was one of the great adventures in the history of the Western Slope. Alternately swimming, climbing, and walking, the two men were swallowed in the shadows of canyon walls which grew higher and higher. By the third day, the Gunnison River had become a foaming, vicious torrent, and the canyon walls had become vertical. On they went, past the Giant Stairway and Painted Wall, through the narrows where the walls of the canyon were only forty-four feet apart, and finally to Red Rock Canyon where Fellows' aide, A.W. Dillon, could finally supply them. The expedition came to an end a day later. For nine days, Fellows and Torrence, totally exhausted, nerves on edge, had looked death in the eye in the Black Canyon, but they had found a good site for a diversion tunnel to bring Gunnison River water to the Uncompahgre Valley.

The United States Reclamation Service, now satisfied that a tunnel could be built under Vernal Mesa, began work on the Gunnison Tunnel. The "Gunnison River Diversion," as it was called, was one of the first five projects undertaken by the Reclamation Service, now known as the Water and Power Resources. Following several surveys, work got underway in 1905. Hundreds of men labored from Lujane or West Portal and River or East Portal in the depths of the canyon. Although the Gunnison Tunnel was only 6.2 miles long through Vernal Mesa, a twisting, terrifying twelve-mile wagon road with twenty-two percent grades was used to supply the workers at River Portal.

Five hundred men labored in the bracing Colorado air on the Gunnison Tunnel from 1905 to 1909. The work was not easy; difficulties included badly fractured rock, concentrations of poisonous gases, underground streams, and hot water seams. Despite good pay and fringe benefits, the work was so hard and dangerous that the average stay for a worker was only two weeks. The cost in lives and money was high. Six men were killed during construction, and the total cost of the tunnel and accompanying canals was $10,541,560. On September 23, 1909, at Lujane or West Portal, the great moment finally occurred for the Western Slope and the people of the Uncompahgre Valley. President William Howard Taft threw the switch which opened the headgate of the Gunnison Tunnel, symbolically releasing the flow of water from the six-mile-long bore into the thirsty valley of the Uncompahgre. The Uncompahgre Valley had been rescued from the desert! The pitch of the tunnel was a little over two feet per thousand; the water capacity was 1,300 cubic feet per second.

Although the Gunnison Tunnel and its canals were constructed to irrigate 146,000 acres, enough water was available for only half that acreage. Since the opening of the tunnel, the total value of all crops grown in the Uncompahgre Valley is slightly over a quarter of a billion dollars. A long recognized need of the Uncompahgre Project was upstream storage of spring runoff so that irrigation water would still be available in late summer. This prompted the construction of the Taylor Park Dam in 1937. The 206-foot-high earthen dam holds back a massive reservoir containing 106,200 acre-feet of water when full. The water in the reservoir is owned by the Uncompahgre water users. For the people of the Uncompahgre Valley in 1909, the Gunnison Tunnel was a dream come true; for the thousands who live there today, the tunnel is life itself.

There were other irrigation projects on the Western Slope which were not so successful. Consider the Montezuma Valley in southwestern Colorado. Nearly 100 years ago, men recognized the financial possibilities in diverting Dolores River water to the warm and sparsely watered Montezuma Valley south of present-day Dolores. The Dolores River makes a big U-shaped bend below the town of the same name; just south of the low divide bordering the bend lay the potentially rich Montezuma Valley. The trick was to get water to the valley. Out on those dry flats, dominated by a magnificent view of the north rim of Mesa Verde, James W. Hanna owned a block of land. During the prosperous and speculative 1880s, when the Western Slope was experiencing a craze brought on by outsiders eager to invest in water schemes, the aggressive Hanna set forth to get water for the Montezuma Valley.

Hanna told his story of potential wealth in Denver and in the financial capitals of the East. He convinced enough people by 1885 that he and his backers were able to incorporate the Montezuma

Valley Water Supply Company. The new company cut a mile-long tunnel under the Divide separating the Big Bend of the Dolores River from the Montezuma Valley. With ample water flowing to the arid but fertile valley, Hanna and his company had hopes of making a fortune.

As part of his contribution to this get-rich-quick scheme, the shrewd Hanna donated some of his land to the water company. The company proceeded to lay out upon the sagebrush flats a townsite they named — what else for a valley called Montezuma — Cortez.[5] By 1889, gravity diversion water flowed into the valley through the tunnel, and hopes were high for a massive occupation of the Montezuma Valley. It did not happen; few buyers appeared. Unfortunately, the panic of 1893 loomed just around the corner, and an agricultural depression already had begun. Farm prices plummeted and the hoped-for eastern investors, who were expected to buy the land at inflated prices, never appeared. Such land promotions had succeeded before and since, but they do not succeed during a depression. The Montezuma Valley Water Supply Company went broke.

The succeeding decades brought new bankruptcies, feuds, and reorganizations, but the Montezuma Valley never saw much water except from subsurface wells. Finally, a conservancy district was established. The new hope of the district was to obtain water for the Montezuma Valley, Dove Creek, and nearby Ute Mountain Ute Indian Reservation from one of the Bureau of Reclamation's projects under the Upper Colorado River Storage Act of 1956. After almost 100 years of failure and disappointment, hope again sprang eternal. Was it possible that the people of the Montezuma Valley and Dove Creek would get a dam and canals to carry life-giving water to the region? The answer was yes; the Dolores Project is currently underway in southwestern Colorado.

Seventy-five miles or so to the north, another ambitious band of pioneers attempted to subdue the land and mother nature in a region just as dry as the Montezuma Valley. The Colorado Cooperative Company, a Denver-based utopian ditch concern, found a site on a little mesa named Tabeguache Park just north of the San Miguel River. In 1894, the colony founders, their worldly goods loaded in lumber wagons, made their way over the Uncompahgre Plateau to Tabeguache Park. The park contained 20,000 acres of fertile but arid land; irrigation water was needed if the colony were to survive and prosper. After a thorough investigation, colony members decided it would be possible to divert San Miguel River water from the San

Miguel Canyon seventeen miles to the southeast. The water would be transported through a ditch and wooden flume to the head of Tabeguache Park.

Following some preliminary work, the colonists established the town of Pinon in the bottom of San Miguel Canyon where Cottonwood Creek ran into the San Miguel. This became the major construction camp for the diversion of the river, but it was not the only one. At least three other camps were established along the route of the diversion. After a decade of work, the ditch was finished in 1905. Most of it was wooden flume because lumber was available and inexpensive. When water began to flow through the ditch, colonists began leaving Pinon for Tabeguache Park. Land was cleared and ditch laterals built. Soon, the park became an agricultural garden with fruit, vegetables, and grain, along with lush crops of hay. The colonists did not want to use up one precious acre for a townsite on Tabeguache Park, and so established a town on a rocky hill above the park. The new town was named Nucla.

As the years passed, the wooden flume began to deteriorate and the residents of Nucla were forced to replace it with a ditch. Most of the work was performed during the winter so it would not interfere with farm work. Maintaining the long ditch has required much work and skill, but it has been maintained. Today, the ditch diverts water to over 6,000 acres in Tabeguache Park. The great diversion ditch insured success to farmers and ranchers alike in the lower San Miguel country.

The Grand Valley, with Grand Junction in its center, is another example where irrigation was necessary for development and growth. If fruit, grain, and hay were to be raised, the Colorado and Gunnison rivers would have to be tapped for water. Grand Junction did not wait long. By mid-1882, only months after the town began, the Pioneer and Pacific Slope ditches were completed. The biggest water diversion, however, was the Grand Valley Ditch, begun in the early 1880s. The ditch was designed to irrigate 50,000 acres of land in the Grand Valley, but the ditch company ran into financial difficulties almost from the start. The Traveler's Insurance Company of Hartford, Connecticut, lost $200,000 financing the original diversion.

The expense involved in constructing the Grand Valley Ditch was enormous, but residents of the Grand Valley, desperate for water, paid the price in money and sweat and, with help from the Bureau of Reclamation, finished the ditch. In 1915, the Grand Valley Diversion Dam of the Grand Valley Water Users Association was built across the Colorado River seven miles above Palisade. The dam made it possible to raise Colorado River water twenty feet; the water was then diverted into the Highline Canal, thirty-eight feet wide and ten and one-half feet deep. The canal carried water to lands north of the Colorado River and ran as far west as the town of Mack. The first water ran through the mammoth canal on January 25, 1917.

Beginning in 1922, the Bureau of Reclamation constructed a siphon across the Colorado River in DeBeque Canyon, just up river from Palisade. Water ran in a concrete bench flume and an open canal to a hydraulic pumping station a mile south of Palisade. From here, irrigation water was pumped to the fertile, but dry, Orchard Mesa south of Palisade and southeast of Grand Junction. It was not long before the mesa lived up to its name, producing bumper crops of fruit. Many other irrigation ditches have been built in the Grand Valley. Today the valley contains the most sophisticated irrigation network on the Western Slope. Without life-giving irrigation water, the Grand Valley would have remained what it was prior to 1882 — a desert.

The Western Slope has been totally dependent upon irrigation water for its existence as a farming and ranching section. In addition to the already mentioned irrigated valleys, every other Western Slope valley capable of grazing cattle or raising agricultural produce has spent great amounts of money to divert water onto arid land. They include the North Fork, Gunnison, Roaring Fork, Yampa, White River, Eagle River, and Animas River valleys, along with some lesser known lands which also made use of the precious liquid. Water was life to the Western Slope and even in the early days, it seemed to flow not downhill, but rather towards money.

By 1922, the opportunity to use Colorado water in Colorado was being imperiled. More people, more irrigated lands, more industry, and especially the growth of California had placed severe demands on the amount of water produced by the Colorado River. Upper Basin states of the Rocky Mountains fought Lower Basin states of the Southwest; the Western Slope of Colorado was at odds with the eastern slope; and farmers, ranchers, municipalities, and industrialists engaged in bitter feuds over water rights. Many of the conflicts over water wound up in court. Two far-reaching cases, Kansas vs. Colorado (1907) and Wyoming vs. Colorado (1922) were decided in the United States Supreme Court. The water users soon realized that court action was not the way to solve the problem; the cases cost much money, took a long time to settle, and after great expense and long waits, one could not be sure of victory. It was time to change tactics.

The Colorado River and its tributaries flow through seven western states. The Upper Basin states of Colorado, Wyoming, Utah, and New Mexico were separated from the Lower Basin states of Arizona, Nevada, and California by Lee's Ferry, located a few miles below today's Glen Canyon Dam in northern Arizona. All the states were interested in guaranteeing water for the future; they all realized that water and their futures were irrevocably linked. Two major questions had to be answered: how much water was produced by the Colorado River; and how should the water be divided among Upper and Lower Basin states? Despite bitter animosity among the seven states, they all sent representatives to Santa Fe, New Mexico, and hammered out one compromise after another before signing the famous Colorado River Compact of 1922. Though all the states feared each other, they feared ultimate federal government control of western water more; this fear led to the compact. The Western Slope, home of the Colorado River and many of its tributaries, obviously was greatly affected by the 1922 act.

Two serious mistakes were made in developing the Colorado River Compact, and both have hurt the Western Slope ever since. The first mistake was made by the Bureau of Reclamation in overestimating the flow of the Colorado River at between 18,000,000 to 20,000,000 acre-feet of water per year. The average flow since 1922 has been only 13,700,000 acre-feet per year. The second mistake was agreeing to allow 75,000,000 acre-feet of water to pass by Lee's Ferry every ten years (an average of 7,500,000 acre-feet per year). The failure of the Colorado River to live up to expectations in water production severely penalized the Upper Basin states and, of course, the Western Slope. If the Colorado River only produced 13,700,000 acre-feet per year and the Upper Basin states allowed an average of 7,500,000 acre-feet to pass Lee's Ferry, that only left 6,200,000 acre-feet for Upper Basin development. If a federal treaty with Mexico, giving away an additional 1,500,000 acre-feet of Colorado River water is considered, the figure is even lower.

The Western Slope was unaware of the approaching water crisis during the years immediately following the Colorado River Compact. Few people lived there and plenty of water was available for irrigation, if the water could be moved from its source to where it was needed. But the Western Slope failed to understand western water law which amounted to: "use it or lose it." If Western Colorado could not make use of its water, then other developing regions of the Southwest and Colorado would. The Lower Basin states and the eastern slope of Colorado were waiting in line and drooling at the prospect of obtaining Western Slope water. Denver and the Front Range were growing and needed water, as did farmers in the South Platte and Arkansas River valleys.

Water diversions from the Western Slope to the eastern slope had begun as early as 1860, when the Hoosier Ditch was built to divert water to placer diggings near the headwaters of the South Platte River on the east side of the Divide. But the first major diversion came in 1939 following the completion of the Moffat Tunnel. The underdeveloped Western Slope was now in danger of losing its water unless it could show it needed it immediately. Another state water war, which has lasted to the present, began as the Western Slope fought for its future. During the long battle, Western Colorado was blessed with some fine torchbearers, including Congressmen Ed Taylor and Wayne Aspinall and Senator Ed Johnson. The battle was long and intense and its story will be told in a later chapter.

From 1870 to 1945, the Western Slope, by hard work, vision, and stubbornness, built dams, canals, ditches, and pumping stations to supply water to an arid land.

> The Montezuma Valley story, the extraordinary community effort that gave birth to the town of Nucla, the grim determination of the men who first explored the Black Canyon of the Gunnison for the Uncompahgre Project — all these things show clearly enough that water has always been recognized as the key element of a satisfactory life between peaks and the desert.[6]

And still the battle continues; it has not stopped or even slackened — it has, instead, become a titanic struggle. But that is the way it has always been on the Western Slope — an arid land doomed without life-giving water.

Farrington Carpenter
The Man From Hayden

He was born in Illinois in 1886 and educated at Princeton and Harvard Law School. After coming to the West for his health in 1900, he fell in love with the wide-open spaces and never left. Today, at ninety-four, Farrington Carpenter still lives on his cattle ranch along the Yampa River, just east of Hayden in northwestern Colorado. He has resided in that section of Colorado for nearly all of the twentieth century and is the state's most famous cattleman and agronomist.

Carpenter was one of six children born to a wealthy shoe manufacturer and his wife in Illinois. At the age of thirteen, he was sent to New Mexico because his mother feared that he might contract tuberculosis. Carpenter became enamored with the cattle industry and the man he worked for, rancher Si Dawson. He devoted his summer vacations to punching cows for Dawson—first in New Mexico, and then in northwestern Colorado. Carpenter loved the Yampa Valley because it was "wide-open and available for homesteading—young man's country." In New Mexico, most of the land was Spanish land grant and was too expensive for a young man to buy.

Upon his graduation from Princeton in 1909, Carpenter took up a 160-acre homestead near Hayden in Routt County. Three years later, in July of 1912, Carpenter, a recent Harvard Law School graduate, hung out his shingle. He recalled: "Hayden had never had a lawyer and didn't need one, but I was determined to supply it with one."[1]

It did not take long for Carpenter to find out what he was up

193

Farrington Carpenter, age 14.

against. One of the few early cases he had involved collecting stud service fees from ranchers in the Hayden area. A Nebraska owner of a Percheron stallion had come to town with his horse to breed the ranchers' mares for a fee, paid in the form of a promissory note. Carpenter wrote to all of the defaulting note signers threatening them with a lawsuit if they did not pay their notes of twenty-five dollars. The day after he sent the letter, Carpenter was awakened from a sound sleep by an angry cattleman. According to the rancher, the deal with the owner of the stallion had been twenty-five dollars for a service which guaranteed a foal, fifteen dollars for one service with no guarantee of foal, and five dollars for "one leap." Although all the cattlemen claimed they had only contracted for "one leap," they all had good foals. So much for Carpenter's bill collecting [2]

Farrington Carpenter's first law office in Hayden was nothing more than desk space in the Yampa Valley Bank. There was not much need for a lawyer in the Yampa Valley when Carpenter hung up his shingle, but that situation soon changed. Sheep were on the way!

The cattle-sheep dispute consumed northwestern Colorado for over twenty years, until the Taylor Grazing Act of 1934 finally established rules for the open range. During the titanic struggle for the open range, Farrington Carpenter was embroiled in the middle of the controversy, first as lawyer for the cattlemen, and later as the first director of the Taylor Act. He proved to be intelligent, tolerant, humorous, and gifted with common sense. For many years, due in large part to his efforts, northwestern Colorado remained cattle country. Later he recalled: "No [livestock associations] were incorporated, and only a few kept any books . . . they came to life when there was a need, and then faded away when the need lessened. The earliest associations offered rewards for wolf scalps . . . When the sheep came, they sprang to life in order to oppose them."[3]

The dispute between cattlemen and sheepmen was primarily economic. There was only so much open range in the West, and both wanted the land to graze their herds and flocks. Conflict was inevitable. The appointment of Farrington Carpenter as first director of the Taylor Grazing Act was a stroke of genius. Despite his long association with cattlemen, Carpenter was considered a fair man and was accepted by sheepmen. By hard work, common sense, and fairness, he made the Taylor Grazing Act very successful; few others could have.

Carpenter knew the prejudices and problems of cattlemen and sheepmen firsthand. For two years, he drove his dusty model-A Ford all over Colorado and other Western states explaining fees, grazing permits, and classifications to thousands of angry stockmen. When he resigned as director in 1938, the bitter struggle involving cattle and sheep was over. It was due in no small part to the small town lawyer and rancher from Hayden.

Farrington Carpenter has seen many changes come to once-primitive northwestern Colorado. He likes to say that he can look south from the porch of his Yampa Valley ranch and see the four eras northwestern Colorado has passed through. In his yard, characterizing the first era of the frontier, is a pile of antlers and horns. The second era is shown by the railroad tracks nearby. The tracks are those of the famous Moffat Railroad, which reached Steamboat Springs in 1908 and Craig in 1913, bringing much-needed transportation to the region. The highway which runs by Carpenter's ranch is a dramatic reminder of the third era—the motor age. The fourth era is characterized by a large coal generated power plant, located just south of the highway. This era marks the rise of energy development, more people, and environmental problems. Carpenter has lived through all four of the eras of northwestern Colorado.

Farrington Carpenter has been a pioneer, rancher, lawyer, politician, bureaucrat, and now is a breeder of fine cattle. He thinks of himself as an agronomist striving to raise cattle with more beef, at less expense, in an effort to show the world one way to eliminate starvation.

Carpenter regards development in northwestern Colorado as inevitable. "I'm not a believer in the view that we can put a fence around us and keep everyone else out." He believes that change has been the one constant factor in the history of northwestern Colorado.

He is a very old man now, but still he looks to the future and not to the past. And he is optimistic. When asked to characterize himself, Ferry modestly replied that he was a little like Andrew Carnegie: "I never knew much but always surrounded myself with people who did." Farrington Carpenter was and is a pioneer in the true sense of the word. He has always led and not followed; he has believed that hard work and dedication would lead to a better life. "I got from my mother a desire to crusade," he told one of the authors in 1979. "Everything I've been in I always wanted to change a little."[4] Not many of his generation and stature are left today; he is one of the last of a dying breed. Too bad for all of us.

13.

"Playground for the Nation"

The twentieth century ushered in a calmer period for the Western Slope. Growth leveled, the astonishing spurts of the earlier mining rushes being a thing of the past. Such steadiness proved desirable, allowing the region time to catch its breath, with less sudden shifts one way or the other. Maturity replaced youthful exuberance in the four decades following 1900.

In the opening decade, the hardcore mining counties (except San Juan) lost population, accelerating the trend begun in the nineties. The farming counties prospered, Delta and Mesa showing the greatest percentage of increase (149% and 139% respectively). Mesa, the big gainer, led the entire Slope with 33,791 residents. Every county gained in the 1930s except San Juan, which was hard hit by mining decline and labor unrest. Although the mining counties showed a percentage jump in the thirties, they actually contained fewer people in 1940 than in 1910. In 1940, a ranking of all Colorado counties by population found only Mesa in the top ten, joined by Montrose, Delta, and La Plata in the first twenty. Most of the Western Slope lay in the bottom half.

These developments reinforced the Western Slope's rural, agricultural image. Without the attractions of new mining districts and communities, urbanization seemed to recede. Only Grand Junction and Durango, urban islands, exceeded 5,000 people, thus maintaining the position they had held since the early 1900s as the largest and most significant of the region's towns.

197

Western Slopers did not change much either. Native-born Americans continued to be the vast majority. Of minority groups, Indians made a statewide percentage impact. Because of the Ute reservations, La Plata and Montezuma Counties contained 69% of all Indians living in Colorado in 1940. Chinese, Japanese, and Blacks were found only in insignificant numbers. The cosmopolitan population attracted by mining, evident in 1910 by the 25% or more foreign-born in the mining counties, had largely disappeared by 1940; national immigration patterns had changed and mining had lost its attraction for many immigrants.

With agriculture suffering from problems common elsewhere in the United States and mining in sharp decline, the Western Slope's economy cried for help. Tourism offered an attractive alternative. Blessed with the most spectacular and varied of Colorado's mountain and plateau scenery, and with a growing reputation among tourists, the Western Slope had a solid foundation for expanding its promotional activities. The stabilization of population actually provided a breathing spell during which tourism could be developed without pressures of urbanization, industrialization, and growth. Fortunately, the Western Slope acquired both national forests and parks early, thereby bringing in the federal government and its resources.

The Western Slope welcomed the coming of national parks and monuments. The region received two-thirds of those established within the state. Efforts to preserve the archaeological ruins and sites at Mesa Verde led to the creation of that national park, the first in Colorado and the Southwest. A group of dedicated women were largely responsible for its establishment. They talked, wrote, agitated, lobbied, and finally saw their labors rewarded. In June, 1906, President Theodore Roosevelt signed the bill. An active conservationist, Roosevelt also championed national forests, setting aside many of the reserves, an action that angered Western Slopers. They were pleased, however, by "Teddy's" hunting trips on the Western Slope and his praise of their land.

Rugged access to Mesa Verde National Park left out all but the healthy, adventurous types. Only 27 tourists visited it in 1906 and a decade passed before 1,000 appeared, hardly an outstanding total for a couple of summer hours today. Mancos, on the Rio Grande Southern Railroad, was the starting point for reaching Mesa Verde. Here one could rent a horse, buggy, and a guide, and be off over country roads that eventually became trails up the mesa to the ruins. Road improvements came later. In 1914 the first automobiles wheezed and coughed up a narrow road, their drivers stopping frequently to take pictures. Mancos liverymen strongly opposed such competition, accurately sensing their day was drawing to a close. Even with improvements, the roads gave the flatland visitor a thrill; the "knife-edge" section was not easily forgotten. A fee of $1 per trip, or $5 for the season, allowed one to enter the park, except when wet and muddy roads prevented travel. Cars sank nearly to their hubs in some of the mud holes.

With the advent of the twenties and Americans' love affair with the automobile, visitor totals mushroomed, reaching 16,000 by 1930. To keep pace, Superintendent Jesse Nusbaum constructed a visitor complex near the well-known "Spruce Tree" ruin. This included administrative offices, museum, bunkhouse cabins, bath house, lodge, and a hospital to treat those sprains, cuts, and minor injuries acquired from scrambling over the cliffs. Stabilization and excavation of sites improved noticeably under archaeologist Nusbaum's direction; he was the first superintendent to reside in the park, establishing park headquarters there, rather than at Mancos.

Initially Mancos gained the most economically from the park and its visitors, although before long Durango, and finally Cortez, came to share the trade. Interestingly, a few small coal mines in the park supplied coal to Cortez. Not until 1931 were these mines closed for being inconsistent with a 100% conservation policy. This minor setback was the only one the region suffered from the park's proximity. Mesa Verde helped advertise southwestern Colorado, promote tourism, encourage better roads, and bring in needed federal and tourist money. These marvelous ruins also encouraged interest in archaeology throughout the region, a study which today is locked into a savage race against destruction by encroaching settlement.

Mesa Verde was not Colorado's best known park. Rocky Mountain National Park claimed that honor, even though nearly a decade younger. Almost overlooked is the fact that part of it lies on the Western Slope. A determined Enos Mills, Congressman Edward Taylor, just starting a long and distinguished career as one of the Western Slope's greatest spokesmen, and others led the movement to create the park. Grand County reacted lackadaisically, and eastern slopers were openly hostile to their efforts. They overcame this indifference and antagonism and, as Mills wrote, saved a rare variety of nature's best, a "place of distinction," a park "established for the benefit and enjoyment of men, women, and children, a playground for the nation."[1] The park's western section remained nearly forgotten until 1932, when the Park Service completed a fine road over the Fall

River pass. This opened the whole park, and charmed visitors discovered Grand Lake just beyond the park's boundaries.

"Playground for the nation"—the sparsely populated Western Slope would become just that, though not for several decades. Once highways and passes were opened for automobiles, the Western Slope provided an escape back to nature for inhabitants from the heavily populated front range. Although it took more time and individual expense, the rest of the United States eventually enjoyed it, too. The question of how to satisfy the demands of growing numbers of visitors without spoiling the playground, and also provide for Western Slope development, has never been satisfactorily resolved. Some locals have never, in fact, adjusted to the playground concept.

Government involvement in making the Western Slope the "playground for the nation" culminated in four national monuments. Dinosaur National Monument, tucked away in the far northwestern corner of Colorado and northeast Utah, protected deposits of dinosaur bones. This also happened to be one of the last "unspoiled" wildernesses left in the country. Man had been there—Indians, the Escalante expedition, and the famed explorer John Wesley Powell—he had just never gained much of a toehold. President Woodrow Wilson set aside the first eighty acres in 1915, and Franklin Roosevelt enlarged it in 1938 to include the scenic Green and Yampa canyons.

In March, 1933, Roosevelt's predecessor, Herbert Hoover, in one of his last official acts, established the Black Canyon of the Gunnison National Monument. Montrose may take a large share of the credit, particularly the Lions Club, which actively worked for a road to the south rim. As early as 1901, a visitor commented that "something should be done to invite tourists and sightseers to look on its wonders."[2] It was done and, with reliable help from Representative Taylor, it succeeded.

Isolated and oft-forgotten Hovenweep, west of Cortez, came into existence in 1923 by presidential proclamation. Featuring a series of Indian ruins on canyon top and bottom, it was the least frequently visited, barely topping 200 visitors per year in the twenties.

Colorado National Monument owes its establishment to John Otto, nicknamed a "self-appointed one-man Chamber of Commerce of Western Colorado." Almost singlehandedly, he preserved, promoted, and developed the site just west of Grand Junction. Slightly eccentric, Otto badgered locals and elected officials in order to create interest in his dream. The monument was proclaimed in 1911, with Otto as custodian. Living in the monument, he continued his one-man campaign until finally he antagonized one official too many. His eccentricity took its toll; his employment was terminated in February, 1927. The ever-loyal booster John Otto had served all that time for $1 per month.

Not to be outdone by Washington, Western Slopers did their best to stimulate interest in their own homeland. That heritage of nineteenth century America, the fair, proved to be a popular way to promote local products, while providing a good time. Here town and country exhibited the "finest, largest and best" of local agricultural and horticultural products, as well as an unlimited variety of other things, including quilts, cakes, and grandmother's favorite jams. Mix in a rodeo, baseball games, parade, races, and perhaps a novelty like an "aeroplane" or "moving picture" and one could hardly resist the temptations. Special trains brought visitors from miles around, infusing the local economy with welcome cash. Durango had the Colorado-New Mexico Fair (with an Indian camp as an attraction), Montrose its Western Slope Fair, Kremmling the Grand County, or Middle Park Fair, Glenwood Springs its Strawberry Days, and so on. Occasionally the fair dates overlapped and squabbles ensued, such as in 1905 between Montrose and Grand Junction. Generally, however, peace was preserved.

Alarmed protectors of public morality monitored these events, ever watchful that sin did not sneak in under the guise of community fun. One year at Kremmling it evaded their guard, but a quick stop was put to "ragging, including the turkey trot, bunny hug and all other objectionable forms of dancing." Nevertheless, fairs promoted towns, counties, and products. Many have long since disappeared or been modified, yet Glenwood Springs continues its Strawberry Days, still a major celebration for the community. In 1925 it was held on June 23-24, with a Ford touring car given away each day to "some lucky visitor." Besides plenty of strawberries to eat, events included a rodeo, baseball games, airplane exhibitions, and other sports, all free.

Strawberry Days proved to be more than just a promotional effort—it helped Glenwood move from the declining hot springs era into a more diversified tourist, recreational, and ranching economy. Glenwood Springs had been a leading "spa," with railroad tracks almost to the pool's edge. In the late 1880s and 1890s, the majestic Hotel Colorado, one of the state's finest, catered to affluent guests. Gracious elegance prevailed, a "Victorian heaven," or as the Hotel Colorado advertised, "one of the most romantic spots in America." The hotel's pamphlet boldly declared that its famous springs, luxurious bath establishment, and bathing facilities "far surpass everything of the kind in America or the Old World."[3] A golf course and polo grounds lured sports enthusiasts from the veranda's ease.

But the old order changed noticeably after World War I, and Glenwood found itself a Victorian has-been, out of step with the new age. Glenwood Springs had to change, and it did. The *Glenwood Post* proclaimed on January 1, 1931, that the visitor would find "Recreation, Rest, Recuperation." It lauded the hot springs, to be sure, then went on to acclaim local hunting, fishing, horseback riding, mountain climbing, and auto trips. By 1941 Glenwood Springs was advertising itself as a resort, a ranching center, and an outfitting point for sportsmen, in anticipation of post-war developments.

The same pattern of promotion was attempted for other "spa" communities, but less successfully. Pagosa Springs, with one of the largest springs in Colorado, met with the least success. Not for lack of trying, it was doomed to failure. A picturesque location and springs certain to cure rheumatism and "stomach trouble, blood and kidney diseases" could not overcome isolation, lack of strong financial backing, and a slow promotional start. Other resorts left Pagosa in their dust, and it never caught up. The same could be said for Hot Sulphur Springs, despite its early prominence, Gunnison's Waunita Hot Springs, Steamboat Springs, and Durango's Trimble Springs. Ouray did all right with its springs until mining declined.

Steamboat Springs most nearly paralleled Glenwood's achievements, adapting easily to recreational needs. Recreation-oriented tourists made their presence felt, particularly in hunting and fishing. Such activities were not, of course, new to the Western Slope, where they had been pursued for the livelihood they provided. Now they became a sport. The Steamboat-Hahn's Peak area offered some of the best hunting and fishing spots available, with convenient access by car or train. Once this land teemed with game; now the deer and elk populations had been reduced to the point of scarcity. The *Steambot Pilot* commented in 1934 that game management was the key to bringing back the big game animals. The paper pushed for development of a "wild game policy" that would not work any hardship on established industries or area occupations. Eventually cooperation between state and local people achieved just that for both the hunter and fisherman.

Fish had been stocked in lakes and streams on the Western Slope for years. In 1914 there were at least ten state and private hatcheries in Western Colorado. The Colorado Fish and Game Department also released new types of game birds, such as Hungarian partridges, and restocked elk on their old ranges. The Western Slope had gained an enviable reputation. Noted author William Raine, in 1911, rhapsodized, "When one speaks of the big fellows, the ten-pounders, he thinks of the Gunnison River." And for the big game, "he very likely has Routt County in mind." Pressure on available hunting and fishing resources nevertheless built up in the thirties and exploded after the war in unforeseen ways.

There appears to be something about traveling on the open road that brings out the worst in people. Grand Junction's *Daily News* finally remonstrated in its May 23, 1923, issue that it was too bad "that there is not some way to train the urbanite in the rules of the outdoors and campfires." He should, the article went on to say, learn the etiquette of the forest, learn when it is wrong to throw down a lighted match or cigarette. Generations of Western Slopers concurred and have their own stories about those atrocious "outlanders."

The tourist activity, both the sightseeing and recreational varieties, was seasonal, limited primarily to the summer and fall. Something had to be done to generate more year-round appeal. One answer was immediately at hand—skiing. Recreational skiing, with long skis, primitive bindings, and only nature-provided slopes, caught on in a few mountain communities in the nineteenth century. The skier usually zoomed down a long slope, hoping not to careen into a pine or spruce, or ski over some hidden obstacle. Then a long hike, or perhaps a sleigh ride, got the skier back to the starting point.

In the twentieth century, thanks to strong Scandinavian influence, skiing attracted more participants. During the Christmas season of 1911 Hot Sulphur Springs held a "winter carnival" that included jumping and cross-country skiing. Jumping soared in popularity; Dillon's winter sports club sponsored a meet on its new course in February, 1919. It attracted some of the "world famed ski jumpers," and the competition produced a then world's record jump of 213 feet. In December, 1941, the Aspen Ski Club was making arrangements to install a rope tow and had scheduled "quite a few important meets" for the coming winter. Other events intervened. The great skiing boom obviously came after the war, but the Western Slope had made a start. With the foundation laid, all that was needed now was promotion and money to develop ski areas and resorts.

Thus tourism and recreation charted development of the Western Slope. Grand Lake, between the lake of the same name and Rocky Mountain National Park, had reached the point of gearing its economy toward visitors, as seasonal as they were then. Elsewhere, tourist camps sprang up in or near many communities, and for those who preferred indoor accommodations, motels met the need. Lodging habits were changing; the stately hotel found itself an anachronism. Convenience, cost, and a new life style contributed largely to the changes. The prime mover, however, was the automobile; it produced demands for better roads, increased tourism, and a whole new industry devoted to servicing this family "necessity."

The first cars chugged onto the Western Slope early in the century, sometimes helped along by their rival, the horse. For example, the first car into Silverton was pulled by a team of horses over the pass it could not climb. Glenwood Springs residents turned out in 1906 to see Barney Oldfield drive through during the first coast-to-coast automobile race. Then there was Aspen's Bob Pipson, who purchased a Star automobile in the spring of 1925 and delighted in speeding around the local highways, making everyone else "eat his dust."

Bob, Barney, and the rest could only go as fast and as far as the highways permitted. The first major impact of the automobile was increased demand for better roads. "Good Roads" conventions, usually held in Denver, promoted statewide efforts. A Colorado automobile club was also organized to pressure for better roads, and finally in 1913 the State Highway Department came into being, replacing the older highway commission. Three years later Uncle Sam dealt himself into the game by contributing road construction funds on a dollar matching basis. Even the smallest towns aspired to a position on a transcontinental highway, as ardently as they had wanted earlier to be on a railroad line. Gradually a state and federal system developed, which satisfied some communities and rang the death knell for others. An example of the highway's impact on one area was shown in Montezuma County. A local historian maintained that no function of county government was more vitally important to the general welfare than county highways and roads.[4] Montezuma grew slowly, as did its county seat of Cortez, until roads improved after the turn of the century. Still, it was 1923 before it had its first gravel-surfaced county road. Tourism lagged, even with Mesa Verde, until improvements came.

Dove Creek, in next door Dolores County, owed its existence to better roads. The construction of a good road from Cortez in the early 1920s completely opened the area and allowed easy access for settlers and convenience in shipping produce. Dove Creek grew enough to wrestle the county seat from declining Rico in a hotly contested election in 1944. Without advantageous road connections, Dove Creek would have remained a country hamlet like many of its neighbors.

Along with better roads and more cars came the demand for improved city streets. The *Grand Junction Sentinel*, April 10, 1902, felt it was high time street repairs were made: "The character and amount of traffic is now so extensive that the question of better and more permanent streets must soon be solved." The question of when a solution would come has persisted from that day to this, particularly during street-destroying spring thaws. With increased traffic came more "fender-benders," serious accidents, and fatalities. The car proved to be a mixed blessing.

All those roads had to lead somewhere, but the mountains stood in the way; their passes had to be conquered. A state road over Wolf Creek Pass came first, followed by new or improved ones over Berthoud, Loveland, Fremont, Monarch, and others. Dust was a nuisance in summer, but the real difficulties came in winter. As late as World War II, the highway department did not attempt to maintain Tennessee, Slumgullion, and Lizard Head passes, among others. Narrow, winding, blasted out of the mountain face, these passes terrified the flatland tourist and challenged even local drivers. But they did open Western Colorado to the motorist. Denver was now an easy summer day's drive from Middle Park or a couple of days from Durango. The impact of these improved mountain roads cannot be overstressed; the Western Slope would never be so isolated again. What many would consider its "good old days" were gone forever.

The real squeeze came in the 1920s, when Western Slope counties simply did not have the financial resources to maintain, let alone build, roads. They turned to the state for help. Typically, the legislature appropriated less for the west than it did for the east. By 1925 the Western Slope had fewer than six miles of state hard-surfaced roads, out of 251 miles completed. Most county and state roads stayed unimproved. Some improvement came in the next decade. In 1935, when Colorado averaged a little better than 50% of its state roads surfaced, Grand County hit the average, La Plata bettered it, Moffat was lower, and "poor little Pitkin had none." Evidence of county financial straits is shown by the fact that, though the whole state averaged about 15% surfaced and 33% graded, Grand and Pitkin had no county surfaced roads, and La Plata had only 3%. Nor were the figures any better for graded; Moffat, for instance, had only 4% even at that level. The rest of the roads were unimproved.

By World War II the counties caught up somewhat, but still lagged, as did state construction. Not until the 1950s would there be more equalization. The more politically powerful eastern slope counties would finally be prevented from helping themselves at the expense of the Western Slope. The feeling of regional exploitation grew, and now Western Slopers had the hard facts, jarred backs, and poor roads to support their contention.

Denver remained a prime suspect. Durango's crusty old Dave Day had suggested back in 1912 that Western Slope fruit growers form their own association and stop dealing with Denver "commission pirates." Others complained of Denver's political power, legislative lack of concern, and what amounted to regional discrimination toward the rest of the state.

To counterbalance this trend and continue to promote the Western Slope, towns and counties collected exhibits, dispatched speakers, and published pamphlets. In 1912 the town of Hayden printed a booklet proclaiming itself the agricultural, mining, and cattle heartland of northwest Colorado. Steamboat Springs, Pagosa Springs, Montrose County, and Moffat Tunnel League, to name a few, followed suit, each promoting its own district and special attractions. Finally, a Western Colorado Chamber of Commerce was organized to advertise the entire area. A Western Slope Historical Association was also formed. Regionalism was beginning to take hold, but the hardships of the depression years put an end to most of these early efforts. Money in desperately short supply could hardly be spent to publish "puffs," when people were out of work and short of food.

The newspapers, those champions of localism, however, continued the fight when occasion demanded. They rushed in at the drop of a hint of criticism or lack of appreciation of the Western Slope and its towns. The *Meeker Herald*, March 1, 1913, was typical in its comment, "Everybody please boost our school and everything that is for the good and advancement of our community. If you can't 'boost,' don't 'knock' — everyone dislikes a knocker."

Western Slopers appreciated their quality of life, as elusive and individual as that term might be. Just what they meant by this was never specifically defined, though a good approximation may be gathered from their comments. Durango, read a 1901 pamphlet, was law abiding, possessed unsurpassed educational facilities, was blessed with a religious and moral atmosphere, and was a well-built city — the "best city of its size in the West." Montrose and Olathe advertised their delightful, healthful climate and abundant water supplies. A Delta man wrote, "There is no place like Delta county" to make money.[5] Mix scenery with climate, add some culture and refinement, a dash of urbanization and modern improvements, and stir with profit, and a quality of life emerges. This might not be today's definition of quality of life, but it met the needs of those times. A Durangoan of 1915 was concerned about the local smelter's odor and pollution — not its existence, but its possible absence. If the stench disappeared, it meant the closing of the town's chief industry and loss of jobs.

As interesting and potentially profitable as the concept of "playground for the nation" appeared to be, most Western Slopers probably were hardly affected by it, economically or in any other way, in the early years of the twentieth century. Simply making a living was the important thing, whether for the citizen of Maybell or resident of Bondad. They read in their newspapers that the state and nation were changing, and whether they liked it or not, that change filtered slowly down to them. Barney Oldfield was interesting to read about — so were those "aeroplanes" — but they were in the future for most Western Slopers.

The first fifteen years of the twentieth century produced an acute awareness of America's problems, and optimistic Americans were convinced they could solve them. In this progressive era, as it was named, a wide variety of issues received attention, from urban government to child labor to conservation. Coloradans ardently embraced progressivism, passing a varied legislative program and sending forth some national leaders. With the notable exception of conservation, Colorado stood foursquare for the movement.

The Western Slope attacked a number of inequities with particular vigor, among them "special interests" that appeared to threaten American democracy. "They" influenced legislation for the benefit of the few, to the disadvantage of the masses, charged the *Dolores Star* on October 31, 1910. The writer went on to support the initiative and referendum amendment as the means to end political corruption and restore power to the people. Dolores and Colorado voters did just that, overwhelmingly, in the state election. Those two major tenets of progressivism received enthusiastic national application as well. Two years later Colorado voters faced a wide choice of thirty-two bills and amendments, twenty of them initiated by the people's concern. Everything from statewide prohibition to recall of judicial decisions came before the voters, who reacted by defeating most, but passing the recall of judicial decisions in an unprecedented step.

On local and individual levels, various issues agitated Western Slopers. Although not threatened by big city political machines or widespread corruption, communities did experiment with new forms of city government, one of them the city manager concept. Meeker phone users castigated Mountain States Telegraph and Telephone for its rates and service. Dissatisfied with the "telephone octopus," they favored establishing independent lines and found support from other

Western Slope towns. Electric companies overcharged their customers, complained one Western Sloper, and there could be no apology for such "bum service." Municipal ownership was the answer to such shenanigans, though it smacked of socialism and would have generally horrified Coloradans in an earlier day. Now, with attacks on "monopolies" a popular pastime, it was taken in stride.

Grand Junction's Chamber of Commerce indignantly protested long vs. short haul railroad rates, which it felt discriminated against Western Colorado shoppers and businessmen. Members telegraphed the Interstate Commerce Commission to ask for a hearing. The railroad, once considered the Western Slope's savior, had been looked upon with increasing disfavor for more than ten years, mostly due to the rate issue. Even Durango and Silverton, which obviously benefited from the Denver and Rio Grande, expressed displeasure toward their benefactor. In 1906, however, Durangoans were more agitated over the charge that local butchers used chemicals to restore color to meat (that was the year of Upton Sinclair's muckraking novel *The Jungle* and its exposé of the meatpacking industry).

Western Slopers became every bit as involved in the progressive era as their big city cousins in Denver and beyond. Americans have a habit of seeking the short cut to the promised land; they prefer to believe that one reform will solve everything. That one answer at this point was prohibition. Crime would surely decrease, the red-light district depart, the poor house be abolished, and juvenile delinquency vanish; those who favored prohibition saw nothing but the rosiest future once the reform took hold.

There was nothing new about the "liquor question." "Wets" vs. "Drys" had been fighting over local option and statewide prohibition for years; even the "drys" showed no unity, some favoring temperance, others prohibition. An early ramification of this struggle had been the Sunday closing issue. Mining communities heatedly opposed such an idea; the farming settlements more readily acquiesced to no liquor sales on the sabbath. The 1912 statewide prohibition amendment went down to defeat. Its supporters, never losing heart, aimed at 1914 for another attempt.

The battle, and it was that, was fought on the speaker's platform and newspaper page. Ignacio, which had gone dry locally in 1908, had some insights to offer. Only a few days in all that time had whiskey or beer not been available, and the editor of the *Weekly Chieftain* concluded that Ignacio had "more drunkenness than ever seen in the average wet town of the same size."[6] The cost of prosecuting bootleggers, whose business flourished, was not insignificant. The editor felt certain these conditions would continue, even if Colorado voted dry. His colleague in Dolores emphatically disagreed and urged his readers to vote yes on the amendment. Mining camp residents were nonplussed at the thought of such action—it seemed to be a denial of another bit of their heritage. With dance halls and gambling gone and the red-light district a pale shadow, what would be left for them? Mountain outposts, however, also had their active WCTU'ers holding the line.

Colorado voted dry in '14. The Western Slope fractured completely on the issue. Ignacio voters, for instance, voted to make themselves a "saloon territory" again, and then turned right around and approved statewide prohibition! The farming/ranching counties (Delta, Mesa, Montrose, Routt) voted dry; most of the mining counties (Dolores, San Juan, Ouray, Pitkin), wet. Mining simply did not carry the political clout it had once mustered.

A certain tranquility pervaded this reform era. The intolerance which characterized the post World War I era had not surfaced, even on the conservation and prohibition issues. Western Slopers took it all in stride and calmly tried to figure out a way to avoid prohibition.

The European debacle was enough to turn one to drink. Newspaper coverage of world affairs improved noticeably after 1900, and Western Slope readers were keenly aware of the European tensions that led to World War I. What they did not foresee was that they would become involved. A few with close ties to the homeland became emotionally involved, but it seems likely that most of them were happy to be where they were. When the United States eventually entered the war, in 1917, they greeted the occasion with songs, cheers, parades, bells, and patriotic addresses. Breckenridge residents were admonished to "produce more; use less—be a patriot." "Thank God we are Americans," said the *Craig Empire*. "Hoist a flag and show your patriotism." On a more somber note, the Hesperus Fuel Company hired extra watchmen for its coal operation. No enemy was going to sabotage the war effort.

Men volunteered from all over the Western Slope; Grand Junction gave its first volunteers a parade and a $25 purse as a sendoff. The boys joined impulsively, ready to get the "Hun," some in a company composed exclusively of Western Slopers. They trained, moved on to active duty, and saw more of the country than many had expected to see in a lifetime. Some did not come back from "over there," and the war took on new meaning for friends, relatives, and hometowns. The home folks joined the Red Cross, planted victory gardens, purchased bonds, loyally observed meatless days, and listened to exhortative speeches. They came to hate the "Hun" and all he stood for, a hate that could not be easily turned off when the armistice came in November, 1918.

Montrose broke into "pandemonium" when the news flashed that the war was over. Citizens crowded into autos and raced up and down Main Street, firing rifles and riddling a dummy of the Kaiser hanging at the corner. Whistles, sirens, fire bells, any kind of noise-maker, joined the din. Breckenridge High School students continued to buy "war savings stamps," and by the end of the school year were near the top nationally for per capita purchases.

That same fall and winter the flu epidemic hit the Western Slope. Hardly a town escaped it, nor was the countryside unscathed. A La Plata County farmer went to California, a Silverton miner fled to Durango. Nothing seemed to prevent its running its course; everything from quarantine to home cures was tried. As mysteriously as it had come, the flu departed, touching more Western Slopers personally than the war had. "Influenza was worse than Hun bullets," said the *Pagosa Journal*.

The progressive era and the war changed the Western Slope, as had the coming of the automobile and the tourist industry. What lasting impact they would have would become evident in the decades that lay ahead.

14.
Bootleggers, Bread Lines and a Desperado of the Far East

The "roaring twenties," a euphemism applied to a decade, conjures up visions of bootleggers, the Charleston, jazz, and a "fast" life. Colorado's Western Slope displayed little of the tinsel associated with those years, perhaps because of its rural setting. When the urban mining frontier disappeared, the region became largely rural by residence and agricultural by occupation. Agricultural villages replaced mining camps as urban exponents, implanting a conservatism and resistance to change that characterized the twenties.

Grand Junction stood as the major urban outpost. Its Chamber of Commerce boasted that "Grand Junction is a metropolitan city in every sense of the word," blessed with an "agreeable climate," recreational opportunities, excellent transportation facilities, shopping facilities equal to Denver or Salt Lake City, and a modern educational system. "The churches, the clubs and the many fraternal organizations all contribute toward a wholesome social life. . . . One can live very economically in Grand Junction."[1] Other Western Slope communities duplicated Grand Junction's pride in themselves. Boosterism was mandated, and descriptive slogans were applied indiscriminately. Paonia set the pace, calling itself "The Core of the Apple Country." 'Twas a privilege to live in Western Colorado.

The flapper and her consort called these pretenders "hicks and rubes," but Western Slopers took it all in stride. They accepted with alacrity certain material goods of the twenties (the car, radio, and movie), eyed dubiously the "Black Bottom," bootlegging, and the

211

liberated woman, and rejected the degraded morality and big city vice. Old time virtues, the wholesome life, held special meaning for them. Their way of life reinforced these attitudes and their isolation sheltered Western Slopers from threatening cross-currents.

Life went on much as it had before. Socially and, to a lesser degree, politically, the lodge, Grange, church, and the new American Legion Post shaped their thinking and fostered their companionship. Fads flared and faded. As it had for years, the weather furnished a continuing topic of conversation — a "genuine old fashioned" blizzard, like that which struck Moffat County in December, 1919, generated hours of reminiscences and speculation. Were those new-fangled "aeroplanes" affecting the weather? Sentimentality, not cynicism, molded their lives. A family Christmas, a heaping table on Thanksgiving, a patriotic Fourth — all were hallowed traditions. A touch of twentieth century Victorianism crept in under the guise of Mother's Day, a combination of the sentiment and commercialism. Breckenridge's *Summit County Journal* was moved on May 8, 1926, to pay tribute to mothers: "But the greatest job in the world is the poorest paid in the matter of dollars and cents. The job of motherhood, the hardest work, the keenest mental anguish, the greatest physical pain, brings the smallest reward in wages."

Lest one imagine that only sentimental rural reactionaries lived west of the Divide, it should be pointed out that the Western Slope attracted its share of Babbitts and others. Prosperity today and profits tomorrow shaped their thinking. An immediate post-war slump had rebounded by the mid-twenties and, as Yampa merchants happily remarked, our people "are happy and contented," as business volume and bank deposits rose in 1924. The flag of "business prosperity" waved proudly in the 1920s. Western Slope leadership only echoed national business attitudes; indeed, many of the local leaders emerged from the business ranks. Business's impact could be seen everywhere: Steamboat Springs folks were advised to spruce up their town to encourage visitors to increase their stay and stimulate business. What benefited business was good for the Western Slope.

Prosperity settled unevenly over the Slope, though without the extremes seen elsewhere. As the *Yampa Leader* observed, January 11, 1924, everyone was about "equally poor and all about equally rich," none ever going hungry. Money to dabble in the stock market, that paper road to the land of two cars in every garage, simply did not exist for most. A certain resignation shaped Western Slope thinking; it was not totally a part of this new age and was willing to settle for what it had.

212

The mountains could not isolate Western Slopers completely from the twenties. The insidious Ku Klux Klan incited some emotions. From Bayfield and Durango in the south, northward to Grand Junction and Steamboat Springs, the sheeted figures marched, recited their mumbo jumbo, and burned their crosses. Customarily, they staged their demonstrations on weekends; one lady remarked that the way to tell who belonged to the Klan was to check clotheslines on Mondays. Not enough Blacks or Jews inhabited the entire Western Slope to warrant their vendetta, so the Klan found other minorities to attack. Catholics and Spanish-Americans became the targets; conveniently, they were often one and the same. Violence marked the KKK path, Grand Junction garnering more than its share when the Klan took on Walter Walker and his newspaper, the *Sentinel*. When Craig's newspaper lost advertisers and subscribers under Klan pressure, the plucky editor retaliated by supporting Catholic and "wet" Al Smith in 1924.

True Klansmen boycotted certain businesses and patronized others, some of which wove the KKK initials into their advertising. They stood staunchly against hiring Catholic teachers, or even clerks, and tried to ferret out anyone unsympathetic to their peculiar brand of Americanism. Western State College in Gunnison landed in the middle when influence was brought to bear to fire Catholic and Jewish faculty members. In the end the college president resigned and the school was left in turmoil for several years.

By the end of the twenties the Klan had disappeared, though not the insecurities and bigotries it spawned. Klan hysteria followed the national pattern, gaining much of its strength in small rural communities. Its forlorn hope of restoring the old American virtues collapsed under its own violence, bigotry, and hatred. The reasons for its existence are found in Americans' uncomfortableness with change, their fear of foreigners, love of exclusive, secret fraternal groups, and the idea of Anglo-Saxon racial superiority. An ex-Klansman (and few admit to having been members) said, "Don't ask me why I joined. . . . But at that time if you weren't a member you weren't anybody, you were on the outside of everything. It's a hard thing to understand now."[2]

The bootlegger pirated his way onto the Western Slope, as law enforcement agencies winked at his activities. The United States went dry in 1920, and Washington busied itself trying to enforce the unenforceable. The "Feds" were hampered by inconsistent local law enforcement. Fish and game officers stumbled upon hidden stills and arrested their operators while searching for poachers. Frequently they filed charges on both counts—bootleggers had a habit of killing game out of season. Elsewhere, outnumbered federal agents were outwitted by determined bootleggers, whose enterprise thrived. Stills were found in abandoned mines near Silverton and in garages in Rifle. Some bootleggers' products achieved local acclaim, and even enforcement agents and elected officials were known to take a nip now and then. Otherwise law-abiding citizens made "home brew" to satisfy their own needs. Thus the ultimate reform failed, a remnant from the progressive age. When the great experiment finally ended with repeal of the Eighteenth Amendment in 1933, Western Slopers rejoiced with everyone else. This attempt to legislate the country's morals proved as unpopular here as it had in Denver or Chicago. Speaking of Chicago, rumor had it that some "big time" hoodlums hid out on the Western Slope until things cooled down at home. Both the Klan and bootlegging reflected national post-war social turmoil, not Western Slope aberrations.

When legislative action failed to promote morality, the schools gained renewed support as the means of inoculating young minds against worldly vices and of instilling middle class virtues. The one-room white schoolhouse of grandfather's day inexorably disappeared with the increase in consolidation of rural schools. Not until after World War II was consolidation nearly completed and then not without the natural resistance which opposed such change. Mesa County was a leader in the consolidation movement in Colorado, and in developing a new high school curriculum that would convince rural parents that continued education was just as necessary for country children as for their urban cousins. The plan succeeded, as more children finished the eighth grade and went on to high school than ever before.

Improved education extended·to all levels on the Western Slope. Colorado State Normal School, later renamed Western State College, opened in 1911, following nearly 25 years of appeals by Gunnison residents for a college in their town. The nearby deserted mining camp of Gothic was converted in the late 1920s into the Rocky Mountain Biological Laboratory, which offered summertime classes in a striking mountain setting. Grand Junction privately supported Mesa College until it received state aid and finally became a state junior college in the late '30s. Far to the southwest, when the bugles ceased to blow at Fort Lewis, it evolved into an Indian school (Grand Junction also had an Indian school, the Teller Institute), then a high school, and finally a junior college. Located in the country, south of the tiny coal camp of Hesperus, Fort Lewis naturally gravitated toward an agricultural curriculum and quickly became associated with the larger Colorado A & M College at Fort Collins. Two junior colleges and one four-year school satisfied the needs of Western Slopers, some of whom still doubted the practical wisdom of all that "book learnin'."

The national binge, known as the roaring twenties, came to an end in the fall of 1929, when the confidence that fueled the fun collapsed with the stock market and the economy. Since the Western Slope had not ridden the crest of prosperity, it did not immediately feel the first aftershocks of the crash. Six months to a year passed before the real tremors hit. The agricultural setting softened the blow somewhat; at least it provided food for the table, if the farmer had enough income to pay his taxes and other living expenses. Many were driven from their farms or city homes when the business failed or the job was abolished. The smelter shut down in Durango in November, 1930, closing that town's major industry and bringing home to the locals what the depression meant. Railroads, with less freight and fewer passengers, laid off workers; construction plummeted. Farmers found their market, not strong for a decade, almost gone. Banks failed, and people who had bought on credit in the 1920s discovered themselves mired in debt. Local relief agencies toppled under the magnitude of distress. To one who lived through these times, the good old days are simply "balderdash." One particular Western Sloper expressed no desire to go back to the hardships he remembered, including the bankruptcy of the insurance company in which his father had carefully saved money in an educational insurance policy; it became simply a worthless scrap of paper.

The depression was something personal for those who lived through it; for those who did not, it is almost impossible to grasp its total impact. The pictures are still vividly etched in people's minds of "Hoovervilles" and shanty settlements outside some Western Slope towns; bank failures and the loss of a lifetime's savings; moving from the home when money was no longer available to pay taxes; attending foreclosure sales — one's own or his neighbor's; eating marmots on the ranch when no other food was available; Christmases when Santa Claus failed to visit. Vivid images that would last a lifetime. In those days a nickel ice cream cone was a long-cherished treat for a youngster.

The first reaction to the depression was typically American — keep a stiff upper lip and muddle through. Do not give up, keep the faith — there is no cause for discouragement or alarm. Western Slopers tried but failed. Relief rolls lengthened, foreclosures mounted. By 1933 the *Steamboat Pilot* devoted eight pages of small print to delinquent property tax lists. Listen to the widow who wrote the Silverton tax assessor, pleading for a reduction, "I am not trying to evade my duties as a citizen — it's just hard to pay taxes. My chief business in life now has become the raising of $165 twice a year for taxes in four counties."[3]

Optimism became a rare commodity by election time 1932. Western Slope voters clearly preferred Democrat Franklin Roosevelt and his vague "New Deal" to four more years of the same with the Republicans and their discredited candidate, Herbert Hoover.

The New Deal enveloped the Western Slope. Federal relief agencies touched everyone and were gratefully welcomed. Western Slopers acquainted themselves with the scrambled alphabet that represented the New Deal agencies. Federal planning and money inundated the Slope. Relief, recovery, and reform, Washington called it.

Immediate relief, desperately needed in town and farm, came in 1933–34. Any job, from raking leaves to repairing schools, was subsidized to get people working to restore their confidence and pride. Then came planning, and under the Public Works Administration (PWA), Ouray, Montrose, and Grand Junction's water systems received needed modernization, Gunnison and La Plata counties secured major construction projects for the Taylor Park, Lemon, and Vallecito reservoirs, the Ute Indian Reservation received aid for repairing a sewer system, road building, and remodeling of a boys' dorm. Glenwood Springs acquired funds to improve its hospital. Much effort was put into improving parks, Mesa Verde using PWA funds to repair and stabilize major ruins, construct a museum addition, and improve its water system. At the Black Canyon, the scenic rim highway was graded. The Agricultural Adjustment Act helped farmers (with over $685,000 in payments) until the Supreme Court declared it unconstitutional in 1936. Even the much maligned National Recovery Administration and its Blue Eagle obtained support and some positive results. The National Youth Administration (NYA) provided jobs for high school and college students, helping them to finance their education. Perhaps the most popular New Deal agency, the Civilian Conservation Corps (CCC), built camps throughout the region, bringing in young men to work on a variety of projects.

Supported by federal funds, the State Historical Society interviewed pioneers and gathered historical data; artists painted murals for public buildings; librarians repaired and bound books; and musicians gave concerts. Jobs were found for white and blue-collar unemployed. Yet the unemployment situation proved more than just a temporary problem; business and industry were unable to absorb the surplus labor supply. Thus the work programs and government involvement continued throughout the thirties. Some Western Slopers could not grasp the underlying meaning of these changes. Slowly the system righted itself and the shock wore off, to be replaced by a quiet optimism. The Western Colorado Power Company, serving a third of the Western Slope, reported to its stockholders in 1936 that business all over its system was improving.

Electricity, no stranger to the Western Slope, primarily served the urban and mining areas. The Western Colorado Power Company, a conglomerate of smaller companies stretching from Paonia, Hotchkiss, Durango, and Silverton into Utah, powered a large region, but few lines criss-crossed the rural areas, where profits languished. It was the same throughout the United States — the one group (farmers) which could clearly benefit from electricity, was left without it. Roosevelt sought a remedy by setting up the Rural Electrification Administration (REA). Farmers were encouraged to form cooperatives, which would erect transmission lines and furnish electricity with the assistance of low interest loans from the REA. By 1941 three REA's had been established on the Western Slope and the competition encouraged older companies to extend lines to the farmer. The car had relieved his isolation, now electricity eased his work and modernized his home; the farmer was slowly catching up with his urban neighbors.

When better times allowed the luxury of criticizing such legislative tampering, it began. A Ouray citizen grumbled about suffering from an overdose of "legislation and regulation." Long-time Telluride and Silverton mine manager, Charles Chase, complained, "I have a horror of organization. We are over-organized." Western Slopers have repeatedly echoed similar sentiments while watching Federal regulation and involvement grow since the days of the New Deal. The *Montrose Press* took time out in 1939 to hammer editorially at the Works Progress Administration for top-heavy administration and a politically motivated payroll. Something else which annoyed the editor was the fact that WPA workers banded themselves into a union, when "they ought to be so thankful to have a job" that they would stick to it as "close as fleas stick to a dog."[4]

In the backs of many minds lurked a fear, perhaps best expressed by a La Plata County resident in late 1940: "When any people succumb to the lure of political coddling and give up their right of private action, even in a small degree, they have taken the first step toward state socialism . . . ."[5] The rugged individualism, presumed to have conquered the Western Slope's elements and land, was not compatible with the New Deal.

The 1932 election sat crusty, conservative Edwin (Big Ed) Johnson in the governor's chair. From Craig he came to Denver with a background of homesteading, teaching, running a farmers' co-operative elevator, and state politics. He had come to Moffat County to regain his health and now was a Western Sloper to the core. He knew the land, that mystical force that shaped his and others' thinking, and his actions, reactions, and words proved his roots were well buried. His Western Slope supporters understood and applauded. Although a Democrat, Johnson split with the New Deal and engaged in a long struggle with that arch New Dealer, Harry Hopkins. A states' righter, Johnson hardened his position as the crisis passed. This was more than just the traditional, parochial, western distrust of the federal government — it exemplified Johnson's and his neighbors' conservatism and reaction toward such basic changes. The Western Slopers' ingrained individualism found the "near socialism" of the New Deal a hard pill to swallow. Big Ed they liked; his success in Denver put him in the United States Senate and reinforced his claim of being the most influential Colorado politician of his day.

Ed Johnson was not the only major political figure to emerge from the Western Slope. No one more steadily represented the region's interests than Edward Taylor, who is nearly forgotten today on the Slope he did so much to shape. Illinois-born, Taylor moved to Glenwood Springs in 1887 to practice law, after brief sojourns in Leadville (where he had been the first principal of the high school) and Aspen. As lawyers often are, he was drawn into politics, first on the state level, then in 1908 he was elected to the United States House of Representatives. Except for one term, this Democrat served continuously until his death in 1941, a Colorado record. Taylor defended and fought for his district's interests, the Fourth Congressional District which at that time comprised the Western Slope. In water rights, dam construction, and national parks and monuments, Taylor was there to represent Western Colorado vigorously. The Taylor Grazing Act was his creation, as was the idea to change the name of the Grand River to the Colorado. He advocated good roads and, as far back as his state legislative days, pushed for what once was known as the "Taylor State Road" from Grand Junction to Denver. In the years before World War II no one better understood or represented Western Slope interests than this veteran lawmaker who died at 83, still serving his constituents.

Western Slopers seemed hypocritical in readily accepting, then rejecting, the New Deal. The first reaction was a deviation brought about by the hard times; the second, a traditional reaction. They were not mere opportunists; their self-help, individualist ethic had failed, and all that they had been taught to admire was teetering on the verge of collapse. Under such circumstances they accepted radical measures, as they had in the 1890s, to preserve their basically conservative way of life. This time, however, they reverted to their traditional paths much more quickly, as shown by their criticism of the New Deal, support of Johnson, and return to the Republican fold by the end of the '30s. Unfortunately for their peace of mind, the questions raised by the depression and the New Deal's response to it would not go away so easily. The old ways would no longer suffice, the clock could not be turned back. Not ones to give up, Western Slopers continued to fight the good fight, retreating slowly before the tide generated by the New Deal.

The New Deal offered only a few crumbs to mining, which had fallen upon hard times in the twenties. Uranium interest picked up again after World War I, but was completely crushed by competition from the extremely rich and cheaply produced Belgian Congo ore. Vanadium production limped along until the depression closed the Naturita Mill and shut the mines. Not until late 1936 did the U. S. Vanadium Corporation resume production in Western Colorado. The company constructed a mill at Uravan, which eventually became the largest in the world; the town was considered a model company town for its day. Situated in a narrow valley on the San Miguel River with the mill's tailings pile towering above, Uravan showed the company's faith in the district's long-range future.

Gold and silver mining declined — low grade deposits and higher costs continued the trend of the past thirty years. Telluride's big producers, the Tomboy and its neighbors, closed or mined only a fraction of their previous output. Silverton, after prosperous war years, followed the same path and nearly collapsed during serious labor troubles in the late thirties. Aspen lived on a hope that put no bread on the table. Breckenridge miners experimented with different methods to save placer gold. None of the processes solved the "mountain's greatest mystery," how to extract the finest placer gold from gravel and sand. Ironically, the depression stirred new interest in the placer districts. Previously scoffed at, dollar-or-two-a-day diggings looked pretty good in those years and the government helped by raising the price of gold. The New Deal went so far as to sponsor classes in the art of panning. Men and women took to the hills, reworking placers hardly touched since the days of '59. Interest soon waned, when jobs became more plentiful; placering was not a bit easier than it had been in the sixties.

Scattered throughout the mountains, small quartz mining operations upheld the industry's reputation — a far cry from the glory days of the previous century. Easterners occasionally gambled their money on untried Western mines, but only disappointment rewarded most of their efforts. The president of the New York-based Pardners Mines Corporation, J. G. Baragwanath, exploded in frustration, writing to Henry Carlisle, his mining engineer. Carlisle, having just examined the La Plata placers north of Hesperus, presented a discouraging picture that completely undermined enthusiastic local reports Baragwanath had received:

> Every now and then I get heartily sick of the mining business and after reading your letters, this turns out to be one of those days. It seems incredible that so few people connected with mining are capable of telling the truth. They either lie deliberately or they kid themselves or what is often worse, they are perfectly honest individuals who are unable to make reliable observations and draw trustworthy conclusions therefrom. It is a hell of a business and I get sick of sitting here listening to stories, ninety-nine percent of which I am convinced are the bunk.[6]

A "hell of a business" it was, and it had not changed much over the years for either westerner or easterner.

If Baragwanath thought he had been bamboozled, he had plenty of company. Americans opened their purses to oil shale speculators in the early twenties. Semi-arid, northwestern Colorado (Garfield, Rio Blanco, and Moffat counties) contained millions of gallons of oil locked in shale. The mere thought of such riches brought gleams to promoters' eyes. For decades a much-discussed potential, it was only prior to America's entry into World War I that oil shale was predicted "to develop into an important industry in western Colorado" in the next four or five years. Companies already in the field experimented with the key to success, economic recovery of the oil. The little settlement of DeBeque, cradled between sand cliffs and the Colorado River, expected to become the shale oil capital of the United States. Time out to "save the world for democracy" delayed the promised millenium. By 1920 "well over" a hundred oil shale companies competed in buying land, patenting claims, constructing reports, and selling shares in this new get-rich-quick scheme. Shale oil promoters claimed they could run your Model T, check the spread of "social diseases," kill weeds, fertilize the garden, and make the best soap that ever cleaned the body. They promised even more than that, but those are sufficient to show what powers shale oil possessed. Stock was sold everywhere; Americans could hardly wait to link up with this prosperity train.

DeBeque eagerly anticipated each new development. By 1923 oil shale excitement reached fever pitch. DeBeque imagined itself to be one of the great commercial centers of the oil industry. Oil was more sought after than gold, the *Shale* proclaimed, predicting a great period of prosperity just around the corner.[7] That corner was never turned.

Simply stated, no process was developed that could compete economically with oil, although a variety of miracle processes tried unsuccessfully. Some actually produced oil from the shale, but not at a marketable price. To make matters worse, the 1920s brought new oil fields gushing in Colorado, Texas, and Oklahoma, depressing the price and dooming oil shale. Wells were drilled in the DeBeque area, without much success. Oil shale schemes, with no other purpose than to defraud investors, blackened the whole industry's reputation and ended its prospects. By the late 1920s quiet had returned to the oil shale cliffs, and a lot of investors, sadder but only questionably wiser, chucked their stocks, as the first oil shale fever subsided.

Not everyone lost hope. Washington, which had set aside oil shale reserves in Garfield County, operated an experimental plant at Rulison for a few years, trying to find an economical method of extraction. During the thirties, Colorado promoted its Western Slope oil shale land as one of the greatest undeveloped natural resources available. Even this promotional pamphlet (1930), however, admitted that the low price of well oil, compared to shale, handicapped prospects.

Fortunately for Western Slope mining interests, molybdenum came into its own at Climax. Molybdenum mining jumped off to a rousing start in the teens, just as oil shale had, but there all similarity ended. A whole mountain of the mineral was discovered at the upper end of the old Ten Mile district. War demands (molybdenum is used to harden steel) generated an unprecedented market. Claims were staked on every little outcrop, claim jumping was rampant, false entries were filed, and the whole mess ended up in the courts, hurting the district for years. Summit and Lake counties became embroiled in a controversy over which one harbored the rich deposits; Summit won.

Armistice and a gutted market killed the molybdenum boom; operations did not resume until 1924, under the control of the Climax Molybdenum Company, which emerged victorious in the claims disputes. The automobile industry came to the rescue, purchasing molybdenum in carload lots. Climax helped, too, conducting a vigorous promotional research campaign into the uses of molybdenum steel.

On top of Fremont Pass, the company laid out and built the town of Climax for its workers. An attempt was made to make it as pleasant as possible, because the labor turnover was almost as high as the elevation, 11,300 feet. Working at that elevation tired one out quickly, lowered efficiency, and affected men in various ways, both physically and psychologically. Although there was a recreational hall (with bowling alleys, billiard tables, and social rooms), ski run, library, dorms for the unmarried workers, and homes for married ones, the altitude, weather, and harsh environment sent a steady number of workers down the hill in search of other jobs.

Through it all the Climax Company persevered, becoming the nation's and the world's leading source of molybdenum. It was Colorado's greatest mining operation from the mid-twenties and, by 1940, had matured into an industrial giant. War-related contracts incited even further development.

The Climax operation epitomized how much mining had changed since the days of the fifty-niners and the ninety-niners. The corporation controlled everything from digging to marketing; nothing was left to chance. Although numerous molybdenum claims were filed at the height of the early excitement. Climax remained the only economically significant Western Slope source during these years. The impact of Climax on Western Colorado proved negligible, however. Located on the far eastern rim, it was allied more closely with Denver and the east than with the west. This exemplifies one of the paradoxes of the Western Slope: major industrial and financial developments, such as Climax, are very often more compatible with outside interests than with local ones.

The thirties forged a bond between eastern and Western Colorado that had not existed since their 1890's woes united them. Highway improvement also promoted cohesiveness. It was now considerably easier to reach Denver from such places as Rangely and Cortez, except in winter when mother nature called the tune, as she had for the past eighty years. A mountain-locked town like Silverton could still be held hostage by snow slides; nothing there had changed. The Denver and Rio Grande was still its main lifeline. In 1927 and again in 1932, slides blocked the tracks for a month or more. Stored food and supplies allowed residents to wait out the siege, while D&RG crews shoveled and plows bucked the snow.

222

The railroad's vitality on the Silverton run belied the industry's declining significance elsewhere. Abandonment was the trend, as freight and passenger traffic defected to automobile and truck. The Moffat Tunnel doomed Gunnison's main line aspirations, and abandonment proceedings in 1936 gave rise to jealous bickering. Gunnison fought to prevent the railroad's relinquishment and was shocked to find that Montrose and Delta favored Grand Junction connections. It was a disruption of half a century of amicable relations, steamed the *News-Champion* on May 28, 1936, "we don't want to be cut off from the rest of western Colorado." The plea failed and the community had to adjust. The railroad steadily decreased its mileage and service, blaming lack of revenue, mounting costs, and high taxes. Silverton did not go unscathed—its three short narrow gauge lines also shut down, leaving only the D&RG Durango tie. The golden age of railroading was well past by 1940.

More mobile, cars could go places the trains could not; faster than the automobile was the newest of wonders, the airplane. With barnstorming and exhibitions the plane proved its worth. During the 1927 Silverton blockade, a pilot flew 400 miles to Silverton and Eureka to parachute diphtheria antitoxin (which proved to be unneeded), reportedly the first plane to fly over those communities. Ground conditions and lack of airfields forced the extended trip; even a decade later only six fields existed on the whole Western Slope. Three of these, Durango, Delta, and Montrose, were municipally owned and the others were auxiliary fields. If this seems inadequate, it should be remembered that Coloradans owned just 67 airplanes in 1936. Denver captured most of the early attention, since the operating airlines flew north and south from there—not west. A plan to develop a Denver-to-Craig, Grand Junction, and Alamosa route was scuttled by the outbreak of World War II. By then there were more airfields, many like Cortez's. Its dirt runway, usable only in dry weather, made service irregular for the few local and transient fliers. To make ends meet, the operator sold new planes and instructed flying.

The airplane supplied the answer to one of the Western Slope's gravest problems, the need to overcome the isolation/time factor. Long travel hours evaporated before the speed of flight, and once ground facilities became available the plane could reach nearly all of Colorado West.

The airplane, for all its potential, touched few Western Slopers' lives directly. Not so the radio—they spent delightful hours laughing with such favorites as Jack Benny and Amos 'n Andy, or listened to

Gabriel Heater and Lowell Thomas bring the news. The radio came to America in the 1920s, to the Western Slope in the 1930s. Local stations operated only in Grand Junction and Durango, although at night a little fiddling with the dial and a lot of patience could bring in Denver or out-of-state stations. Battery-operated sets pioneered with a crackle and hiss; spreading electric power doomed them with the far better plug-in models. Western Slopers loved their radios; by 1940 seventy-five percent of them owned one. More than any other factor, the radio broke the communications isolation with the rest of the state and nation. Not even the best metropolitan newspaper provided such instant coverage, from politics to sports to fashions.

Add the telephone, which stretched into the rural areas via the "party line," and the average Western Sloper was more in touch with his neighbors and up-to-date with the changing world than his father ever dreamed of being. Newspaper coverage improved, too. However, that old-time personal journalism was replaced by more wire service news. The disappearance of the old-style editors and the flavor they imparted to their writing was the price paid for modernization and radio competition. Nationally syndicated writers and cartoonists superseded local efforts; it was cheaper, faster, and more "modern" to rely on them. Readers demanded more national coverage and special features (e.g., photographs and Hollywood columns). Adventures of comic heroes, such as Red Ryder and Alley Oop, beguiled young and old. More often than not, the sports page, rather than the front or editorial page, was the first stop for the male reader.

By 1940–41 the Western Slope had pulled out of the depression and returned as nearly as possible to the "good old days." The economy perked up, tourists reappeared (1941 was the biggest travel season in years for Ouray), and conservatism triumphed. The Western Slope restored confidence in itself. Meanwhile, newspapers carried thorough accounts of Europe's problems, but they seemed a long way away. When war broke out in 1939, Western Slopers held fewer emotional ties abroad than they had in 1914.

Farmers and ranchers drove to town for Saturday shopping and visiting. The debris from a busy Saturday worried Montrose more than the blitzkrieg in Poland. Clean it up, pleaded a concerned writer, for the sake of the town's impression on visitors and Sunday worshipers. In December, 1941, Montrose expected to have a merry Christmas, highlighted by the Lions Club-sponsored home yule lighting contest. The lights would never be festive that year.

The "day that will live in infamy" caught Western Slopers unaware. Disbelieving that war had come to the United States, they joined other Americans in listening to their radios that Sunday afternoon. The impact of the war, like the depression, is not easy to describe:

> *War* with all of its awful *human woe and suffering* is upon us. The *calmness* and *sacredness* of a beautiful Sabbath Day (Sunday, Dec. 7, 1941) *was desecrated* by that desperado of the Far East, the island empire of Japan.
>
> . . .
>
> *Visitors* to power plants, dams, sub stations, etc., should be *scrutinized carefully. Give out no information,* unless properly authorized. All *suspicious characters* or movements or people whom you have reason to suspect should be *reported* to your foreman or Dist. Supt. promptly.
>
> *Be Alert. Analyze. Scrutinize.* [8]

Frenzy and hate, fear and dismay hit Western Slopers all at once that Sunday and Monday. War's impact was brought home quickly — local boys were stationed at Pearl Harbor. People heeded the admonition to "Be Alert," for who knew what might be the target of sabotage. On December 18, Aspen's mayor warned all citizens to be on the lookout, although it seemed highly unlikely that the Japanese could be blamed for the seven street lights that were shot out during the previous two days. The press and radio bombarded the public with war slogans; "Buy U. S. for Christmas" was one of the earliest. Within weeks youths were out gathering scrap metals, the Red Cross was collecting war relief funds, and everybody was buying defense stamps and bonds. Before it was over, many of the old mining camps and mine sites had been picked bare of any scrap, thereby removing the residue of the frontier's litter.

The draft started to take its toll in 1942, and letters home told of adventures in boot camp and overseas, provided they got past the company censor. Rationing became a fact of life, along with price freezes and shortages. Tourism collapsed amid gasoline and tire rationing and the unavailability of new cars; tanks and planes had a higher priority. Scrap metal and waste paper drives enlisted school children, clubs, churches, individuals, and communities to help in the war effort. The visit of a recruiting officer was a reminder of the continued need for men and women. Women were actively sought for the services to free men for overseas duty; the WACs (Women's Army Corps) were particularly vigorous in their efforts.

For youngsters the war was some hazy, faraway thing. Many of their comic book heroes went to war, victoriously conquering every conceivable Axis enemy. Children played guns against Japs and Germans, rather than combatting outlaws and Indians. They turned on the radio, not to hear the latest war news, but to listen to the adventures of the Lone Ranger or Jack Armstrong, the all-American boy. Scrap drives and buying stamps toward a bond were their greatest involvement.

For homefront parents and other adults, it was four years of anxiety over relatives or friends in service (17,724 Western Slopers), shortages, the war's outcome, and such related ulcer producers as the zooming divorce rate of "draftee marriages." Adjusting to wartime shortages and demands required patience and a dose of humor. Even on the Western Slope rumors spread like wildfire, and the appearance of a military vehicle could set a town humming. Life on the homefront was not quite as restful as a boy slogging through a Pacific jungle, fighting off mosquitoes and malaria, imagined it to be.

The homefront did have its lighter moments, however, as when the Pagosa Springs PAG WO Club sponsored a barn dance and raffled a "ration" free beef for $1 per ticket. The return of a son or daughter was a joyous moment, made even better by tales of exotic places, such as those related by one of the Piedra River Valley boys of his duty on the Fiji Islands.

And there were always the "slackers." A few homefronters dealt in black market activities, but far more grumbled about the wartime speed limit of 35 miles per hour. The vast majority, however, accepted shortages and war-related problems with equanimity. Unlike 1917–18, the war did not generate the hate toward neighbors of German or Japanese ancestry. Unfortunately, though, racial prejudice against Mexican-Americans persisted. An ugly incident at Camp Hale, involving construction workers, proved that such attitudes died hard. Not until pressure was brought to bear were Mexican-Americans given equal barracks and mess halls with other workers.

Indecision and doubt hampered some New Deal efforts, but now Western Slopers rallied behind President Roosevelt, even the die-hard New Deal haters. Fruitful results inspired confidence, as the tide of war turned toward victory in 1943. As it dragged on, however, the casualty lists rose, leaving no town or county unscathed. Determination to back the boys and see this war through to total victory was evident in the repeated success of bond drives. Counties organized and boasted, as Rio Blanco did, of going "over the top as it always had and always will." Towns, service clubs, and others set quotas for themselves and tried to surpass them. In January, 1944, during its fourth bond drive, Meeker sponsored a dance and convinced the local theater to give a free pass to everyone who purchased a bond. One of the few communities that had a USO for the servicemen was Glenwood Springs. Young ladies maintained the club and sponsored a variety of activities in the Legion Hall. The Western Slope had gone to war.

Mining went to war also. Desperate for war-needed minerals, Washington controlled this industry as never before. Gold and silver mines, rated nonessential, were shut down and miners shifted to copper, zinc, and other minerals. Non-ferrous metal miners received deferments, and Uncle Sam paid for transportation and provided housing for miners moving into strategic mining districts. To improve transportation, the 1941 Defense Highway Act provided for the construction, maintenance, and improvement of access roads. The Bureau of Mines examined mines to see if they contained sufficient minerals and approved building roads to over fifty mines in Western Colorado. Coal mining, which had been slumping for more than a decade, losing out to natural gas and oil, received a boost. Seldom had Western Slope coal mines produced as they did now, especially in Routt County.

In the frantic quest for more oil, the Rangely field was finally developed in 1944–45. The first well had been drilled near this isolated, sleepy supply town forty years before, but lack of a pipeline and insufficient demand terminated the effort. Now all that was past. The Iles field in Moffat County, which had been Colorado's big producer in the '30s, flagged and Wilson's Creek (Rio Blanco), a field brought in in 1937, surpassed it to become the leader. Other smaller oil fields, such as Hiawatha, Tow Creek, Powder Wash, Price, and Moffat, attracted new attention under wartime demands. The Western Slope was the state's oil capital, and a real boom was not far off.

On the plateaus beyond Montrose and Grand Junction, the government quietly pushed a diamond drilling program and purchased uranium for unstated purposes. Vanadium also prospered until 1944, when increased imports cut the need for domestic production and lowered the price.

The Western Slope's only military base, Camp Hale, located below Tennessee Pass in the Eagle River Valley, housed the Tenth Mountain Division. Chosen because of its elevation and mountainous setting, Camp Hale's unique purpose was to train and harden troops for combat in severely cold weather and high mountain terrain. Deactivation came in the fall of '44, and the site today shows few signs of its history as a military post. From the group that trained there came a nucleus of men who developed several ski areas after the war; they had fallen in love with Colorado and returned to Aspen,

Vail, and other mountain communities.

By 1945 the war against Germany—they called them Huns in Montrose, mindful of 1917—was nearly over, and Japan was reeling under Allied attacks. People still collected funds for war-torn areas and books and magazines for servicemen. They planted gardens to free food "for the boys" and cut down shortages at home. Canning gained a respectability it had not known for years. Although the trend had slowed, skilled workers continued to be drawn away from Western Colorado to work in defense plants and shipyards on the West Coast. This drift had worried Chambers of Commerce since 1940, and they tried without success to obtain defense contracts for their cities. Durango's attempt to convert its half dismantled smelter into an ammunitions factory came to naught; an attempt to open a tool works was also unsuccessful. Previous lack of industrialization and transportation distances precluded such efforts. Never more than barely industrialized, the Western Slope had only two counties (Mesa and Delta) which produced over $1,000,000 worth of manufactured products in the last pre-war year, 1939.

By the summer of '45, Germany was vanquished and only Japan remained. The "Men and Women in Service Column" grew shorter, and, with more optimism, people watched Hollywood's winning of the war in movies like "Objective: Burma," featuring Errol Flynn accomplishing the feat. Westerners retained their hold; Gene Autry rode the range and righted wrongs in the traditional fashion in "Springtime in the Rockies."

Wartime sacrifices and shortages began to take their toll, and Western Slopers anticipated the end of the conflict. Towns like Craig, county seat of oil and coal-prospering Moffat County, suffered more than others because of increased population pressures. The editor of the *Craig Empire Courier* described the congestion and inconveniences, and complained that Craig was suffering from growing pains, "and I mean suffering." The end came in August, when two atomic bombs, no doubt carrying Western Slope uranium, were dropped on Japanese cities.[9]

The war was over; most Western Slopers returned home (473 did not), and the home folks breathed a sigh of relief. Any wish to return to the "good old days" was wasted. The mystique of the mountains could no longer shield them. The depression, New Deal, and the war had changed the people and the region too much. The time of waiting was over—a new age dawned.

IV
Years of Bonanza, Times of Tribulation 1945-1980

Not all farmers were fortunate enough to benefit from irrigation and they resorted to dry land farming, which in good years paid well, but only tightened the belt in others. This 1977 scene near Cortez captures the sweep and loneliness of much of the Western Slope, which is still basically rural. *Courtesy Richard L. Gilbert.*

The years from 1945 to the present have been years of transition for the Western Slope. The 1920s and 1930s were slow years involving little growth. However, following World War II, changes, slow at first, but eventually building to a crescendo, shocked the region. Water projects and problems, energy development, increased population, and environmental concerns divided Western Colorado.

15.
Energy Frontier Ouches

Peace came. The Western Slope's mining industry longed for a return to the good old days. But the splendor days of hardrock mining were so long past they existed only as a memory, a story told by old-timers, who themselves were fast slipping away.

Young David Lavender rode into Ouray on a bitter cold January day in the late 1930s, surveyed the scene, and captured forever the flavor of the faded mining community:

> It was a gloomy little town, with down-at-the-heel brick buildings lining main street, an astonishing rococo hotel, and rows of widely spaced, once-handsome frame houses radiating out from the remnants of the business district. Over it all hung the ineffable sadness of departed wealth.[1]

Ouray's plight mirrored that of Breckenridge, Aspen, Pitkin, Telluride, Gothic, and all the rest of the former boom towns. An exodus to a new promised land had been underway for decades. Then the infamous, impersonal, wartime government Order L-208 shut down non-essential mines and forced the miners into other jobs in industry, war-related mining, or into service. However, gold and silver mining had never completely disappeared. By the 1960s, it was making a comeback of sorts, helped immeasurably by the federal government's decision to free the price of these two metals. Silver rose to the $4 an ounce level, and gold eventually reached $200 an ounce before declining to the mid-hundred range. By the late 1970s, silver peaked at $15 an ounce, while gold evened out at a fantastic $650 an ounce. Imagine what this would have meant to production at the Tomboy,

Mollie Gibson, and Amethyst. It would have made Ashcroft into the city its boosters imagined it would be, developed Lake City into a booming metropolis, and enriched the Western Slope ten times over.

As it was, no new rush unfolded, because mining had become too expensive. In a day, miners could make what they used to earn in a month or more, and the cost of machines, power, and smelting had risen tremendously. Instead of many smaller operations, large companies completely dominated: Standard Metals at Silverton, and Idarado at Telluride. They often mined gold and silver as by-products of copper, lead, and zinc and were at the mercy of a volatile world price and market. By 1970, San Juan (Standard Metals) and San Miguel (Idarado) produced over 80% of Colorado's $1.3 million in gold. Although these were small amounts compared to peak years, the Western Slope was still producing, whereas such famous districts as Cripple Creek and Central City were reduced to tourist handouts.

Gold and silver, the glamour metals, no longer reigned supreme; Western Slope excitement centered on oil and the more exotic uranium and oil shale. One more rush, reminiscent of years gone by, spilled into parts of far Western Colorado, triggered by post-war demands. Permanent peace had not come to the world after the war, despite enormous sacrifices of resources and manpower. Instead, a cold war chilled the globe, as two conflicting powers and ideologies contested. Never in world history had such power been in the hands of rival governments; the atomic bomb blasted the world into a new era. The United States developed the bombs and wanted more. The key to success was uranium, and the Colorado Plateau, western San Miguel, Montrose, Mesa and north to Moffat County, held a monopoly of the major reserves known to the noncommunist world.

This rush proved to be like the old-time ones only in that it offered the possibility of sudden wealth, the hard work of prospecting, rewards for a few, and disappointment for many. Uncle Sam came along as a partner this time; he was the buyer and kept the lid on all activities. No one wanted the "commies" to know what was transpiring on the Western Slope. The scene of this excitement was the same as that for earlier uranium mining, the semi-arid plateaus and rock-ribbed canyons beyond Telluride, Montrose, and Grand Junction, and edging over into Utah. Once again prospectors trooped into this uninviting land, carving roads, and establishing base camps. The mechanized mule of World War II, the jeep, and its lineal descendants, made travel easier. A few of the more adventuresome prospected from the air. All carried geiger counters, whose beeps and whines, flashing lights, and jumping needles announced the presence of radioactive material. Jeeps, planes, geigers, scintillometers, diamond drills, precision instruments — the grizzled prospector of yesteryear would have been agog over such accouterments.

"Uranium has become a magic word for many Americans in the past few years," proclaimed a pamphlet. Neophyte prospectors learned from the manual how to locate and file a claim and use a geiger counter. The pamphlet gave geological hints about what to look for and advised that a folding cot or air mattress "may be found very serviceable."[2] They found from actual experience that work with a pick, ax, and shovel offered few romantic interludes.

Controlling all activities was the federal government, via the Atomic Energy Commission, established in 1946. The AEC kept a finger on everything. It withdrew land to be leased to uranium mining companies, established price schedules, built roads, and allowed buying stations and processing plants to operate only with AEC contracts. The agency underwrote other incentives, including raw material and exploration programs.

Grand Junction prospered as it had not for several generations. Here the AEC opened an office and many of the mining firms located. In the late forties and fifties business went on around the clock in the belief that fame and fortune lay just a pick stroke away. Uranium fever produced the same tawdriness as the gold rush; somehow, though, trailer courts and junked cars seemed less appealing than the false-fronted buildings of earlier years.

For the less adventurous, stock speculation offered a shortcut to wealth. Potential investors asked few questions once the excitement gathered momentum in the 1950s. Promotional literature promised the familiar "pie in the sky," and Barnum was again proven right — "a sucker is born every minute." "Experts" were to be found on the streets of any uranium-crazed community. Even with the Securities and Exchange Commission keeping watch, the unwary found themselves holding an empty bag, just as they had before.

The action was not centered solely in Grand Junction. Dove Creek, Uravan, Naturita, Nucla, Gateway, Durango, and Egnar were all either jumping-off places for prospecting, milling towns, or supply points. Farmers and ranchers found new markets, businessmen new customers, and even the old mining town of Rico new life. The need for sulphuric acid in uranium processing profited the Rico Argentine Mining Company and a local sulphuric acid plant.

Before the excitement waned, uranium mills opened or were renovated in Rifle, Uravan, Slick Rock, Maybell, Durango, Gunnison, Grand Junction, and Naturita. Durango's experience epitomizes the pattern. The smelter had closed down in 1930 and, despite plans and wartime expectations, had only briefly reopened. Across the river from the town sat the decaying plant, once the community's principal industry and employer. The AEC and Vanadium Corporation of America put it back into production, and by 1953 it produced more uranium concentrates, at a faster rate, than any other mill. AEC contracts kept it active; the tailings pile at the base of Smelter Mountain grew again and smelter smoke drifted over Durango. The last contract expired in 1962 and early the next year milling operations were transferred to Shiprock. Once more the smelter fell silent. Dismantled and abandoned, the remains still scar the slope, and the radioactive tailings have been bandaged by a partial covering of grasses.

What happened in Durango also occurred elsewhere. Gradually the needs and fears of the cold war changed. By 1956 the AEC relaxed security measures and began to make public the tonnage figures, reserves, and other pertinent facts. Montrose County could finally claim its place as Colorado's leading uranium area with over 130 producing mines. As the uranium stockpile grew larger, the government's needs diminished. During the sixties the AEC reduced purchases and changed its price support schedule. Production and exploration declined; the uranium boom had ended. Like its predecessors, it left behind debris that had been ignored during the excitement and overlooked in the abandonment. Radioactive mine dumps and tailings piles, and miners facing unknown health dangers for having worked in these mines, were problems unique to the uranium excitement. For a while more jobs, higher prices, expanded markets, and increased taxes sparked the region's economy, but they all faded and quiet returned to the scarred Colorado plateau. However, interest in uranium is still high and there are those who hang onto their claims, waiting for its resurgence.

Less excitement, but more wealth, came from Western Slope oil. In the post-war years Rangely fulfilled its promise and emerged as the oil capital of the Slope. Well into the 1970s the Rangely field dominated Colorado, and Rio Blanco County became *the* oil producer (76% of the state's 1976 production). Geologists and oil company crews traversed all possible oil lands, ready to drill at the slightest sign of success. The Oak Creek field in Routt County, for instance, which opened in 1949, quickly "watered out," but not before triggering an extensive search that opened several new fields in the county.

Several significant factors finally led to the development of these isolated fields. Wartime demand for petroleum did not abate when peace came, as American cars, homes, and industry gulped it with an insatiable national thirst. Isolation, which had killed interest for so long, was no longer a hindrance, with better roads and, more important, pipelines to ship the crude to refineries and markets. In addition, older fields were no longer producing as they had earlier, leaving a larger share of the market to newcomers.

The town of Rangely, once "merely an outpost in a desolate area,"[3] prospered as never before or since. The oil companies and crews transformed its main street and residential district, and before they were through, the town had even gained a junior college. Oil wells pumped right in town, framed by yards full of equipment and stacks of piping, making the "desolate area" seem congested. The *Rangely Driller*, proclaiming itself a servant of "the Last Frontier," monitored all the activity. It heralded the opening of each new oil and gas field which added to the county's tax base and enhanced the town's importance. In the end, Rangely quieted and the excitement waned, but the oil pumps kept working and the geologists continued searching.

Other towns prospered as well. Craig celebrated "Oil Progress Week," in October, 1952:

> We doff our hats to the oil men of the Moffat County, rough necks, the financiers, the pump jockey and the distributor, the geologist and the rodman, the companies and the lease hounds, all of whom have had a part in the progress of the development of oil in the Craig quadrangle. We salute them for their contributions to the economic life of this community and for their active interest in the life of our community. The part they have played in the development of Craig as an oil center and the part they have played in the improvement of Craig has been important through the years.[4]

In the southwest corner of the state, Durango blossomed as an oil company town, not so much from neighboring wells, although gas fields were discovered, but as the exploration headquarters for New Mexico and Utah. Throughout the 1950s and into the mid-60s the impact was noticeable in many ways. More jobs were available at higher wages, subdivisions opened, and housing prices jumped; new merchants were attracted to town, and oil people organized clubs, served on the city council, pushed for civic improvements, and even helped promote a mosquito district to eliminate those pesky little devils who had made life miserable north of town. A new spirit was infused. More tax money meant new schools, better roads, more services. The total impact so changed Durango that it started a growth period that has not ceased. By the 1970s some of these same oil people were moving back to retire in a community and region they fondly remembered. The oil era, though, actually ended in the early sixties, when the companies gradually left for other possibilities in other places.

Most exotic and fickle was oil shale. Its potential had been suppressed by its long-held secret—a method of economical retorting—to produce oil at a competitive price. In fact, as long as the oil fields prospered, there seemed little hope that shale could profitably compete.

The federal government and private companies never conceded, however. Uncle Sam began building the Anvil Points plant near Rifle in 1945, starting limited operations in 1947. The shale mined in the nearby federal oil shale reserve was shipped to the demonstration plant and refinery. In the last half of 1949, the plant went into full operation, producing diesel oil, gasoline, and burner fuels. Again hopes soared, it "will open up a great new industry for Colorado and particularly for Western Colorado," predicted the *Colorado Yearbook* in 1947. Experiments were also conducted to discover the best methods of drilling, mining, and hauling. It was all to no avail, however; Congress, appalled at the rising cost and seeing little immediate need, suspended research at Anvil Points in 1956 and put the plant on stand-by basis. Until the cost of well oil rose to match shale and put the two on a more competitive basis, shale would remain at a disadvantage.

The intriguing possibilities of shale seduced private companies to try to succeed where the federal government had failed. Union Oil built a pilot plant near Grand Valley in 1957, only to suspend operations within a year. In 1964 a consortium of companies leased Anvil Points and had little better luck.

The government, meanwhile, took off on another track in 1960, when the AEC exploded 1,100 pounds of explosives to test the feasibility of releasing oil directly underground with a nuclear blast. Eventually this led to the Rulison Project in 1969, in which an atomic charge was detonated to determine if natural gas could be freed in this manner. Thus the Western Slope partook of its first atomic explosion, probably involving ore from its own mines. In 1973, this was followed by the Rio Blanco Project, which exploded three special bombs to tap a deep-lying natural gas formation. The AEC hoped to launch a period of exploration and mining, only to harvest outraged public protests and a citizen-initiated law to require a statewide referendum to approve future underground nuclear blasts.

Technically, Rulison had succeeded; economically, it had failed.

238

The Rio Blanco blast failed totally. In 1976 both wells were plugged with cement, the ground seeded and graded, and the sites abandoned.

Even as these experiments failed or proved economically unfeasible, the impact of a possible oil shale boom on the Western Slope concerned farsighted individuals. In 1957, then Colorado Governor Steve McNichols warned that paralleling any growth of oil shale development would be the considerable problems of land use for highways, town and industrial sites, and water. One of the main ingredients of shale refining was water, a scarce item in northwestern Colorado. The governor went on to point out the total impact of a shale boom on existing communities and counties, including the need for more schools, water, and sewer systems. It would require careful forethought, programming, and money, he cautioned, and Coloradans must not approach the problems with a "narrow or chauvinistic" point of view. With prophetic foresight, McNichols warned of declining reserves and gluttonous consumption by the free world, particularly the United States. "It does not appear that the United States can expect to consume the lion's share of these essential metals indefinitely."[5]

Others have repeated these concerns and warnings, but not until the oil crisis of 1973 was the message brought home. Nor has the required planning been done, even as we enter an expansion era, brought on not by oil shale, but by coal mining.

The post-war years brought little encouragement for Western Slope coal mines, as home consumption of cleaner oil and natural gas replaced coal-burning furnaces. This conversion did wonders for clean air but not for miners' jobs. The number of mines steadily decreased; only strip mining managed to hold its own. Routt County, the Western Slope's major coal producer, receives the blame for initiating (in 1946) that potential environmental nightmare — strip mining. By 1963 nearly all of the county's production came from two large strip mines; the coal was used for electric power generation. The Western Slope held billions of tons in estimated coal reserves; the day loomed near when they would be needed.

The same patterns, discernible in coal and gold and silver mining, were evident elsewhere in Western Slope mining. Molybdenum continued to be the preserve of the AMAX Company, which remained by far the largest and wealthiest mining operation. In 1970, for example, its $114 million production ranked first among Colorado's metal, nonmetal, and mineral fuels producers. It had long since emerged as the Western Slope's most productive and valuable mineral resource. The Climax Mine made quite an impact on American mining history when, in 1964, it detonated 417,000 pounds of explosives to break loose 1-1/2 million tons of molybdenum. The blast was felt on seismographs throughout the nation and echoed as far away as Yellow Knife in Canada's Northwest Territory. Zinc mining has always seemed prosaic to the public; nonetheless, the Western Slope maintained state domination of this mineral with the New Jersey Zinc Company in Eagle County the leading operator, followed by Standard Metals and Idarado.

Mining in the seventies can be summarized by describing production—in a word, higher. From 1970 through 1976 molybdenum production increased by 60%, silver and zinc doubled, and coal and gold quadrupled; oil wells pumped nearly five times as much and natural gas zoomed up almost seven times. Only uranium prolonged the downward slide begun in the sixties. Although these are statewide percentages, the Western Slope reflected the overall pattern. Thus mining was better off than it had been for years, if production can serve as an indicator.

During these same years, mining had changed more than it had in the previous seven decades, thanks to mounting public concern over the environment and pollution, and the sudden awareness of potential shortages. No longer could the industry operate outside the realm of public concern; forced into the limelight, mining found itself uncomfortably situated. Nor could it be isolated on the Western Slope — mining was part of the national and the world scene.

The change was obvious everywhere. As recently as Dave Lavender's day at the Camp Bird, muckers' qualifications were rumored to be a "size-forty shirt and a number-two hat." The old-timer miner would have found life strange in the highly mechanized, government-regulated, well-paid world of his 1978 counterpart. Better educated and trained, the modern miner still faced hard, dangerous work, about the only common bond with his predecessor. Where once whiskey was taboo in the mines and the bane of many a miner, now marijuana proved more of a problem.

Never in the old days had the mining industry encountered the problems it faced now. For instance, Colorado Westmoreland hoped to lease some coal on federal land near Paonia. The Bureau of Land Management scheduled a three-hour hearing in July, 1977, which attracted nearly 1,200 people. Supporters and opponents argued passionately, generating a lot of heat and only a little light. Jobs, environmental impact, and the local economy received attention during the course of the debates. Not until December did the Secretary of the

Interior approve offering the lease for sale. A sign of the times was the fact that Colorado Westmoreland needed the coal to supply the Northern Indiana Public Service Company of Hammond, Indiana. This and similar examples raised a fundamental question about the use of Western Slope resources for local, regional, or national demands. No easy answer has or will come forth, and the specter of the rape of western resources to benefit outside groups still haunts the region.

Another warning of the changing times was the $40,000 fine levied against Standard Metals Corporation in October, 1977, by the Colorado Water Quality Commission. Mill tailings had been accidentally released into the Animas River two years before. The company quickly moved to stop the seepage and establish new tailings ponds to prevent further water pollution; consequently, the Commission suspended two-thirds of the fine, provided Standard Metals continue its efforts. Years before, the Animas had been virtually a dead river because of mine and mill dumpings, but it had been cleaned up, and environmental issues now ranked equally with the issues of jobs and mining.

Standard Metals received another setback in June, 1978. Lake Emma, under which the company was mining, suddenly broke into the workings and flooded the mine, bringing operations to a halt. Providentially, it happened on a Sunday when no one was at work. Flood waters, muck, and mine timbers shot out the portal and eventually found their way into the Animas River. Environmental protests were heard all the way from New Mexico. The besieged company went to work to reopen the mine, carefully monitored by the government to prevent further damage. Environmental issues had nearly as much to say as ore reserves and cost in determining whether mining would be resumed.

Some of the older mining companies saw their era ending. The 154 miners of the Eagle Mine at Gilman received notice of its closing just before Christmas, 1977. This mine had been worked off and on since 1879. The New Jersey Zinc Company had worked the mine since 1915. Plans called for a complete shut down early in 1978. The mine was a victim of declining zinc prices, reduced ore reserves, higher mining costs, and the expense of new health and safety regulations. The layoffs immediately affected Red Cliff, Gilman, and Minturn, and promised long-term problems for the people and their communities. What happened here could be repeated, warned Norman Blake, Director of the Colorado Division of Mines, "This is just the beginning of what's going to happen to the mining industry in Colorado. We're going to lose a lot of them."[6] He feared for small operations whose owners could not afford to implement the stringent health and safety standards established in 1977. Uncle Sam's role in Western Slope mining had become that of a not-so-silent, nearly equal partner.

Neither the large nor the small mining companies were going to have free reign to develop as they saw fit. Environmental impact studies were required, and the words "land reclamation" became part of the miners' vocabulary. A large firm, such as AMAX, employed environmental control engineers whose job it was, among other things, to prevent water pollution and supervise revegetation·and reclamation of the land. Environmental efforts did not involve only sites no longer operating. At their big new Henderson Mill and mine, AMAX's environmental planning started with the development of the mine—for example, in reclaiming and reusing water. The program, known as "experiment in ecology," tested the premise of whether a major mining operation could operate within the demanding confines of environmental concerns and regulation.

AMAX was also involved in exploring a major new molybdenum find near Crested Butte. This old precious metal and coal camp, with a long mining history, had recently attracted attention as a ski resort. AMAX, which started exploratory drilling in 1974, conducted a comprehensive series of technical, economic feasibility, and environmental studies. Crested Butte residents quickly divided themselves into two schools of thought with respect to this economic windfall that seemed ready to descend upon them. Old-timers generally favored the idea; newcomers, who had come for the skiing and scenic beauty, opposed it. Ex-City Manager Bruce Baumgartner clearly put his finger on the problem: "The real issue is whether a tourist-based economy can coexist with a mine without damaging the environment. The majority of the people here have left the cities and high-paying jobs and are pretty protective about their lifestyle."[7] AMAX countered by working closely with local officials, conducting studies, and trying to fulfill state and federal requirements. The whole issue was clouded further by the fact that the area is a national historic district, which the Forest Service insisted be considered when weighing future mining or milling permit requests. Discussion among the company, residents, and officials continues. The nineteenth century miner would have shook his head in disbelief and cursed the day that had brought such things to pass.

Oil shale and oil companies found themselves under the same gun. The gas shortage of 1973 and steadily mounting gasoline prices finally placed shale on a nearly competitive economic basis. Research and testing continued, but development still lagged. One commercial mine was being opened south of Meeker, after four years of off-and-on planning by the Occidental and Ashland Oil companies. Other projects languished in the planning stage. No plans were approved, however, unless they called for careful monitoring of environmental impact, with corrective provisions. The Western Slope's flagging oil-shale industry seemed about ready to come into its own, a point it had reached several times before.

Nothing was more suspect to environmentalists than strip mining for coal; the fear was well-founded, if its track record were any indication. But as oil and natural gas reserves declined and new sources appeared to be few and far between, interest turned to the nation's abundant coal reserves. Billions of tons of coal underlay the Western Slope from Durango to north of Craig. Cheaper and faster strip mining held more potential for profit than underground operations, but it had a history of producing environmental nightmares.

By the mid-seventies forecasts predicted a tremendous impact on certain areas. Thousands of new jobs and a rapid increase in growth were anticipated. All this cried for advance planning. Local, state, and federal officials wrangled and accused, while precious time evaporated and development proceeded. As the first waves of the predicted boom swept in, no one seemed to be ready for them. Craig, the center of the "energy frontier," is the best example of this unpreparedness. Environmentally, the companies were regulated, but the poor community found no such help for the growth which inundated it and strained local services. A newly-appointed high school principal resigned, stating that purchasing an expensive house "in a boom town was an awfully big risk." Most, unwilling to take that same risk, crowded into unsightly, "ticky-tacky" trailer courts which mushroomed around Craig. Traffic congestion became a problem, even with one-way streets; construction proved unable to keep pace with demands. The Craig *Empire-Courier* saw little relief in sight, predicting an eventual population of 25,000-30,000. "That is going to create a lot of ouches; it's going to change a lot of things that people are not going to want changed. These people will need homes, stores, facilities and schools and that will cause a lot of ouches."[8] If that prediction is true, it is an understatement, and Craig's problems have just begun.

Mining is making a strong comeback on the Western Slope in the seventies and those "ouches" have just begun where its impact is being felt. The free-wheeling days are as dead as the nineteenth century frontier. Perhaps it is just as well; few today want to leave such an environmental heritage to the future as was left to them, despite its romantic connotations. Without question the mining industry will play an increasingly significant role on the Western Slope throughout the remainder of the twentieth century. Ready or not, with it are coming changes and great demands on water, quality of life, natural resources, and scenery. And tourism still lurks on the horizon.

16.
The Good Life:
Dreams and Dilemmas

September, 1945, World War II was finally over. For the young men of the Western Slope, the lucky ones returning from around the world, thoughts turned to cool breezes, the bright yellow of the aspen, the mountains with their dusting of white forecasting another winter, and home. From France, Italy, North Africa, Saipan, Australia, New Guinea, Germany, and a thousand other places, they would soon be on their way home. Home again to the mountains! It was great to be young and alive and heading back to the Western Slope!

To men returning home to ranches, farms, and small towns, it did not seem that things.had changed that much. The Normandy beaches and Solomon Islands seemed a long way from Main Street. A hundred home towns, from Hayden to Pagosa Springs and Granby to Gateway, looked pretty much the same as they always did when the GI's came marching home. Yet, subtle changes, barely perceptible, were already taking place. The changes came slowly at first, picked up momentum in the 1950s and then burst in the '60s and '70s like a deluge from the sky. To a region which had not shifted gears much during the previous half century, the changes were staggering. The consequences of change since 1945 have been enormous; the entire character of Western Colorado has been altered forever.

Throughout the years since World War II, everyone has recognized that change must occur and has occurred. But what kind of change? Therein lies the rub. And so, we have had land developers, water boards, ranchers, skiers, the federal government, miners,

245

tourists, industry, and many other groups engaged in heated debate over the direction Western Colorado should take. All are concerned about their own self-interests. One wonders how many care about the interests of the region.

Western Colorado slumbered, a sleeping giant in the years immediately following World War II. The population was sparse, skiing had not yet arrived, and transportation was tough and expensive. The age of recreation had not yet dawned. However, it was only a matter of time before the sensational hunting and fishing, mountains and majestic scenery were discovered by the masses. The opening of the Rangely oil field in the 1940s brought northwestern Colorado into the public eye. But the discovery of uranium in Gunnison, San Miguel, Mesa, and Montrose counties after World War II brought boom conditions back to the region. This time, miners looking for uranium scorned mules and picks; instead they used jeeps and geiger counters.

The jeep, used with great success by the United States Army during World War II, had an enormous impact upon the Western Slope. With four-wheel drive and seemingly indestructible, the vehicle was tailor-made for the mountains, canyons, and plateaus. Soon, thousands of residents and tourists were scouring the hills with Broncos, Scouts, Toyotas, Land Rovers, Jeeps, and other four-wheel-drive vehicles and getting into places impossible to reach in the past. As more and more people traveled farther into the back country, they became aware of what they had missed. High lakes, great stream fishing, mountain climbing, old ghost towns, and the lure of adventure were there for the taking. Today, so many people with four-wheel-drive and two-wheel trail bikes flock to Western Colorado that they have made themselves a nuisance. Driving over easily-damaged tundra, tearing lumber from old buildings and creating their own roads, many four-wheelers have caused irreversible damage to the high country.

"Nature can giveth and nature can taketh away." That ominous warning haunted the Western Slope psyche after 1893. Blessed with great mineral resources, many towns languished after the turn of the century either because the resources had been depleted or because there was no more demand. At the eleventh hour, however, with the age of metals seemingly coming to an end, the age of snow began to dawn.

Western Colorado had long been a skiers' paradise. Skiing on nine to fourteen foot-long skis with a guide pole for balance, early miners used skis for transportation. They used them for recreation, too. In the Gunnison country in the 1880s, races were held between miners from the surrounding mining camps. Flashing down mountains at better than sixty miles an hour, men like Al Johnson and Charlie Baney became famous. The silver panic of 1893 not only killed mining camps, it also damaged the early day ski industry. Skiing after the turn of the century was hard work. One might climb a mountain for four or five hours for the pleasure of one run.

The 1930s saw the rise of ski clubs on the Western Slope. The Gunnison Ski Club sponsored Marshall Pass ski trains. The club hired the Denver & Rio Grande to run a skiers' special to the top of 10,846-foot-high Marshall Pass forty-five or so miles to the east. After the skiers schussed to near the bottom of the pass, the train picked them up and returned them to the summit for another run. It was wonderful fun skiing, and then singing songs, dancing, and drinking on the return trip to Gunnison. It kept alive the hope that skiing might revive in Western Colorado.

There were also skiing enthusiasts in Aspen during the 1930s. Led by Billy Fiske, Tom Flynn, Ted Ryan, Andre Roch, and others, the people of the decaying silver town sensed a revival. In 1938, a crude "boat tow" ski lift was constructed from mining equipment. Powered by a motor, it carried a limited number of skiers part of the way up Ajax Mountain. In 1941, the National Alpine Championships were held in Aspen, giving a major boost to the ski industry in that community.

World War II put a temporary halt to the fledgling Colorado ski industry, but the famed 10th Mountain Division ski troops, who trained at Camp Hale just northwest of Leadville, kept the tradition alive. On weekends some of the ski troops traveled to Aspen, slept on the floor of the Hotel Jerome, skied, and livened up evenings by drinking a concoction called "Aspen Crud" — a tall, thick milkshake spiked with five or six slugs of 90 proof whiskey! Skiing was helping to bring Aspen back from four decades of stagnation. The town had barely stayed alive during the Depression of the 1930s. During that decade, a disgusted Aspen businessman asked a drowsing prospector in front of the Hotel Jerome: "Pop, what makes this town so slow?" Opening his eyes, the old fellow growled: "The people's mineralized, that's what. They got silver in their hair and lead in their pants."[1]

From a half-dead, struggling old mining camp down on its luck, Aspen was reborn in 1945. The man behind the amazing transformation was Walter Paepcke, a millionaire and chairman of the Chicago-based Container Corporation of America. Initially, Paepcke was interested in Aspen as a cultural oasis where men and women could come to "recharge their batteries." He thus founded the Aspen Institute for Humanistic Studies. Business and corporate leaders were brought in for two-week conferences with brilliant moderators like Walter Reuther and John Dos Passos. The seminars gave the businessmen a chance to examine their beliefs. Adding to the Institute were music and art festivals, design conferences, and film festivals. Because of Paepcke, Aspen achieved an international reputation as a cosmopolitan community.

Paepcke did more than just make Aspen into a cultural mecca amidst beautiful surroundings; he also started one of the world's great ski resorts. The Aspen Ski Corporation, heavily backed by Paepcke, began carving out ski runs and building lifts on Aspen Mountain in 1946. On January 11, 1947, Aspen officially opened. Soon it was on its way to international acclaim as a ski resort. As the years went by, the ski industry transformed Aspen into a progressive and prosperous community. The population quadrupled, the economy brought back memories of the glorious 1880s, and optimism pervaded Bleeker Street. By the late 1960s, Aspen had four major ski areas—Aspen or Ajax, Highlands, Buttermilk, and Snowmass.

The growth of Aspen created serious problems, native to most other Western Slope ski areas. Too many people, pollution, lack of good zoning, tremendously high real estate prices, and the raping of the beautiful Roaring Fork Valley created a "dreams and dilemmas" atmosphere. What did Aspen want—continued growth and development or a return to the quiet and tranquil days of the '40s and '50s, when one could buy a good "skiers special" at the Red Onion for two dollars and drink beer with the old timers at the Hotel Jerome? Today, it is clear that Aspen cannot have both.

Despite its current problems, Aspen is still a magical town. The high mountains, Victorian buildings, tremendous skiing, and the history of the old silver camp give it a unique quality. Ruthie's Run, Face of Bell, Hotel Jerome, Red Onion, Chair One, Wheeler Opera House, and Tom's Market reek of history and nostalgia. In the 1960s, writer Neil Morgan got a glimpse of what Aspen meant to those who wished to be free of the shackles of society. He wrote of "a family who had all but abandoned themselves to nature, and who seemed among the happiest of people. . . . My last glimpse of them was as they skied off at the summit of the highest ski lift above Aspen into the dazzling, limitless blue and white of the Rockies."[2]

Along the Continental Divide in the Fraser River country, Winter Park sprang into prominence as an early West Slope ski area in 1940. First known as Idlewild Stage Station and then West Portal following the completion of the Moffat Railroad Tunnel in the late 1920s, Winter Park became a haven for Denver ski enthusiasts during the next decade. The snow was deep, the Denver & Rio Grande provided easy access to the great park, and railroad construction shacks became instant warming houses. There were no lifts then; one walked to the top of the high park and skied down. The evolution from abandoned railroad camp to ski area was underway.

By 1940, Winter Park became a non-profit recreational ski area, owned by the city of Denver. A T-Bar was the original lift and day tickets were sold for one dollar. By 1950, lodges had been constructed, more lifts built, and Winter Park became Colorado's largest ski area, a position it held into the '60s.

A unique feature of Winter Park is the famous Denver & Rio Grande ski train which runs from Union Station in Denver, through the Moffat Tunnel to the ski area. The train runs on weekends and carries 650 eager skiers for six dollars and fifty cents a round trip, leaving Denver early in the morning and arriving shortly after the lifts open. On the trip to Winter Park the camaraderie of the skiers on the train is a sight to behold. Accordians and harmonicas are played; singing and stories appear and disappear. On the return trip, the mood is subdued after a hard day on the mountain. The old days are not gone after all. Today Winter Park is going strong as a unique non-profit ski area. Only Aspen and Vail handle more skiers per year than Winter Park.

West of Denver by 100 miles, jammed into a narrow canyon at the southern end of the Gore Range, Vail Village rose from the valley floor in the early '60s. Pete Seibert, a veteran of the 10th Mountain Division, and Earl Eaton of Eagle first became aware of the tremendous open bowls of snow in the Gore Range in 1954. By 1959, a major ski area was in the planning stages. In 1962, a tyrolean-type village was built at the base of the mountains. Vail formally opened as a ski area in 1962 and, unlike most other ski areas, prospered from the beginning. Lacking space in the narrow valley to expand horizontally, Vail has shot upward. It is a stunningly beautiful region, with no cars allowed in the village, great powder skiing in the back bowls, and some spectacular ski runs like Riva Ridge, Prima, and Blue Ox.

Created out of what Pete Seibert called "a wasteland at the foot of a nameless mountain," Vail has become the second largest ski area in Colorado. By the end of the decade it handled 350,000 skiers a season, had a total investment of $70,000,000, and boasted one high-priced condominium development after another. During the 1977–78 ski season, Vail recorded over 1,000,000 skier visits, and building and expansion have continued. Vail was an instant town and ski area, successful from the beginning, blessed with great terrain and snow and enormous amounts of money. Yet, Vail has not been without its problems. Pollution, congestion, high prices and taxes, and environmental difficulties have concerned many. Beaver Creek, another mammoth ski area just west of Vail, will begin operations in the '80s, worrying environmentalists who see more growth, pollution, and congestion in the pint-sized valley. There seems to be no real end to expansion in sight.

Long before Vail was even heard of, the great mining town of Telluride, located below Bridal Veil Falls at the head of the San Miguel River in the beautiful San Juan Mountains, had already started a rich skiing tradition. During the 1920s, Swedish and Finnish miners working at the Black Bear Mine high above Telluride to the east rode the tram buckets to work in the morning and skied the precipitous terrain into town after work just before sunset. The skiing tradition was continued by school teacher Bruce Palmer, who sponsored races from Camel's Garden west of town down a steep powerline to Telluride. The width of the run was 30–50 feet, the slope was 50 degrees and the vertical drop was 2,500 feet. Shades of the early day racers!

During the 1930s, '40s, and '50s, rope tows run from jacked-up automobiles made their appearance in Telluride, enabling youngsters like Billy Mahoney (later Telluride's mountain manager) to ski the steep terrain of the region. As early as the late 1930s, races were held from Camel's Garden to town. Racers came from as far away as Aspen to compete. A skiing tradition had begun. In 1968, millionaire Joe Zoline came into town, liked what he saw and began plans for a ski area which opened four years later in 1972. Today Telluride has enormous potential as a major ski area. The scenery is magnificent, the amount of skiable terrain is enormous, the snowfall is heavy, and some of the runs are already legendary. The Telluride Plunge (appropriately named) and the Spiral Stairs are two of the great ski runs in the United States, snaking through the trees 3,100 vertical feet from the top of the mountain to the San Miguel River below. Like Aspen, Vail, and Crested Butte, Telluride has important decisions to make today. Land values have sky-rocketed, condominiums have shot up and high taxes have placed a burden on people who have lived in Telluride all their lives. Recreation does have its price.

The heyday of the ski industry in Western Colorado began during the 1960s. During the 1950–51 ski season, only four daily ski areas existed in Colorado—Arapahoe Basin, Winter Park, Aspen Mountain, and Loveland Basin. This all changed during the sudden and dramatic rise of skiing in the 1960s. Skiing had been a sport for the few and had never gotten out of the flappy pants, wooden ski, and lace boot stage. In the 1960s, however, a tremendous skiing boom, the like of which had never been seen, hit Colorado. The boom did much to revive a stagnant Western Slope economy. During that decade and the 1970s, Crested Butte, Monarch, Purgatory, Telluride, Copper Mountain, Keystone, Steamboat Springs, Breckenridge, Powderhorn, Aspen Highlands, Aspen Snowmass, and other Western Colorado ski areas came into existence. Some, like Crested Butte, Telluride, and Breckenridge, had been long dead mining camps given a new lease on life by the powder snow and mountains which had not always been their friends.

The ski industry in Western Colorado grew to enormous proportions by the 1970s. One found it hard to believe that skiing had once been only a means of travel and that not so long ago skiing had involved walking and not riding a lift to the top of a mountain.

During the 1950–51 ski season in Western Colorado, 175,000 lift tickets were sold; during the 1978–79 season, 5,600,000 tickets were sold. Western Slope ski areas accounted for over eighty percent of all alpine skiers in the state of Colorado in 1978–79. The outstanding ski conditions in Colorado had led to its title of "Ski Country U.S.A." The economic impact of skiing upon Western Colorado is staggering. The ski-related income of seven Western Slope counties—Pitkin, Summit, Eagle, Routt, Grand, Gunnison, and San Miguel—ranges from 14% to 85% of the total county income.

The mid-1970s saw a slowing of the skiing express. The winter of 1976–77 was one of the most disastrous on record, with record low snowfalls reported across the Western Slope and the entire state. Many ski areas are still recovering from that terrible winter. In addition, it has become much tougher to build ski areas. The Forest Service, environmental agencies, and local governments have taken tougher stands on new ski area development. All have come to realize that ski areas create growth in regions that are ill-equipped to handle it. Environmentalists are concerned with water and air pollution, four-lane highways, and the blighting of beautiful valleys like the Roaring Fork and Gore. Only Beaver Creek, not far from Vail, seems destined to become a ski area on the Western Slope in the near future. Adam's Rib, a proposed area near Eagle, has been put on the back-burner while Governor Dick Lamm, the Forest Service, and local residents take a closer look at the implications of still another ski area. And many people in Western Colorado, tired of long lift lines and high prices for equipment and lift tickets, have turned to cross-country skiing and touring.

Therein lies another success story. If the story of the '60s was alpine skiing, then surely the decade of the '70s was marked by a tremendous boom in nordic skiing. The guru of nordic skiing was and is Sven Wiik. Born in Sweden, Wiik emigrated to the United States in 1949 and spent the next nineteen years as ski coach at Western State College. Wiik's heart was always in nordic rather than alpine skiing and he held one camp after another promoting the sport. Finally, in 1968, he left Gunnison and moved to Steamboat Springs where he established his famed Mount Werner Training Center which further promoted nordic skiing.

As the 1960s gave way to a new decade, nordic skiing began to take hold. Citizens' races like the Frisco Gold Rush, Keystone Capers, Butch Cassidy Bank Run, and others drew hundreds of competitors. Families discovered the joy of skiing together in the tranquil and beautiful mountains and high parks of the Colorado Rockies. The success of American skier Bill Koch in the 1976 Olympic Games further heightened interest. Today, one can gauge the success of nordic skiing by the higher cost of equipment, by the number of races held every year, and by the thousands of Western Coloradans who skim over the snow from November through April. Nordic skiing has gone the way of alpine skiing and become a multimillion dollar a year business.

Skiing is easily worth over $100,000,000 a year, one of the major industries in the region. It has come a long way from the days when hardy pioneers spent most of the day walking to the top of a mountain or when Aspen, Winter Park, or the old Pioneer ski area in the Gunnison country were young. We have but memories of those glorious days now, but what memories!

A postscript must be added before we leave skiing. No coverage of skiing on the Western Slope would be complete without a mention of that region's favorite son, the ill-starred "Steamboat Cowboy," Buddy Werner. He was a much-loved figure not only in Western Colorado, but around the world. Born in Steamboat Springs in 1936, Werner was the greatest alpine skier ever produced in the United States. From 1954 to his tragic death in an avalanche at Val Selin, Switzerland, ten years later, he was the backbone of the American ski team. Buddy Werner was the heart and soul of United States skiing and was the idol of many a young boy in Western Colorado. Adieu, Buddy.

252

Tourism, which one can trace all the way back to the 1860s, spread like wildfire in the '50s and '60s and became one of the top three industries of the region. No longer were the tourists traveling by train on sightseeing expeditions; no longer were they confining themselves to Mesa Verde, Rocky Mountain National Park, and other usual tourist attractions. No, now they were mechanized and many wanted to "get off the beaten track." During the past quarter of a century they have arrived in, or have brought with them, every kind of conveyance including:

airplanes, ordinary automobiles, monstrous campers and home-made trailers, off-road four-wheel-drive vehicles of various types, motorcycles, trail bikes, power boats, and, in winter, ear-splitting snowmobiles. Rafts of synthetic rubber and easily handled kayaks of fiber glass course the rivers in increasing numbers. Lightweight backpack frames, sleeping bags and tents, freeze-dried foods, and the excellent topographic maps available . . . enable young parents to take even tiny children into remote alpine basins once visited only by a hardy few. The . . . effect has been to 'miniaturize' the mountain areas available for recreation — to make the same amount of space seem both smaller and more crowded than it once was.[3]

Associated with tourism has been a craze for homes in the mountains, especially near ski areas. A tremendous land boom began in the 1960s and has reached frenzied proportions in the 1970s. Real estate developers have multiplied like rabbits, pushing whatever land they can to an often unsuspecting public. "Don't be sorry tomorrow that you didn't buy today," they chant. Subdivider after subdivider has taken advantage of those city dwellers who want to exchange the chaos of the city for the peace and tranquility of the mountains. Everywhere one goes he can see the developments — Tamarron near Durango, Crested Butte, the Roaring Fork Valley, Avon, Telluride, Steamboat Springs, and, of course, Summit County. Once rural and sparsely populated areas have been transformed into rapidly growing year-round recreation areas.

Summit County is the best example of unchecked growth. The construction of the Eisenhower Tunnel in the early 1970s changed Summit County forever. With the elimination of nightmarish Loveland Pass between Denver and Frisco, Denverites flocked in record numbers to the Dillon Reservoir, Copper Mountain, Keystone, Breckenridge, and Vail ski areas and the pristine beauty of the mountains. Many fell in love with that region of the Western Slope and yearned to build a vacation home or condominium there. Summit County became known as the "hottest county in the state." A rash of houses and condominiums soon covered the surrounding hills, ruining much of the beauty their owners hoped to find. Retail sales increased more than six times from 1970 to 1977.

Throughout much of the Western Slope, good ranch land was transformed into subdivisions in the 1960s and 1970s. One could hardly blame the ranchers. After surviving the Depression and experiencing low cattle prices more often than not, they were offered insane, unbelievable prices for their land, only to learn after the sale that a whole pie is not nearly as rich as one subdivided into many pieces. If real estate developers were not pressuring ranchers and other owners to sell with the lure of instant gold, coal companies, chain-stores, and recreation industries were.

Extensive building and a burgeoning population created a dilemma. On one hand, expansion and growth created jobs, raised the tax base, and revived dying communities. On the other hand, prices and taxes soared, the peace and tranquility of the past were shattered, and it became painfully obvious that the mountains simply could not sustain large numbers of people. Heavy snows, below zero temperatures, geological faults, and the prevalence of air pollution in the narrow mountain valleys soon exposed the ignorance of those who believed the mountains could be conquered by modern technology. Water proved to be scarce, septic tanks did not work, water pipes froze, and adequate fire protection was often not available. No matter, people continued to flock to the mountains, lured by the fast-buck, unethical developers, and real estate salesmen.

West of Aspen, in the beautiful Crystal River Valley in the early 1970s, combined real estate developments called for a population of 33,000 with homes to be built in a known mudslide and avalanche area. In addition, the Marble Ski Area was planned, when only a half hour down the road one could be skiing at any one of the four great Aspen areas. It was sheer folly and, unfortunately, this type of development was not confined only to the Crystal River Valley. Although protests against unplanned growth, the raping of the environment, and sky-rocketing real estate prices came in the mid-1970s, the reaction hardly dented the problem. It remains a problem with which Western Colorado must eventually come to grips.

The hordes of tourists continued to cross the mountains in the 1970s. They never even broke stride. Some are hunters anxiously awaiting the deer and elk season in the fall. They come from everywhere and are anxious for action. During the twenty-four hours before dawn of opening day, Western Slope towns and highways are jammed with campers, station wagons, pickup trucks, and jeeps as the hunters maneuver for position in the mountains. Some are slobs, littering the land with beer cans, leering at waitresses in restaurants, warming up their guns by shooting at road markers, and generally making fools of themselves. Most, however, are serious and are in the mountains for camaraderie with friends, to get away from it all, and to put some meat on the table.

For the fisherman, Western Colorado is a virtual paradise. The stream fishing is among the best in the world, with streams like the Roaring Fork, Gunnison, Fryingpan, Taylor, Fraser, and others luring fly fishermen to their banks seeking rainbow trout like the legendary Geronimo, an estimated fifteen pound giant of the Gunnison River. When the willow-fly hatch occurred on the Gunnison River around June 1 to June 10 every year before dams were built, fishermen from all over Colorado flocked into Gunnison and nearby resorts for some of the finest fishing anywhere. Farther north, President Dwight Eisenhower was a frequent visitor to the clear waters of the Fraser River. Today, with more fishermen and more dams, the stream fishing is not quite so good. However, in the winter, thousands of fishermen, armed with a saw, a chair, and their own lucky bait or lures do pretty well ice-fishing at such bodies of water as the Blue Mesa Reservoir, Lake Granby, Reudi Reservoir, Dillon Reservoir, and Grand Lake. During the summer, the fishermen troll the waters of some of the large bodies of water with good results.

The fast-running rivers of Western Colorado have increasingly lured thrill-seekers to their waters. River-running with kayaks and rubber rafts has become a popular sport in the spring of the year when the rivers run full. The Dolores River with Snaggletooth Rapid, the Yampa with Warm Springs, and the Green with the famous Canyon of Lodore, provide some of the most challenging white water in the country. Before the Morrow Point Dam was built on the Gunnison River in the Black Canyon below the town of Cimarron, there was a nine-mile stretch, which included Deadman's and Leap Frog rapids, that, pound for pound, was probably the toughest section of white-water anywhere; it was all white in that stretch. For the unwary who do not treat the rivers with respect, sudden death is the result. Every year during the spring, naive river-runners in inner tubes or inferior rafts without life preservers drown. The roaring rivers take no prisoners.

Two-fifths of the fifty-four mountains of Colorado which rise to 14,000 feet are in Western Colorado, including the San Juan, Elk, and San Miguels. Hundreds more are above 13,000 feet in elevation. The prevalence of the many mountains, the popularity of four-wheel-drive vehicles, and more leisure time have spawned another recreational boom. From age seven to seventy they come, climbing the crags and peaks. Most mountain climbing involves only a long walk to the top of the peak. Some mountains, however, like Capitol Peak and El Diente, are tougher. With the tremendous increase in mountain climbing and hiking, sporting goods and alpine mountaineering firms have profited handsomely from sales of backpacks, tents, hiking boots, sleeping bags, and other equipment. Today, it is not uncommon to see hundreds of people a day climbing the same mountain or to observe outdoor enthusiasts rapelling off the side of a cliff. Everyone, it seems, is bent on his or her own form of freedom.

When fall comes, it serves as a magnet for even more tourists. They come especially to the San Juan and Gunnison countries where the mountains are high and the colors bright. Autumn seems to have a magical character and splendor about it on the Western Slope. The frost on the ground in the morning and the chill in the mountains belies the magnificent warmth one feels physically and mentally. The blaze of colors as the aspen leaves turn, the occasional glimpses of deer and elk, strong now as they enter the winter months, and the stunning panorama bring renewed optimism to one's heart. For tourists from everywhere with picnic baskets, cameras, zoom lenses, and tripods, fall in Western Colorado is truly a magical time.

Wilderness areas, national forests, and national monuments have been great drawing cards for tourists, especially since the expansion of the recreation boom about 1960. The Flat Tops, Maroon Bells, Snowmass, and West Elk Wilderness areas have drawn thousands of people, usually for days at a time. The hikers have come to fish, climb, and be off by themselves. Unfortunately, the tremendous increase of hikers has taken the wilderness out of wilderness areas. It simply is not any fun to "get away from it all" and run into 100 hikers following the same trail.

The San Juan, Uncompahgre, Gunnison, Grand Mesa, White River, Routt, and Arapaho National Forests with their streams, lakes, and mountains also lure tourists. Hundreds of thousands of people every year visit Dinosaur, Colorado, and Black Canyon National Monuments and Mesa Verde and Rocky Mountain National Parks. The unique rock formations, ancient cliff dwellings, and deep canyons have never stopped weaving their spells on unsuspecting tourists and hikers. They want to return again and they will.

Perhaps the biggest and most underrated tourist attraction in Western Colorado involves the 200 or so ghost towns which dot the mountain and valley landscape in nostalgic fashion. The long-dead

256

mining camps stand as isolated sentinels to the past glories. Once, hundreds, occasionally thousands, of miners graced their streets, but following the silver panic of 1893, almost all withered and died. Yet, they have remained a romantic tie to the past. From Dunton to Hahn's Peak and from Ashcroft to Red Mountain, the ghost towns are irresistible attractions to tourists. Alas, the advancing years and destructiveness of vandals who tear old boards from buildings and dig up garbage dumps have signaled the end of the ghost towns. Soon we will only have memories.

Another major attraction for visitors is the many hot springs. Once, not so long ago, Indians, weary miners, and health-seekers with every sort of affliction bathed in the springs in the hope of relieving their injuries or curing their diseases. Today, thousands come for recreation to such spas as Glenwood Springs, Hot Sulphur Springs, Pagosa Springs, Ouray, Waunita Hot Springs, Steamboat Springs, and others.

From out of the past, a railroad whistle screams its cacophony against the canyon walls, and a narrow gauge engine, panting as it pulls its heavy load, creeps along the Animas River. The narrow gauge railroad lives — another link with the past. Between Silverton and Durango during the summer months, the Denver & Rio Grande Railroad runs a tourist train above and along the snaking Animas River. Tens of thousands of tourists compete for reservations on this train to yesterday. The trip is inspiring and one's imagination soon takes over. It is not hard to imagine the snorting little narrow gauge engines run by men of legend operating in the tight canyon almost 100 years ago. For the tourist, it is an unexpected trip into the past, one they will never forget.

Even Hollywood recognized the beauty and movie possibilities of Western Colorado in the 1960s. *True Grit* was filmed at Ridgway, much of *Butch Cassidy and the Sundance Kid* was filmed near Durango, *Cheyenne Autumn* had scenes filmed near Gunnison, and *Molly Brown* was filmed, in part, at the edge of the Black Canyon. Hollywood producers are eyeing the Western Slope as a great new area for moviemaking; if they decide to go ahead with their plans, many Western Colorado communities will benefit economically.

If mountain climbing, sailing on Grand Lake or the Blue Mesa Reservoir, and river-running are of recent vintage, rodeos are as traditional and as old as apple pie. Ninety or one hundred years ago, rodeos were held out in open fields or in large corrals and little or no money was involved. Today, many Western Slope towns have rodeos in the summer months, complete with prize money and much fun and frolic. Some of the great bucking horses like Steamboat and General Pershing and great riders like Kid Vaughn and Isen Dart, along with many unknown horses and cowboys, laid the basis for modern-day rodeos.

So success has seemingly come to Western Colorado. Thirty years ago the region had many fewer people; many of its communities were barely staying alive; industry was non-existent; and travel was tough at all times and almost impossible in the winter. Then came the "sell Colorado" campaign. Large amounts of money were spent to advertise, the skiing industry became big business, and energy development appeared. Everything had changed. The Western Slope was called "the ultimate fringe benefit" and made to look like paradise by the Colorado Division of Commerce and Development. They declared in one of their bulletins:

> Live where others vacation. Here, you are in the midst of scenery and recreational opportunities that delight millions of visitors each year. You get to know dozens of ski areas, from world-famous resorts like Aspen, Vail and Steamboat Springs to uncrowded local family areas. Hike and camp, hunt and fish, explore old jeep trails . . . with sites catering to car and trailer camping as well as to wilderness backpackers. See some of the most spectacular scenery in the country in Rocky Mountain National Park, Dinosaur National Monument. . . . Delve into the past, in the cliff dwellings of Mesa Verde. . . . Ride the Durango-Silverton narrow gauge railroad. Poke around in ghost towns and visit pioneer museums. Sail in regattas under the peaks at Grand Lake, Dillon Lake or Reudi Reservoir; or boat, fish and water ski on the large reservoirs. . . . Enjoy internationally-known concert artists at the Aspen Music Festival, and the Film Festival at Telluride. . . .[4]

Sound fantastic? It is. The question today remains: should we continue to sell Western Colorado or have we had enough? Tourism is already one of the major industries of the region. There is a nagging suspicion that growth advocates might already be strangling the goose that laid the golden egg. Tourists will not want to visit if the air and water are polluted and the roads and trails are jammed with travelers. Too much civilization will kill the tourist industry, and yet that is exactly what is happening today. Western Colorado's population has jumped to 230,000 and is headed far beyond that figure; boom towns with their ugliness are springing up, streams are being dammed, and major coal and uranium mines are starting. Freedom and solitude are threatened.

Faced with change and rapid economic development, the Western Slope is bracing for an unprecedented assault on its resources.

Old timers vs. new arrivals, industry vs. environmentalists, tourists vs. natives, the federal government vs. local control—little has changed, but this time the stakes are higher. Not so long ago, the land was sparsely peopled and quiet. All that has changed. Today, the sound of the bulldozer, tram wheels on ski lifts, airplanes, and especially the real estate speculator, mine companies, and federal government can be heard. The new life may not be as good as we once thought and more will not be better.

Silverton, in the valley beside the Animas River, was very famous as a mining town in the last century and is now practically a ghost town. Macomber Mountain in the background is one of the many 12-13,000 foot peaks that surround the town. *Courtesy U.S. Forest Service.*

17.
Water: The Future
Is Now

John Wesley Powell was impressed. The year was 1867 and the great surveyor of the American West had, for the first time, seen the headwaters of the Grand River (renamed the Colorado River in 1921) on Colorado's Western Slope. The awe-struck explorer exclaimed:

> All winter long, snow falls on its mountain-crested rim. . . . When the summer sun comes, this snow melts and tumbles down the mountainsides in millions of cascades. A million cascade brooks united to form half a hundred rivers beset with cataracts; half a hundred roaring rivers unite to form the Colorado, which rolls, a mad, turbid stream, into the Gulf of California.[1]

Churning up the ground like a giant bulldozer, the mighty Colorado roared out of its birthplace in Western Colorado, crashing through anything in its path, down more than 10,000 feet to the Gulf of California. Today, because of a stunning increase in population in Arizona and southern California, and an accompanying need for more water, the once-mighty Colorado has been tamed by dam after dam. A shadow of its former self, the great river now resembles a series of lakes.

Most of Western Colorado's water problems since the 1940s have been caused by rapid growth in the Southwest, and later, along the Front Range of the Colorado Rockies. The Colorado River Compact of 1922 guaranteed the Lower Basin states 7,500,000 acre-feet of water annually for their development, but what of the increasing water demands of Colorado's eastern slope cities, farmers, and industrialists? The answer was trans-mountain diversion.

Following the completion of the Moffat Tunnel by the Denver & Salt Lake Railroad in 1927, the Denver Water Board leased the pioneer bore of the tunnel. The pioneer bore was the small tunnel driven first and from which the main tunnel was excavated. From 1929 to 1932 the Water Board nonchalantly began to enlarge and line the tunnel. Then it happened. Little snow fell during the early winter months of 1932 and the Water Board grew worried. Up went larger crews of men to the bitter cold of the Divide to finish lining the tunnel and to build the necessary collection works on the west side. The feverish work ended early in 1933 when a six and a half foot snow on the Divide guaranteed water for the following summer.

Because of the scare of 1932–33, the Denver Water Board decided to push through a major trans-mountain diversion. Financially independent and non-elected, the Water Board had traditionally spent all its revenues on water projects, and the Moffat Tunnel was no exception. With its usual careful planning and foresight, the Water Board had purchased water rights on the Fraser River of the Western Slope. Work on the tunnel proceeded unabated during the next few years, and in June, 1936, Western Slope water made its way to the eastern slope. Forty-three thousand acre-feet were diverted, and even though the cost ran into the millions of dollars, the Moffat Tunnel was worth it, for now Denver was, at least for the present, insured a stable water supply. The Moffat Tunnel was not the first trans-mountain diversion in Colorado and it would not be the last, but it was the biggest up to that time.

East of the Continental Divide and north of the Moffat Tunnel, in the Poudre and South Platte River valleys, a combination of drought and economic depression had devastated a once-prosperous region by 1933. Nathan Meeker and his Union Colony had irrigated 12,000 acres along the Poudre River sixty years before. Other irrigation projects soon followed, using water from the South Platte and Big Thompson Rivers and St. Vrain and Boulder creeks. However, by the late 1920s and early 1930s, there was despair and bankruptcy in the South Platte Valley, caused by a drought-created shortage of water in the irrigation ditches. The solution to the problem once again was Western Slope water.

As early as 1889, residents of the South Platte Valley dreamed of tapping the headwaters of the Grand River for use on the eastern slope. Forty-four years later, Charles Hansen, editor of the *Greeley Tribune,* rolled up his sleeves and went to work on what would soon be known as the Colorado-Big Thompson Project, the largest trans-mountain diversion of water ever attempted. Hansen faced formidable obstacles. The Depression had made money scarce, Coloradans were suspicious of federal projects, the Western Slope opposed water diversion and Lower Basin states feared a loss of future water. But Hansen was not discouraged. He organized the Northern Colorado Water Conservancy District in 1937 and began turning his critics into supporters. To those who questioned the cost of the gigantic project, he replied that hydroelectric plants and water fees would pay for the "Big T." He promised conservationists that the pristine beauty of Estes Park would be preserved. For the Western Slope and its powerful champion, Representative Edward T. Taylor, he promised the huge Green Mountain Reservoir near Kremmling on the Blue River as a holding reservoir for downstream irrigators.

Finally the great day was at hand. On December 21, 1937, Franklin Roosevelt signed the bill authorizing the Colorado-Big Thompson Project. Although the "Big T" was supposed to cost $44,000,000 and be finished in five years, World War II ruined those plans. The Bureau of Reclamation began construction of the giant project in 1938 at the Green Mountain Dam. One of the essential keys to the "Big T" was the building of the largest man-made lake in the state, Granby Reservoir in Middle Park. Water from the reservoir would be lifted by pumps into the smaller Shadow Mountain Lake nearer the Divide. From Shadow Mountain, the water flowed into the beautiful Grand Lake and from there was carried 3,800 feet under the Continental Divide by the 13.1 mile Alva Adams Tunnel. On the east side of the Divide, the water ran into the Big Thompson River near Estes Park.

As the diverted Colorado River water descended 2,900 feet from the tunnel under the Divide to the foothills below, it became part of a maze of power plants, transmission lines, siphons, conduits, dams, reservoirs, and tunnels. Major deliveries of water to the eastern slope through the Adams Tunnel began in 1953. The entire Big Thompson Project was completed in 1959 at a cost of $169,000,000; $125,000,000 more than expected. The Big Thompson diversion was designed to divert 310,000 acre-feet of water annually to the eastern slope, but has only averaged 230,000 acre-feet per year.

Thus was the famous "Big T" built. The project was very large and costly, but even so, proved that such a mammoth task could be accomplished at a profit. Its legacy was many future trans-mountain water diversions. And a postscript. Even though the "Big T" diversion was not named for Charles Hansen as it should have been, he died with the knowledge that the people of the South Platte Valley would never forget him.

Not content with the Moffat Tunnel and the planned Colorado-Big Thompson diversion, the eastern slope, by the end of the 1930s, was soon on the prowl again in search of more Western Slope water. Southeastern Colorado water interests proposed the giant Gunnison-Arkansas Project to divert Gunnison country water through the Divide to benefit the drought-ravaged Arkansas Valley. The project was first proposed in the early 1930s, but the success of the Moffat Tunnel and the "Big T" gave it further impetus toward the end of the decade. If the Gunnison country could not use all its water, then why not divert it to Colorado people in need?

The Gunnison-Arkansas Project, proposed by the Bureau of Reclamation after extensive surveys, would have taken 600,000-700,000 acre-feet of water from the East and Taylor rivers north of Gunnison and the Lake Fork, Cebolla, and Cochetopa rivers west and south of the community and moved the water to Sargents, a small railroad town at the western foot of Marshall Pass. The water would have been collected from the spring runoff and taken by huge laterals or open ditches by gravity flow to the base of Marshall Pass. There a twelve mile tunnel under the Continental Divide would have carried the water, again by gravity flow, to the eastern slope. From the east side of the divide, the water would be transferred into the Arkansas River and sent downstream to Pueblo and agricultural lands to the east.

The Western Slope, led by its champion, long-time Fourth District Representative Ed Taylor, was outraged at this power-play by Eastern Slope interests. Taylor raged:

> This is a bold, brazen, buccaneering fight to deliberately steal the summer water of the Gunnison country and the Taylor Park reservoir. . . . I will say . . . that after spending ten years to secure that Taylor Park reservoir, I will never permit any bunch of promoters to get away with it as long as there is a spark of vitality left in my body. . . . [But] it is not at all any easy fight that I am up against in trying to protect our most priceless birthright.[2]

The Gunnison-Arkansas Project would have taken over half the total water produced by the Gunnison River and its tributaries and seriously affected any future growth of the region. Determined opposition by Taylor and Western Colorado interests and the coming of World War II killed the Gunnison-Arkansas Project.[3] When east slope interests tried to revive the project after World War II, they were forced to accept the smaller Fryingpan-Arkansas Project.

Having beaten back the Gunnison-Arkansas Project, Western Colorado was threatened with yet another trans-mountain diversion immediately following World War II. The post-war boom had nearly doubled Denver's population and, along with recurring droughts, had forced severe water rationing for the city. The far-sighted Denver Water Board, recognizing the critical water needs of Denver then and in the future, put a $75,000,000 water bond issue before the voters in 1955. The bond issue was approved and the money was used to finance the Montezuma Tunnel, soon to be known as the Roberts Tunnel (named for Harold D. Roberts, Denver Water Board lawyer who was instrumental in getting approval for the lateral under the Divide).

Token digging had begun at the east portal in 1946, but not until a decade later, when the Water Board was sure it could divert Western Slope water, did the work begin in earnest. On paper, the Roberts Tunnel was an awesome project. The plan called for the diversion of Blue River water near Breckenridge into the giant Dillon Reservoir downstream near the present town of Frisco. The reservoir would cost nearly $20,000,000 and hold 262,000 acre-feet of water. From the Dillon Reservoir a 23.3 mile tunnel, one of the world's longest, was constructed under the Continental Divide to the little town of Grant, on a fork of the South Platte River on the eastern slope. From there, the water flowed by gravity to Denver.

Six hundred men worked from the east and west portals of the Roberts Tunnel for three and a half years before the crews met each other early in 1960. Four more years were needed to complete work on the diversion, but in mid-July, 1964, water from the Blue River flowed into the Dillon Reservoir and, from there, continued through the much-anticipated tunnel to help supply Denver's water needs. The Roberts Tunnel and Dillon Reservoir cost $80,000,000, but furnished Denver with 47,000 acre-feet of badly needed water every year.

Despite the best efforts of Western Colorado, that region continued to lose more and more of its most valuable resource to the more populous eastern slope. No longer was irrigation the only justification for diversion; power and domestic use for a growing population along the Front Range were now also considered.

As the Roberts Tunnel was being completed, still another trans-mountain water diversion was getting started. This was the Fryingpan-Arkansas Project, the remains of the still-born Gunnison-Arkansas Project of the 30s and 40s. Once eastern slope interests realized that the Gunnison-Arkansas diversion would not succeed because of heavy costs and a lack of water, they set their sights on a more moderate proposal — the Fryingpan-Arkansas Project. In 1953, following a complete investigation, the Bureau of Reclamation put the new project on paper. Negotiations between West and east slope interests involving the diversion went on throughout the 1950s. Wayne Aspinall, who played a major role in the negotiations, later recalled: "The Fryingpan-Arkansas Project came into existence only because the interests of Western and eastern Colorado were able to get together and sign an agreement which was satisfactory as nearly as possible to the interests of both Slopes." Recognizing the changed atmosphere of the past ten years regarding diversions, Aspinall laments: "It would be impossible to authorize such a project today."[4]

The Fryingpan-Arkansas Project was authorized by Congress in August, 1962, as a multi-purpose water development in central and southeastern Colorado. The bulk of the project was designed to bring irrigation water to drought-plagued farmers in the Arkansas Valley east of Pueblo. For years, they had been without late season irrigation water. Now, suddenly, there was hope. The water to be diverted east of the Divide was taken from the headwaters of two Western Slope streams — the Fryingpan and Roaring Fork rivers which tumbled off of Hagerman and Independence passes near Basalt and Aspen. Before the Western Slope would agree to the project, it demanded the building of a new compensatory storage reservoir west of the Divide, similar to the Green Mountain Reservoir of the Big Thompson Project. The result was the Ruedi Reservoir located east of Basalt on the Fryingpan River. Completed in 1969, the Ruedi Dam, 287 feet high, backs up 102,360 acre-feet of water for use on the Western Slope.

Above the Ruedi Reservoir, collection systems divert and carry West Slope water to the inlet portal of the Charles Boustead Tunnel. The 5.4 mile tunnel under the Continental Divide carries 69,200 acre-feet of water annually into Turquoise Lake five miles west of Leadville. The lake, at capacity, holds 129,432 acre-feet of water. From Turquoise Lake, power canals carry water to the Mount Elbert powerplant at Twin Lakes, ten miles south, and to the Otero power-plant at the Clear Creek Reservoir, another three miles farther south. From the Clear Creek Reservoir, the water is deposited into the Arkansas River and begins its journey to the huge 357,000 acre-foot Pueblo Reservoir west of Pueblo. Water from the Pueblo Reservoir will ultimately be sent all the way east to Lamar on the Arkansas River and north to Colorado Springs via Fountain Creek.

Water from the Fryingpan-Arkansas Project provides supplemental irrigation for 280,000 acres in the Arkansas Valley, as well as generating a large amount of power. It may also eventually provide municipal water to Aurora, Colorado Springs, and towns east of Pueblo, but that will involve the diversion of additional water and is a story to be told in the future. The Fryingpan-Arkansas Project will cost a staggering $563,000,000 when completed in 1983. Because of inflation, the amount of money expended by that time will probably be greater. Yet, the cost in dollars may only be minor compared to the cost of reduced stream flow, tampering with deer and elk herds, and the harm done to future development of the Western Slope.

In any case, Western Colorado probably has not seen the last of trans-mountain diversion. The Denver Water Board has the Eagle-Piney Project waiting in the wings. This project, approved by Denver voters in 1973, plans to take water purchased by the Denver Water Board from the headwaters of Piney Creek, just north of Vail, and from the Eagle River for use on the eastern slope. The water would be moved via tunnels into the Dillon Reservoir and from there taken to Denver via the Roberts Tunnel for domestic use. This project, if built, would cost hundreds of millions of dollars and divert an additional 170,000 acre-feet of scarce West Slope water.

The eastern slope, with ninety percent of Colorado's population, was, and still is, full of plans for taking water from West Slope streams. However, all its diversions put together did not equal the cost, dams, and implications of the greatest river storage project in Rocky Mountain history. The federally-sponsored Colorado River Storage Act of 1956 was and is a gigantic project, both in cost and in the implications it holds for Western Colorado. In 1949, the Upper Basin states signed the Upper Colorado River Basin Compact, which declared their intent to make full use of their share of the total flow of the Colorado River system assigned to them in 1922 by the famed Colorado River Compact. In 1922, it was thought that the Upper Basin's share would be 7,500,000 acre-feet per year.

Prior to 1949, the Upper Basin states had developed irrigation and municipal uses for only forty percent of their allotment. In the 1949 agreement, the Upper Basin states allocated 51.75% of their water to Colorado, 11.25% to New Mexico, 23% to Utah, and 14% to Wyoming. To avoid the mistake made in the Colorado River Compact of 1922, percentages were adopted instead of acre-feet allotments because of uncertainty over how much water would remain after the Upper Basin had met its commitments to the lower states. The Lower Basin states, especially California, had grown much more rapidly than their northern and eastern neighbors and had won the construction of the Hoover Dam in 1936. The dam provided water for irrigated lands and hydroelectric power and allowed California to use much more than its share of water. This fact put pressure on the Upper Basin states; either they would increase their need for water or face a demand from the Lower Basin that they give up rights to the millions of acre-feet they were not using—a hard and fast rule of Western water law.

To make use of their water, the four Upper Basin states proposed the Colorado River Storage Project of 1956, which was to have an enormous impact on Western Colorado. Passed by Congress that same year, the giant project called for the construction of six major dams, most of them in Western Colorado, to supply water for irrigation and power, and eleven smaller dams for irrigation alone. The reservoirs created by the dams would provide for the use of a great amount of the water assigned to the Upper Basin states in 1922.

The debate over the Colorado River Storage Act contained the beginnings of the environmental movement in Western Colorado. Environmentalists were outraged at the location of one of the dams in Echo Park within Dinosaur National Monument in northwestern Colorado. The proposed new dam would be 525 feet high and "would flood Lodore Canyon as the water backed up the Green [River] for sixty-three miles and up the canyon of the Yampa for forty-four miles to create a 43,400 acre lake and produce a billion kilowatt hours of electricity annually."[5]

Despite support from Senator Ed Johnson and Congressman Wayne Aspinall, a storm of protest forced the deletion of the Echo Park Dam from the project. This indirectly led to the building of three dams on the Gunnison River, to make up for the power lost at Echo Park.

Six major dams were constructed as part of the Colorado River Storage Project: Glen Canyon on the Colorado River in Arizona, Flaming Gorge on the Green River in Utah, Navajo on the San Juan River in New Mexico, and three dams on the Gunnison River of the Western Slope which made up the Curecanti Project—Blue Mesa, Morrow Point, and Crystal. These dams were constructed to store water for downstream water commitments. Eleven other dams in the Upper Basin, including five in Western Colorado, referred to as "participating projects" would store water for use by the Upper Basin. Additional participating dams were authorized later. With the exception of the Crystal, all of the primary dams were constructed during the 1960s.

The cost of the total Colorado River Storage Project was estimated at $1,400,000,000, but delays and inflation have driven the cost higher today. Since the 1960s, the Western Slope has seen one water project after another built. The Paonia Project on the North Fork of the Gunnison River, Bostwick Park Project near the head of Cimarron Creek, Smith Fork Project near Crawford, Florida Project near Durango, and the Silt Project near Rifle are examples of participating projects built under the Colorado River Storage Act.

As more dams were built in Western Colorado, opposition to them stiffened because of soaring costs, damage done to beautiful river valleys, and a low cost-benefit ratio. The Sierra Club, Wilderness Society, Friends of the Earth, and many other environmental organizations began challenging West Slope water projects through public opinion, court tests, and steadily increasing federal agencies. Once it had been easy to build water projects in Western Colorado; those days passed into oblivion in the late 1960s.

During the 1970s, environmental protests against dams and water projects in Western Colorado reached crescendo proportions. The Denver Water Board, Bureau of Reclamation (referred to as the "Bureau of Wreck" by opponents), and real estate developers, who hoped to take advantage of new water supplies, were severely criticized by the press and environmentalists. They were doing only what they had always done—bringing water to an arid land and its people—but now the rules of the game had changed.

In 1962, prior to the authorization of the Central Arizona Project, a $1,400,000,000-plus project to provide 2,800,000 acre-feet of irrigation and municipal water to arid central Arizona, Colorado's Wayne Aspinall, powerful chairman of the House Committee on Interior and Insular Affairs, gained an important concession for Western Colorado. Aspinall demanded and got approval for several reclamation projects within Western Colorado and the Upper Basin to guarantee water during drought periods. This was done in the Colorado River Basin Project Act of 1968. The projects which were guaranteed in Western Colorado included the "Five Fingers" reservoirs. From the "thumb" in west-central Colorado to the "little finger" which extends into northern New Mexico, the projects include West Divide, Dallas Creek, San Miguel, Dolores, and Animas-La Plata. The Five Fingers projects, if and when built, will provide 719,000 acre-feet of water annually for irrigation, municipal, and industrial use.

The Animas-La Plata project, near Durango, will provide 139,000 acre-feet of irrigation water for ranchers and farmers in the La Plata River drainage, plus providing industrial and municipal water for Durango, and Farmington and Aztec, New Mexico. The estimated cost of the project, not yet begun, is in the neighborhood of $150,000,000.

Northwest of Durango is the site of the Dolores Project which will create a giant reservoir near the town of Dolores to provide water for Ute Mountain Indians, farmers, and stockmen in the area. The Dolores Project will cost $186,000,000 and will irrigate 81,000 acres with 120,800 acre-feet of water. Farther north along the San Miguel River, the San Miguel Project has been proposed with a dam below Placerville and canals running west. Water from the San Miguel will provide 77,800 acre-feet of water to irrigate 39,000 acres of land near Nucla and Norwood. The project, which is not yet under construction, will cost $125,000,000.

The Dallas Creek Project currently under construction after a long debate over whether it should be built will provide 60,300 acre-feet of water for the irrigation of 23,620 acres and for municipal water for Colona, Montrose, Olathe, and Delta. The project will dam up the Uncompahgre River between Colona and Ridgway and provide water for the Tri-County Conservancy District. Water will be used for irrigation as well as for domestic and industrial purposes. The cost of the Dallas Creek Project will be close to $75,000,000.

The West Divide Project, not yet started, is located south of the Colorado River between Rifle and Glenwood Springs. At a cost of $200,000,000, plans are to irrigate 39,920 acres of land by pumping 115,600 acre-feet of water annually out of the Colorado River up to West Divide Creek.

Two other major water projects, not part of Five Fingers, have been authorized for Western Colorado development. The Fruitland Mesa Project, long controversial, is located just north of the Blue Mesa Reservoir on Soap Creek in the Gunnison country. The $87,900,000 project would dam up Soap Creek and divert the water to 12,000 acres of land near Crawford. Only sixty-nine landowners would be benefited at a cost of $1,200,000 per landowner. The Savory-Pot Hook Project involves both Colorado and Wyoming along the Little Snake River, which runs into both states. This project, which would cost nearly $80,000,000, would directly benefit 106 farms and ranches in southwestern Wyoming and northwestern Colorado.

Following his election in 1976, President Jimmy Carter dropped a bombshell on western states by excluding from recommended appropriations eighteen major water projects, including two—Savory-Pot Hook and Fruitland Mesa—in Western Colorado. In addition, Carter suggested that additional studies should be made of other water projects on the Western Slope previously approved, but not yet funded, including West Divide, San Miguel, and Animas-La Plata. This was a break with history. Ever since the turn of the century, one American president after another had approved western water projects. This was heresy. After all, water was life in the West and Western Colorado; without it, farmers, ranchers, industry, yes, even towns and states, were doomed to a bleak existence. Just who was this peanut farmer from Georgia to tell people of Western Colorado they could not build dams to keep water that was rightfully theirs? Under the Colorado River Basin Project Act of 1962, the federal government had promised to build five additional participating water projects in Western Colorado. Now Jimmy Carter wanted to renege.

The federal government wanted Western Colorado's energy — coal, uranium, and perhaps oil shale; Lower Basin states and the eastern slope wanted its water. The environmentalists wanted the region left as it was, with no future development. Major corporations, mostly energy companies, land developers, and recreational firms, their eyes glazed with dollar signs, also flocked into Western Colorado with the calm assurance that plenty of water was available. Various interest groups were pulling and tugging at the Western Slope and the natives did not like it. Direction was needed, and fast.

The history of Western Colorado water development has been exciting. The successful attempts of farsighted men to tame the rampaging Colorado River and some of its tributaries make a heroic story of pioneers who would not admit defeat. As David Lavender, historian of the American West, has stated:

> It is the story of a continuing attempt by a remarkably persistent set of people to wrest a living from tempting but unpredictable lands — lands that lie pinched between an oasis too high for growing anything except timothy hay and spruce trees on one hand and on the other, a desert too dry for much besides jackrabbits and sagebrush.[6]

"The history of the West," said John Wesley Powell nearly a hundred years ago, "will be written in acre-feet of water." And so it has been in Western Colorado. Fights over water have been the rule rather than the exception. Irrigation water and hydroelectric power played an important part in the settlement and history of the Western Slope, but with the passage of time, dramatic changes came in water development. The first irrigation works were constructed by private parties as a part of the pioneering process because of expected high returns. However, the aridity of the land and canyon-locked rivers soon forced the federal government to enter the arena with the creation of the Bureau of Reclamation in 1902. Since that time, the federal government has built all major water developments in Western Colorado.

The day came when people realized that towns and industries used much less water than agriculture, while yielding a higher return. Soon came a demand for water transfers. After all, most of the good dam sites were already taken; accessible and low cost water projects no longer existed. For this reason, today Denver keeps an envious eye on Western Slope and South Platte Valley agricultural water.

Changing social values have also played a role in establishing water priorities, particularly the emphasis placed on protecting environmental values during the past two decades. Today emphasis is on the preservation of free-flowing rivers, the maintenance of deer and elk herds, and the preservation of the pristine beauty of the Western Slope. Dams, water diversions, and the increased population which follows water development are opposed. It is a difficult decision; how can recreational and esthetic values in an urban society be measured against agricultural and industrial demand?

When one adds up all the pluses and minuses surrounding water development on the Western Slope, he finds that there are no good guys and bad guys. Honorable men are involved in dam building and also in trying to stop dam building. Those who favor continued water development and dam building in Western Colorado make the following points:

1. Water development has been enormously successful for farmers, ranchers, towns, and industry in Western Colorado. Without water and the courage of the pioneer who developed and used it, the region would still be a barren wilderness.

2. More than seventy percent of all the water in the Colorado River originates on the Western Slope. Why not make use of water that rightfully belongs to that region instead of allowing it to be diverted to the eastern slope or sent downstream to Lower Basin states?

3. Western Colorado is on the verge of becoming one of the energy capitals of the West with coal, molybdenum, uranium, natural gas, and possibly oil shale as major sources. An Interior Department report of 1974 indicated demands on the Colorado River for energy projects could include 125,000 acre-feet of water a year for coal-fired power plants, 351,000 acre-feet for other non-consumptive electrical generation units, and 388,000 acre-feet for oil shale

and coal gasification facilities. To develop the energy supplies in Western Colorado, additional water supplies will be needed.

4. Reservoirs created by dam construction have greatly increased recreation and tourism on the Western Slope. The Blue Mesa Reservoir, for instance, is the second largest tourist attraction in the entire state.

Those who oppose dam building on the Western Slope counter with the following arguments:

1. Almost all good damsites have been taken in Western Colorado; this, plus the fact that prospective irrigable land is at a premium, has led to a very low cost-benefit ratio involving water projects. Refusing to accept this reality, the Bureau of Reclamation now concerns itself with such risky and marginal projects as the Teton Dam, Central Arizona Project, and Fruitland Mesa. Moving deeply canyoned, cantankerous streams out of their normal channels at a cost the user can pay is impossible today without extensive money from the federal government. In short, it is not financially feasible to build new water projects in Western Colorado.

2. Western Colorado is an arid land demanding great amounts of water to raise crops. Why not accept the obvious and leave agriculture in the hands of states with enough water to support it cheaply? The notion that food production can be greatly increased by "making the deserts bloom" is erroneous. Evaporation losses alone require many times the water used in humid regions.

3. Dam building has destroyed some of the finest fishing in the world along the Gunnison River and other West Slope streams, has destroyed much of the beauty of Western Colorado, and has shown little regard for animal life. Environmentally, dams are disasters.

4. Water used for irrigation picks up soluble salts from the earth across which it is conducted, leading to a reduction in quality. Dams check the natural flushing action of rivers, leading to a very serious salinity problem for downstream water users. The salt beds in the Paradox Valley through which the Dolores River flows, are open and notorious. The valley adds the equivalent of 14.3 railroad boxcars of salt to the river every day according to the Bureau of Reclamation. The problem is so serious that the Bureau of Reclamation has on the drawing boards sixteen projects designed to eliminate salts, plus a $120,000,000 desalting plant in southern California. The more dams that are built in the future, the greater the salinity problem will become.

5. Water development brings in more people and they in turn demand more water, which leads to more water development, which leads to more people and the vicious cycle continues à la the present situation in metro Denver. With limited water available, Western Colorado cannot afford a large population; a lack of water would slow population growth.

The water picture in Western Colorado as we enter the 1980s is not good, and important decisions are long overdue. It is almost a virtual certainty that a significant amount of Western Slope water will be reserved for the Southern Ute Indians and Ute Mountain Utes because of the decisions rendered by the United States Supreme Court in *Winters v. U.S.* in 1908 and *Arizona v. California* in 1963. The Court ruled that at the time Indian reservations were created, the United States, by implication, reserved whatever water rights were necessary for the land's economic development.

For some years now, water experts have realized that the architects of the Colorado River Compact drew their conclusions from erroneous statistics, collected during a period of abnormally high precipitation. Since 1922, the Colorado River has produced an average of only 13,700,000 acre-feet of water per year, far short of the thought-to-be normal 18,000,000 acre-feet. Tree-ring studies covering over 400 years seem to confirm that the average annual flow of the Colorado River is 13,200,000 acre-feet. This is not good news for Western Colorado development.

The most sobering fact about Western Slope water is that there is not enough to satisfy all the demands for it. When downstream and Mexico water commitments are taken out of the 13,200,000 acre-feet produced by the Colorado River, 4,900,000 acre-feet are left for the Upper Basin states. Colorado gets a little over 51% of that, for a total of approximately 2,500,000 acre-feet. Already nearly 500,000 acre-feet are diverted to the eastern slope via twenty trans-mountain water diversions. There are at least four or five other proposed diversions which would divert another 2,000,000 acre-feet to eastern Colorado. When existing and proposed domestic, agricultural, and industrial water rights on the Western Slope are taken into consideration, one concludes that the Colorado River is dangerously over-appropriated.

Partly because there is not nearly enough water produced in the Colorado River to satisfy every demand, the previously sacred western water doctrine of prior appropriation is under fire, its days perhaps numbered. Prior appropriation made sense in the early days of Western Colorado; individuals simply took whatever water they needed—hoarding was not permitted. To maintain the right, one had

274

to use the water continuously for a beneficial use. Once all the water in a stream was appropriated, newcomers had a choice; they could either buy the water rights or move elsewhere. Water rights must still be put to beneficial use, otherwise they may be lost. Thus, prior appropriation encourages one to use — indeed waste — his full entitlement rather than conserve it. Water rights are not a matter of public record. It is not known how much water previously used by farmers and ranchers has been sold to energy companies and municipal interests who can afford to pay top dollar. Also, not until 1973 was a state law passed guaranteeing minimum stream flow to preserve fishing and esthetic values. The public is not adequately protected by a water law which allows those with the most money to control the water with only profit as their guide.

In the 1978 gubernatorial election in Colorado, Republican challenger Ted Strickland proposed to file suit against the Colorado River Compact to gain additional water for the state. The suit would have been disastrous and would have led to dissension among western states. Wayne Aspinall, one of the chief architects of western water policy and a strong defender of the use of Colorado water by Coloradans, was shocked. Declared Aspinall: "Colorado's use of . . . Colorado River waters will permit the citizens of Colorado to use such water providing some 'dumbbell' doesn't . . . start a suit with the Lower Basin. When that occurs . . . the Federal Courts . . . will take over. . . . This means that where the political might is, there is where the water will finally be diverted."[7]

The future of Western Slope water projects suffered a damaging blow in 1972, when partisan redistricting of Congressional Districts within Colorado borders saw powerful Wayne Aspinall defeated by Alan Merson in the Democratic primary and not returned to the House of Representatives. As Chairman of the Interior and Insular Affairs Committee, Aspinall was most responsible for Western Colorado water projects. Since his defeat, the coalition of western and southern states which favored water development in the West has been broken. With the passing of Aspinall and the coalition, new water projects in Western Colorado appear to be a thing of the past.

Despite the critical nature of Western Colorado water today, there are ways to make better use of the water available. Far too much water is used to irrigate crops; fields do not need to be flooded. Trickle irrigation could save thousands of acre-feet of water annually. Today, 95% of all Colorado water is used for agriculture; 3% is used for municipalities and 2% for industry. If we hope to gain additional water, much of it will have to come from the elimination of poor irri-

gation practices. Cloud-seeding, although fraught with legal, political, and environmental problems, is another way to increase moisture
on the Western Slope. The practice has been used the past three years
in Western Colorado. Some say cloud-seeding could increase the flow
of the Colorado River by 1,000,000 acre-feet per year, but too little is
known about how this would affect precipitation patterns in other
parts of the country.

The mammoth and expensive NAWAPA (North American
Water and Power Alliance), first proposed in 1964, is another answer
to Western and Western Colorado water needs. This tremendous
project, which would cost an astounding $150,000,000,000, would
divert Alaskan, Canadian, and northwest rivers to the arid Southwest
of the United States, where water is needed. Canadian opposition
and the staggering cost make this project a long-shot at best. Recent
suggestions from studies made by the Massachusetts Institute of
Technology indicate still another way to help solve Western Slope
water needs. By recycle and reuse, it may be possible to cut water
consumption to one-tenth of what is currently needed to produce synthetic fuels from coal and oil shale in Western Colorado. This would
satisfy critics of such production who argue that badly needed water
would be taken from agriculture and commerce if large-scale oil shale
and coal production becomes a reality.

With agriculture making use of most of the water in Western
Colorado, it might be wise to abandon crops which demand much
water and substitute those that are more compatible with to arid
lands. Less than ten percent of the population in Western Colorado is
engaged in agriculture and ranching. In many regions of the West,
agriculture has been supplanted by more profitable economic activities such as mining, manufacturing, and tourism. The hand-
writing is on the wall; either Western Slope agriculture gets more
profitable and conservation minded, or it will be replaced by more
profitable economic activities.

Barring a scientific breakthrough, Western Colorado must
recognize the inevitable; that it is arid and not capable of supporting
large numbers of people. With tourism a major industry, tremendous
energy development near, and the great quality of life offered by the
Western Slope, people are sure to come. What should we do? The
time is already very late. We have no water policy in Colorado or in
the United States, just as we have no energy policy. Yet, water is the
key to life in Western Colorado. The drought of 1976–77 was nature's
way of telling us to face up to the facts of life. Western Colorado
cannot support more people or development without water conser-

vation and planning. Postponing this realization with meaningless gestures is ostrich-like behavior at its worst.

The state of Colorado must find out how much water it actually has, who currently owns the water rights, and decide how the water should be used. In short, Colorado must state its priorities; it must develop a plan and soon — the future is now. Provincialism and boosterism must be scorned. Western Colorado is proud of its pioneering heritage and with good reason, but those days are now gone. This is the time for planning and cooperation and decisions. It is not a time for quarreling, vacillation, and doing nothing. Indeed, it seems crucial that we recognize the demand limits to West Slope development until we are sure of how much water is available and what damage might be done to a beautiful land.

Wayne Aspinall, 4th District Congressman, 1949-1973.

The Pioneer Spirit
Wayne Aspinall

He is eighty-four years old now, but one can still see in his eyes the fire and fervor of youth and the optimism of the pioneer. During his twenty-four years in Congress, the last fifteen as Chairman of the House Interior and Insular Affairs Committee, he was responsible for many Western water projects and courageously defended the interests of Western Colorado.

Environmentalists detested the bills which passed through his committee and called him a "flinty curmudgeon." His own committee members were awed by his iron-fisted rule. Phillip Burton, Democrat from California, declared that he ran the committee "like a kindergarten. You have to raise your hand to ask to go to the bathroom." That may have been true, but there has rarely been a more effective Congressman in the history of the nation's capital.

Wayne Aspinall was and is a pioneer. It is in his blood, in the marrow of his bone. He was born in Ohio in 1896, but, because of his mother's ill health, the Aspinall family moved to Palisade on Colorado's Western Slope in 1904. He was graduated from the University of Denver in 1919, briefly taught school at Palisade, and then returned to Denver, where he earned a law degree in 1925. Aspinall was first elected to the Colorado House of Representatives in 1930. Eight years later, he was elected to the State Senate. Aspinall served continuously in the Colorado Legislature from 1931 to 1949, save from 1935 to 1936 when he did not seek re-election.

By 1948, when he was elected to the federal House of Representatives from Colorado's Fourth District for the first time, he was the most widely known person in Western Colorado. He knew many of his constituents by their first names. Even then he had a reputation for hard work and fairness. Aspinall became Acting Chairman of the powerful Committee on Interior and Insular Affairs in 1958 and replaced Clair Engle as permanent chairman the following year.

During his years as head of the Interior and Insular Affairs Committee, Aspinall was responsible for the reporting out of over 1,000 bills, all of which became law. Gifted intellectually, Aspinall soon gained a reputation as a hard worker who came to the office early and left late and rarely missed a roll-call vote. He personally knew every president from Truman to Ford, and all sought his advice. Aspinall became the father of the famed Upper Colorado River Storage Act and was instrumental in passing water, wilderness, park, and statehood legislation.

Environmentalists opposed him as an enemy, but the National Wildlife Federation named him "Conservationist of the Year" in 1964. Aspinall has little use for environmentalists, referring to them as "extremists who always opposed everything we tried to do in my committee to gain wise development of our public lands." Aspinall believes that recreation is an important use for public land, "but you don't lock up whole areas because of it." The West, with its resources, is important to the future of the country and those resources must be developed. "Life isn't always an either-or situation. You have to compromise and allow the public lands to be used by all."

In the Democratic primary of 1972, because of redistricting, Aspinall was defeated by environmentalist Alan Merson, later the Regional Director of the Environmental Protection Agency. The primary was bitter, with Aspinall accusing his opponent of outright lies. So, after twenty-four years in the Congress, Wayne Aspinall came home to Palisade to practice law again and serve as a consultant on water and energy. Still spry at eighty-four, he speaks out often on the importance of water to the West.

Aspinall does not have much use for President Jimmy Carter. In fact, he supported President Gerald Ford in the 1976 election. He calls the Carter Administration "the most provincial and uninformed federal administration in this century." When Carter vetoed Western water projects in his famous "hit list" of 1977, Aspinall denounced the action as the worst kind of regional politics. He declared: "I start with the premise that usable water has been heretofore, now is, and shall continue to be in the future, Colorado's most valuable natural resource. It is truly our life's blood—the most precious of all nature's blessings."

Wayne Aspinall was a little to the left of center when he entered Congress, a little to the right when he left. "The early people of the Western Slope," he declares, "were frontier men and women knowing what the existence of life depended upon. They were striking out anew, trying desperately to conquer the land and make a good life for themselves." The new arrivals of the Western Slope "are affluent and want to save the land by putting a fence around it."

Perhaps Glenn Saunders, the great Denver Water Board lawyer and Aspinall antagonist, described his long-time foe best. He declared: "Wayne Aspinall had and has a strong sense of moral obligation. That sense of morality bred in him a sense of loyalty to the community he lived in and the area he represented, so he protected it as a father protects his family." Both friend and foe came to realize that Colorado's Fourth District Representative was shrewd, practical, and hard-headed. He believed in and loved the work ethic and the old time values of the past — patriotism, personal honor, and duty.

Wayne Aspinall's life has spanned the twentieth century on the Western Slope. He has been a farmer, teacher, lawyer, and politician and has watched his region expand and grow. He has known good times and bad, victory and defeat, but, through all the years, he has not changed. Some say he has been around in Western Colorado so long that he is the only man who can reminisce about the future. He has always been an honest man — a man of honor who spoke out on the issues. Agree or disagree with Wayne Aspinall, one always has to respect the man.

A long talk with Wayne Aspinall in Gunnison in the summer of 1977 showed that the memory and spirit of the Western Slope pioneer still burned brightly. He reminisced: "Other than the pioneering spirit of those first settlers in the West — the guts and intestinal fortitude of those hardy settlers who have built this great country — the desire and ability to effectively use our water resources has been the determining factor of our success." And what inscription should be placed on his gravestone? "Just say that people were good to me."[1] And the people of the Western Slope would certainly echo: "Wayne Aspinall was good for us."

18.
Yesterday, Today and Tomorrow 20th Century

Change and continuity, new fads and old fashionedness, progressive and reactionary—the Western Slope and Slopers showed these traits and more in the twentieth century. Change which had long been forecast for the region and its people came in surprising ways and times. Yet, through all decades, ran themes nearly as old as the mountains themselves. Some people clung to the familiar, as a rock in a storm, others preached modernization. As the land became more settled, change was bound to come and it did, certainly not without protest and occasional violent reaction. Few would defend the thought that the Western Slope today is like its turn of the century counterpart. Regardless, among the factors beckoning people to come and settle are "old fashioned" virtues and a rural setting, both of which hearken back to an earlier age. This paradox remains one of the region's fascinating themes. A cursory glance or brief visit will not allow the visitor to understand either the land or the people.

The photographic essay which follows is an attempt to capture the nearly impossible—the Western Slope and the people of the twentieth century. Consider the photographs carefully for they speak volumes about the changing times.

Upper and lower left. Only eight years apart chronologically, these photographs represent two different eras of urbanization. Hahn's Peak never went beyond the small mining camp stage and then slumbered into the twentieth century. Grand Junction started with numerous advantages including railroad connections, a mild climate, agricultural land nearby, and plenty of water. It parlayed these to become the largest community on the Western Slope, a future this 1924 scene showed clearly. *Courtesy U.S. Forest Service.*

Upper and lower right. The overall importance of the railroad did not diminish until the 1930s. Winter weather, no matter what year, created problems. The engine was bucking snow in 1916 near Eureka, a mining camp which bloomed at this time, thanks to war related needs for zinc and lead. Perhaps no single railroading event can surpass the building of the Moffat Tunnel for drama and significance. Its importance to northwestern Colorado can not be over stressed. Engine 200 is shown coming out of the West Portal. *Courtesy Martha Carr and Denver Public Library, Western History Department.*

284

Upper left. As the railroad had doomed the era of the mule, so the automobile trimmed the significance of the train. By the 1920s cars were improving and tourists were coming; so were trucks as this Meeker scene shows. Several spare tires were needed in this day of many flats. *Courtesy Colorado Historical Society.*

Lower left. For a while it seemed that much of the Western Slope would be ideal for peaches, apples, and other fruits. Then reality set in and many of the orchards fell victim to isolation, climate, and disease. This hearty group of peach pickers stopped work momentarily on September 18, 1909 to have their picture taken. *Courtesy North Fork Historical Society.*

Above. Fairs have always been a popular way to show the bountiful harvests of the Western Slope, and also promote the region. The Horticultural Hall at Hotchkiss indicates an abundant 1909 harvest. *Courtesy North Fork Historical Society.*

287

288

Upper left. In the days before refrigeration, the ice house remained a feature in many communities, as was the iceman making his rounds. Cutting ice is a skill that has vanished along with the horse on the farm. *Courtesy North Fork Historical Society.*

Lower left. Before the days of the fire truck, horse-drawn carts manned by firemen answered the alarm. This Telluride team ran into a railroad car and survived, but finally proved too spirited and was "ranched out" to Norwood. Fire, an ever present threat, ravaged many communities. *Courtesy Homer E. Reid, Telluride.*

Above. Mining continued on in a much reduced manner after World War I. The easily recoverable deposits of gold and silver were gone, so too the days of the prospector and his burro. Ahead would be only one more rush, the uranium excitement of the 1950s. This is the famous Camp Bird Mine near Ouray in 1937, well past its $2,000,000 per year peak production; limited operations continued into the 1970s. *Courtesy U.S. Forest Service.*

Upper left. Few Ku Klux Klan photographs survive. The Klan paraded and burned crosses throughout much of the Western Slope in the 1920s. From Bayfield and Durango on the southwest to Steamboat Springs, pictured here, they spread their hate before passing unmourned from the scene. *Courtesy Colorado Historical Society.*

Lower left. Many more happy days occurred than nights of Klan marching. A holiday parade signaled communitywide involvement. Both the old and the new took part with a truck carrying the lovely ladies and a mule-drawn float just emerging at the right in this Ouray parade. *Courtesy Martha Carr.*

Above. In the days before television and when movies and radio were just in their youth, entertainment proved more of the homegrown variety. It could become quite physical and certainly involved a great deal of action as does this potato race at Norwood. *Courtesy First Federal Savings.*

292

Upper left. In the twentieth century, football challenged baseball in popularity. Only a few town teams emerged; most of the action involved high school and eventually college elevens. Even as early as 1927 athletics were a big part of college life as shown by the number of cars lined up for this Western State-Greeley game. *Courtesy Hazel Calkins, Gunnison.*

Lower left. "Come Josephine in My Flying Machine." Nothing solved the isolation like that 20th century wonder, the "aeroplane," as it was early called. It is 1920 and the first plane has landed in Gunnison, attracting a curious crowd. *Courtesy Mrs. John Zugelder.*

Above. Isolated Rangely caused oil companies transportation problems until after World War II. This certainly was true in 1920 when this convoy of pipe and other material was hauled by teams and wagons. Somebody rode in the car at the left. *Courtesy Mabel White.*

293

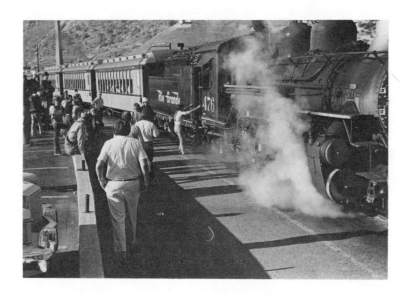

Upper left. Reclamation projects represented a major federal government involve-ment on the Western Slope after 1900. Offering irrigation, power and water storage, plus recreation, the dams and reservoirs promised much. As the century passed, water emerged as the most controversial issue with arguments over inter- and intra-state sharing and conservationists' concerns. Shown here is the Taylor Park Dam in the middle of construction, 1936. *Courtesy U.S. Bureau of Reclamation.*

Lower left. All 'board! Get ready for a trip into yesterday on the narrow gauge, run-ning from Durango to Silverton. Tourism is a vital part of the region's economy. The Western Slope is blessed with national parks, monuments and forests, and a range of scenery from desert to mountains which lures more and more visitors each year. *Cour-tesy Richard L. Gilbert.*

Above. All the dams and all the reservoirs could not withstand the drought of 1977. The Gunnison River runs free and the old D&RG railroad bed re-emerged from a watery grave on this October day, looking west over the site of Blue Mesa Reservoir. *Courtesy Duane Vandenbusche.*

295

"Effie," the pride of the Energy Fuels operation, working in 1979 twenty miles south of Steamboat Springs and west of Oak Creek. The largest dragline in the world, Effie was capable of moving 55 cubic yards in one shovelful. Strip mining, however, raised environmental questions which have not been resolved. *Courtesy Gordon Wren.*

Cross-country skiing steadily gained in popularity in the 1970s, returning in a sense to the "snowshoeing" of the 19th century. Free from long lines, high costs, and crowds of the popular ski resorts, the skier can enjoy the beauty and solitude of the valleys and mountains. *Courtesy Duane Smith.*

Ore dump and mill plant of the Bulldog Mine at Creede. *Courtesy Homestake Mining Company.*

19.
Where Do We Go From Here?

Today, the Western Slope of Colorado is a land alone, cut off from the eastern slope by the Continental Divide and historic bitterness, and separated from neighboring western states by desert. It has lived in a state of siege for nearly a decade, fighting rear guard action against a nation which wants its energy, against other more populous western states which desperately want its water, and against the eastern slope of Colorado which has always looked upon it as a colony to be exploited.

Energy development, tourism, recreation, and real estate promotion have placed Western Colorado on a roller coaster many call success. It is fast, with many ups and downs and even more surprises. There is no doubt that Western Colorado is changing rapidly today. Something unique in that region's character is passing—perhaps forever. The cattle ranches are diminishing. Gold and silver mines are being replaced by uranium, molybdenum, and coal mines. But most of all, the people are changing. They are not as self-reliant as before and lack the sense of community that once existed. Many residents seem interested only in exploitation and profit; they care not at all for the land they rape and the people they exploit.

During the last decade, control of the Western Slope has increasingly passed into the hands of outside interests. Control now rests with the federal government which owns over half of the region, major energy companies which have bought up leases and staked thousands of mining claims, absentee real estate developers, and young, affluent newcomers who have attempted to prevent anyone from following to their Utopia.

"The only thing we learn from history is that we learn nothing from history." This old refrain characterizes the Western Slope today. For it is true in Western Colorado that "the more things change, the more they stay the same." One hundred years ago, it was beset with problems involving Indians, water, mining pollution, lack of political clout, and growth. Today, the problems are almost exactly the same; nothing has changed but time.

A century ago, mining dominated Western Colorado as the San Juan, Roaring Fork, and Gunnison countries were dotted with scores of promising gold and silver camps. The silver panic of 1893 and mineral exhaustion wiped out most of those dreams, and aside from limited coal production, and a brief uranium boom in the 1950s, big-time mining seemed a thing of the past. But then along came the energy crisis in the 1970s, and mining was back in business. This time the emphasis was on coal and lots of it. Molybdenum also looked promising with the huge Henderson Mine operating near Berthoud Pass, a proposed mine on Mount Emmons near Crested Butte, and many other potentially promising deposits scattered throughout Western Colorado. Although large deposits of both uranium and oil shale exist, their futures are clouded because of environmental problems.

Traditionally, mining has been characterized by a boom-bust cycle. Today, the Western Slope is in the vanguard of the biggest mining boom in its history. Coal, molybdenum, and possibly oil shale and uranium will easily surpass the glory days of mining before the turn of the century. The energy crisis facing the United States makes that an absolute certainty.

Mining is not the only industry that has courted, wooed, and then seemingly abandoned Western Colorado. To a lesser degree, the lumber industry followed the same pattern. Never as glamorous or big, its industrial pattern was similar. From Pagosa Springs north, numerous abandoned townsites and logged out regions trace timber development. The town of McPhee existed from 1924 to 1948 on the Dolores River near the town of the same name, while its loggers worked the nearby timber stands. Once the site of the state's largest, most modern lumber mill, nothing remains today except a few foundations, and those will soon disappear under water if the Dolores Project is completed. Unlike mining, the lumber industry does not appear to have as bright a future.

Tourism, a relatively clean industry, and a major economic

pillar, may be in trouble with the dawning of the 1980s. From Dinosaur National Monument in the north to Mesa Verde in the south, and from the Colorado National Monument in the west to Aspen in the east, several million tourists every year have flocked into Western Colorado. The lure has been the mountains, skiing, fishing, hunting, giant reservoirs, and the stunning beauty of a pristine land. A large-scale mining revival and population increase would certainly cut into the tourist industry, eliminating some of the reasons that tourists enjoy coming here. In addition, the energy crunch has already diminished the numbers of tourists coming to the Western Slope. The scarcity of gasoline and its rising cost have made it increasingly difficult for those who live a thousand or so miles away to travel to this vacation land.

Everything in Western Colorado centers around water or the lack of it. "Water is blood in Colorado," wrote John Gunther in *Inside U.S.A.* "Touch water and you touch everything; about water the state is as sensitive as a carbuncle."[1]

"Water, water, everywhere nor any drop to drink," is the lament of the Western Slope today, as most of its water leaves the region for California via the Colorado River or for the eastern slope via diversion. Water is the single most important commodity. Without it, mining, agriculture, urban development, recreation, and almost any growth is doomed. The drafters of the Colorado River Compact of 1922 would be chagrined to learn that the major beneficiaries of their work today are not farmers, as they intended, but rather cities and industry. They would be annoyed to learn that the dams they envisaged have contributed to serious pollution.

Although Western Coloradans were outraged when President Jimmy Carter vetoed several water projects in 1977 and 1978, it was becoming painfully obvious that massive dams and reservoirs had become relics of the past. Most were not cost-productive, good dam sites were increasingly hard to find, and local rivers were seriously overappropriated.

By refusing to accept mild growth restrictions and by its insatiable thirst for water, the eastern slope has created an immediate and devastating effect on Western Colorado. Western Slope growth, energy development, economic diversification, and esthetic beauty are being sacrificed on the altar of an elitist, large tract, smog-inducing urban sprawl from Fort Collins to Pueblo. Further diversions of West Slope water should be prohibited, and tough land-use restrictions should be imposed on the cancer-like growth along the Front Range in eastern Colorado. Whatever happens, the water question has been, is today, and will be in the future, the most critical problem confronting Western Colorado.

Pollution, once thought to be a problem native only to the eastern slope's Front Range, has begun to infest Western Colorado. New Mexico's coal burning power plants cloud the skies of southwestern Colorado. The problem is not confined just to pockets where power plants exist. Small, mountain encircled valleys like the Roaring Fork, Gunnison, and Gore have days when a dirty haze hangs in the air above. Meanwhile, the great polluter, the automobile, does not run any more efficiently in Grand Lake or Pagosa Springs than it does in Denver, and there seem to be many more of them lately. Too many automobiles, too many fireplaces, and too many people in a very fragile geographic location have caused the pollution. Tragically, the problem is only in its infancy as more and more people flock to the mountains.

During the past 100 years, from the booming mining days of the 1870s and 1880s until the mid-1970s, the Western Slope touted its virtues and craved growth and development in a sparsely populated land. Local chambers of commerce more often than not stretched the truth about weather, water, and mines. "Watch us grow" was seen on more than one billboard on the outskirts of small communities. By the mid-1970s, however, the environmental movement came, and massive water projects, uranium mines, oil shale development, and large scale growth were questioned. But the past and traditional values die hard.

The argument that growth cannot be slowed or at least controlled or planned for is a blatant lie, unfounded in fact. It has been controlled in many areas of the United States and it can be controlled in Western Colorado, if less than courageous state and local politicians will hammer out a state-wide growth policy instead of going from crisis to crisis using the current provincial policy of no plan at all. The growth problem is compounded by sleazy land developers interested only in a "fast buck" on one hand, and, on the other, militant and provincial environmentalists who oppose any development in rural Western Slope valleys which they discovered last month.

With proper planning and courageous leadership, growth can be accommodated in almost all areas on which energy and recreation have had an impact. But problems become monumental when planning is done by short-sighted and provincial no-growth advocates in constant confrontation with profit-motivated businessmen, land owners, and major energy developers.

Craig, a booming coal town along the Yampa River in northwestern Colorado, is the best example of unchecked growth on the Western Slope. Sadly, it may be an indication of things to come. The town has been unable to keep up with ever-increasing demands. One observer notes:

> Confusion is the order of the day. When will growth come, how much will the town grow, when will it stop? . . . Confusion is a significant part of the problem in a community such as this. The coordination of information between local government, federal and state government and private industry is replete with lack of coordination, bureaucratic stumbling and missed guesses.[2]

Despite Craig's problems, many local people see only jobs and money for the economy. The Craig *Empire-Courier* called it good fortune when the Yampa Valley was selected as the site of another power-generating unit in 1978. Why, it meant more people and more money for the economy. ". . . Here they come. Welcome! Good fortune is still smiling."[3] The boomers and boosters of 100 years ago would have cheered them on.

The Western Slope specifically, and Colorado generally, desperately needs a plan to slow down and control growth. Water, pollution, population, and minerals have already created serious problems and must be dealt with. Politicians who do not legislate, leaders who do not lead, and special interest groups who do not see beyond their bank accounts are dangerous and can no longer be tolerated. Time is running out; Western Colorado needs action and action now! It is not accurate to say that growth is good and "more is better." Someone must speak for the wildlife, the environment, and the beauty and serenity of Western Colorado; otherwise it will be lost forever. We need a vision, an ideal of what the region should be. That ideal is a land with clean air and water, no great numbers of people, and a land free of the ravages and dangers caused by uncontrolled energy or recreation development.

Politically, the Western Slope has been treated as a "country cousin" on the state level. Eastern slope legislators have always held the political power within the state and have treated their western neighbors as a minor and unimportant political force. Out of the one hundred members of the General Assembly, approximately ten come from the Western Slope. Once, not too long ago, Western Slope legislators aligned with other rural counties to exercise some clout. No more. As Colorado has increasingly become urbanized, the Western Slope has lost whatever political clout it had.

Rarely has Western Colorado been an important force in gubernatorial elections. In 1978, the region cast only 9.9% of the state's

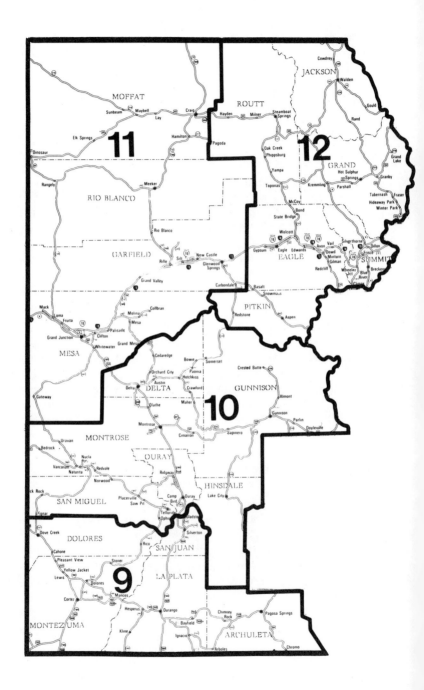

Western Slope Population by State Planning Region 1970, 1979 and 1985 Projection

	1970 (Census)	July 1, 1979 Estimates	% Change 1970-79	1985 Projection High Series
Region 9	37,356	47,900	28.2	62,115
Region 10	44,927	56,300	25.3	93,060
Region 11	80,562	111,200	38.	155,833
Region 12	28,858	57,300	98.5	76,056
Western Slope	191,703	272,700	42.2	387,064
Colorado	2,207,259	2,716,000	23.	3,436,231
Western Slope as % of State	8.6%	10%		11.2%

Source: Colorado Division of Planning, "Population Estimates," Series CP-26, June, 1979. "Population Estimates and Projections," Series CP-25, August, 1979.

Leading Western Slope Mineral Fuels Producing Counties, 1977

	Coal	Gas	Petroleum (millions of $)	Total
Rio Blanco	$	$ 23.3	$208.6	$231.9
Routt	103.9		1.6	105.5
Moffat	18.3	16.7	5.8	40.8
Gunnison	22.2			22.2
La Plata		22.1		22.1
Pitkin	15.4			15.4
Colorado	197.3	133.2	374.1	704.6
Western Slope as % of State Total	81.0	46.6	57.7	62.1

Source: Colorado Division of Mines, *A Summary of Mineral Industry Activities in Colorado, 1977*, Part II, June 15, 1978.

Almost exactly a century after it was first settled, the Western Slope of the Rockies is once again facing change and rapid economic development.

Western Slope Employment Profile 1970 and 1976

	Western Slope 1970	Western Slope 1976	Colorado 1976	Western Slope as % of Colorado 1976
Total wage and salary	52,300	83,700	1,003,400	8.3%
Mining	3,000	4,700	21,100	22.1
Contract construction	2,700	6,900	55,100	12.5
Manufacturing	4,500	5,500	144,500	3.8
Trans, Com, and Public utilities	3,000	4,800	60,000	8.0
Wholesale & retail trade	12,300	22,200	249,100	8.9
Finance, insurance, real estate	1,800	4,100	57,700	7.2
Service	10,100	17,200	196,500	8.7
Government	14,100	18,300	219,500	8.3
All other non-agricultural	8,700	12,800	89,700	14.2
Agricultural	10,700	8,300	45,100	18.3
Total employment*	75,600	113,400	1,140,500	10.0

Source: Colorado Division of Employment, *Colorado Planning Region Summary*, Summer 1978

*Columns do not add to totals because wage and salary figures are on the basis of jobs by place of work, other than on the basis of labor force.

Courtesy: The First National Bancorporation, Inc.

total vote and had a minor impact on the election outcome. Governors from the Western Slope have been few in the past 100 years. Frederick Pitkin of Ouray, Davis Waite of Aspen, Ed Johnson of Craig, Dan Thornton, a transplanted Texan from Gunnison, and John Vanderhoof of Glenwood Springs have held that office.

Nationally, the Western Slope's subordinate political position within the state is best seen by the fact that only Ed Johnson of Craig has ever held a United States Senate seat. On the other hand, until just recently, it exercised some real power in the United States House of Representatives. The Fourth District had traditionally belonged to the Western Slope. From 1912, when Ed Taylor won his first race, to 1972, when Wayne Aspinall was beaten in the democratic primary, Western Colorado was a force to be reckoned with on the national level. Both men became powerful committee chairmen and were instrumental in influencing water, farming, and energy legislation. Alas, post World War II growth forced redistricting, splitting the district among more populous eastern slope counties so that congressmen would more nearly represent equal numbers of voters. Southwestern Colorado found itself in the Third District dominated by Pueblo; the rest of the region remained in the Fourth District, now dominated by eastern slope suburban areas. So much for Western Slope political power.

One of the major problems facing Western Colorado today is the lack of unity and the internal bitterness within that region. The Western Slope has not grown evenly since World War II. Instead, growth has been centered in urban pockets—near energy sites, ski areas, and fertile valleys. Urban centers like Grand Junction, Craig, and Durango have little in common with smaller and more rural communities. Bitter water battles, environmentalists vs. developers, old-timers vs. newcomers, town vs. farm and ranch, and rivalries between communities have made unity hard to come by. Only emotional issues such as threatened trans-mountain water diversion or President Carter's hit list bring Western Colorado together. In more ways than not, the Western Slope is its own worst enemy.

As one looks at the Western Slope today it is hard to be optimistic about the future. The problems are many and complex. Some of the gravest concerns include:

1.) *Water.* Although 69% of all of Colorado's water originates on the Western Slope, most of it goes downstream to satisfy water commitments or is diverted to eastern Colorado. It is now very clear Western Colorado will not get all the water to which it is entitled.

2.) *Energy.* Major energy companies like Exxon, Atlantic Richfield, Shell, and many others have descended on the region like a plague. Consultants, surveyors, claim markers, helicopters, and well paid lawyers are never out of sight or sound. Uranium, coal, oil, and oil shale are the treasures worth prospecting for. The assault by the energy Goliaths has threatened the very nature of Western Colorado.

3.) *Mining* (other than energy). Along with energy companies, Western Colorado has also been inundated with other major mining concerns. The San Juan country, with Standard Metals above Silverton, Ouray's Camp Bird Mine, and the Idarado mine near Telluride have always had a mining background. But now, other regions evidently laden with molybdenum and vanadium are being carefully examined. A case in point is Mount Emmons, three miles west of Crested Butte, where one of the largest molybdenum deposits in the world has been discovered. AMAX, a billion dollar company, is in the process of developing the mine, complete with huge tailings ponds, disruption of wild life, a population increase of 4,000–5,000 (a minimum estimate with most living in Gunnison, twenty-eight miles south), and all the social and physical upheaval that comes with such a large project. Idyllic Crested Butte, caught up in forces beyond its control, will lose its character and never be the same again.

4.) *Population Growth.* Western Colorado has already seen its population soar during the last decade, but in pockets rather than evenly. And much of the building and growth have taken place on flood plains, mancos shale, and in fragile geological regions. Future floods, mudslides, and other natural disasters may make the expanding population pay a savage price for living there. It is a truism to say, that despite current growth, the Western Slope never has been able to, is not now able to, and will not be able in the future to sustain a large population. The aridity, numbing cold, heavy snows, and fragile ecology will see to that.

5.) *Federal Government.* The federal government, owner of much of the land in Western Colorado, has always played a major role in the development of the region and will continue to do so in the future. The Forest Service, Water and Power Resources Services, Bureau of Land Management, Soil Conservation Service, Bureau of Mines, and National Park Service affect the lives of all residents in some way. Bureaucrats in Washington, D.C. will continue to make decisions on coal leases, grazing lands, dams, water rights, ski areas, mineral resources, and land reclamation. Like the last 100 years, the Western Slope will not have much influence in those decisions.

6.) *Absentee Ownership.* Since the opening of the Western Slope over 100 years ago, it has been treated as a colony to be exploited.

The mines, railroads, and banks were traditionally owned by Eastern or foreign money. Not much has changed today. Many decisions affecting Western Colorado's future are made in boardrooms in Washington, D.C., New York, Pennsylvania, and Texas. Witness the federal government, Homestake, Atlantic Richfield, AMAX, Exxon, and other giant organizations who own the land, minerals, energy, and water. Never the master of its own destiny, today the Western Slope is in danger of losing what little control it did have.

7.) *Environment.* During the past twenty years or so, Western Colorado has been ravaged for the benefit of special interests, a trend that has rocketed out of control today. Streams have been dammed up and diverted, water has left the state in ever-increasing amounts, wildlife has been forced out of traditional haunts, the land has been torn apart by bulldozers and giant cranes, land agents have created housing developments where they have no business being, sections of towns have been built on radioactive mill tailings, and the once-pure air has been polluted.

The dawn of the 1980s is at hand and Western Colorado is in the midst of another boom period, much like a century before. It is still a fantasy land, a unique geographic entity, and a state of mind. It has survived crises, growth, and devastation of its land before. But as the Western Slope moves into the next decade, the forces that threaten to overwhelm it are much larger, wealthier, and more dangerous than at any time in its past. Leadership, planning, and tough environmental controls are needed now more than ever before.

This has been the story of the Western Slope of Colorado, a section influenced historically by its rugged and unyielding geography and elements, and today buffeted by the winds of change — change which has accelerated tremendously. The changes began innocently enough in the 1960s, but during the '70s built to a crescendo, threatening to overwhelm Western Colorado. The energy boom, new hordes of people, water diversions, and serious environmental problems face Western Colorado today. The quality of life is threatened as never before. Growth, pollution, and tremendous numbers of people are all too common in our society; clear air and water, beauty, solitude, and the wild are important too, and need to be preserved. One can only hope that big money, growth, and an insatiable craving for energy will not destroy that idyllic land for, sad to say, there simply are not a hundred more years of plunder remaining in Western Colorado.

Endnotes

Chapter 1

1. Arthur Rohn, *Mug House: Wetherill Mesa Excavations* (Washington: National Park Service, 1971), p. 261. See also 94–109 & 260–63.

2. *Ibid.,* p. 257.

Chapter 2

1. Herbert E. Bolton, *Pageant in the Wilderness* (Salt Lake City, Utah: Utah State Historical Society, 1972), p. 7.

2. LeRoy Hafen, *Mountain Men and the Fur Trade,* II (Glendale, California: A. H. Clark Co., 1966), pp. 63-64.

3. Frank Waters, *The Colorado* (New York: Holt, Rinehart and Winston, 1946), p. 177.

4. John Rolfe Burroughs, *Where the Old West Stayed Young* (New York: Bonanza Books, 1962), p. 7.

5. LeRoy Hafen, "Fort Davy Crockett, Its Fur Men and Visitors," *Colorado Magazine,* (January, 1952), p. 19.

6. *Ibid.,* p. 18.

Chapter 3

1. Gwinn Harris Heap, *Central Route to the Pacific* (Glendale, California: The Arthur H. Clark Co., 1957), p. 270.

2. Richard Bartlett, *Great Surveys of the American West* (Norman, Oklahoma: University of Oklahoma Press, 1962), p. 196.

Chapter 4

1. Dan De Quille, *The Big Bonanza* (Hartford: American Publishing Co., 1877), p. 116.

2. Daniel Conner, *A Confederate in the Colorado Gold Fields* (Norman: University of Oklahoma Press, 1970), p. 74, 76, & 79.

3. John Dyer, *The Snow-Shoe Itinerant* (Cincinnati: Cranston & Stowe, 1890), p. 143. See also 125–26, 140, 142, & 144. Isaac Beardsley, *Echoes from Peak and Plain* (Cincinnati: Curts & Jennings, 1898), pp. 244, 254, & 255.

4. Conner, *A Confederate,* p. 117.

5. *Miners' Record* (Tarryall), Sept. 14, 1861, p. 2.

6. Rossiter Raymond, *Statistics of Mines and Mining* (Washington: Government Printing Office, 1870), pp. 342–43. Samuel Bowles, *Our New West* (Hartford: Hartford Publishing Co., 1869), pp. 138 & 187.

7. Frank Fossett, *Colorado* (New York: C. G. Crawford, 1880), p. 564.

8. Isaac Beardsley, *Echoes from Peak and Plain,* pp. 337-40. Bowles, *Our New West,* pp. 116–19.

9. Bayard Taylor, *Colorado: A Summer Trip* (New York: G. P. Putnam & Son, 1867), p. 115.

Chapter 5

1. *Engineering and Mining Journal* (New York), June 28, 1879, p. 461.

2. Dan O'Connell, "The Old Time Prospector," *Colorado Magazine* (March, 1924), p. 106.

3. Homer Hastings, "Pioneers of the Uncompahgre Plateau," *Colorado Magazine* (Winter, 1964), p. 36.

4. Clarence Mayo to Sister, July 30, 1882. See also, Mayo to Ned, Feb. 5, 1882; Mayo to Mother, Aug. 13 & Dec. 12, 1882; Mayo to Father, July 2, 1881 & Nov. 11, 1882; Mayo to Sister, Aug. 7 & Nov. 6, 1881, Oct. 29, 1882, Clarence H. Mayo Letters, Henry E. Huntington Library.

5. George Root, "Reminiscences of White Pine, Colorado," *Colorado Magazine* (May, 1936), pp. 115-16.

6. Helen H. Jackson, "O-Be-Joyful Creek and Poverty Gulch," *Atlantic Magazine* (Dec., 1883), p. 760.

7. Elizabeth Roller, "Life in Montezuma, Chihuahua and Sts. John," *Denver Westerners Brand Book* (1965), pp. 66-67.

8. *Rocky Mountain Sun* (Aspen), May 27, 1882, p. 2.

9. David M. Hyman, "Romance of a Mining Venture," copy in the Western History Research Center, University of Wyoming.

10. Warner A. Root, "The Mining Camp," quoted in Frank L. Wentworth, *Aspen on the Roaring Fork* (Denver: Sundance, 1976 reprint), p. 66.

Chapter 6

1. *Annual Report of the Commissioner of Indian Affairs for the Year 1872* (Washington: Government Printing Office, 1872), pp. 209 & 291.

2. *Annual Report of the Commissioner of Indian Affairs for the Year 1873* (Washington: Government Printing Office, 1874), p. 86.

3. Sun Dance Chant, Collected by Kenneth Periman.

Chapter 7

1. John Bartlett, *Familiar Quotations* (Boston: Little, Brown & Co., 1968), p. 1023.

2. Robert Athearn, *The Denver & Rio Grande Western Railroad: Rebel of the Rockies* (Lincoln, Nebraska: University of Nebraska Press, 1977), p. 101.

3. *Annual Report of the Denver & Rio Grande* (1886), p. 6.

4. Athearn, *Rebel of the Rockies,* p. 163.

5. Len Shoemaker, *Roaring Fork Valley* (Denver: Sundance Limited, 1973), p. 112.

6. Athearn, *Rebel of the Rockies,* p. 100.

7. Gordon Chappell, Robert Richardson, and Cornelius Hauch, "The South Park Line: A Concise History," *Colorado Rail Annual,* No. XII (1974), p. 9.

8. Mac C. Poor, *Denver South Park & Pacific* (Denver: Rocky Mountain Railroad Club, 1976), p. 203.

9. Dow Helmers, *Historic Alpine Tunnel* (Denver: Sage Books, 1963), p. 31.

10. *Ibid.,* p. 30.

11. Mac C. Poor, "How Come, Why and How I Wrote 'Denver South Park & Pacific,' " *Denver Westerners Brand Book* (1965), pp. 354–55.

12. Mallory Hope Ferrell, *Silver San Juan: The Rio Grande Southern* (Boulder, Colorado: Pruett Publishing Co., 1973), p. 5.

13. John J. Lipsey, *The Lives of James John Hagerman* (Denver: Golden Bell Press, 1968), p. 105.

14. Richard Ronzio, "The Uintah Railway: The Gilsonite Road," *Denver Westerners Brand Book* (1959), p. 46.

Chapter 8

1. *Mining Record,* May 8, 1880, p. 444.

2. Tomboy Material, James D. Hague Collection, Henry E. Huntington Library.

3. Edward S. Pierce, "Telluride in 1900," *Pioneers of the San Juan* (Durango: Durango Printing, 1952), vol. III, p. 30. See also T. A. Rickard, *Across the*

San Juan Mountains (New York: Engineering and Mining Journal, 1903), p. 13.

4. Thomas Walsh, "Commencement Address," *Quarterly of the Colorado School of Mines* (July, 1908), p. 16.

5. Carroll H. Coberly, "Ashcroft," *Colorado Magazine* (April, 1960), p. 103. See also, pp. 88-90, 91, 93, 94 & 102.

6. *Montrose Enterprise,* May 16, 1901, quoted in Thomas McKee, "Early Discovery of Uranium Ore in Colorado," *Colorado Magazine* (July, 1955), p. 196.

7. *Silverton Standard,* July 6, 1893, p. 3.

Chapter 9

1. *Gunnison Review-Press,* January 25, 1884, p. 2.

2. *Harper's Weekly,* XXVIII (February 16, 1884), p. 111.

3. Gilbert Lathrop, *Little Engines and Big Men* (Caldwell, Idaho: The Caxton Printers Ltd., 1955), pp. 229-30.

4. Gerald R. Armstrong, "Miss Josephine Roche, President the Rocky Mountain Fuel Company, 1927-1951," Annual Meeting of the Shareholders, Rocky Mountain Fuel Company, April 14, 1975, p. 1.

5. *Pueblo Chieftain,* Oct.-Nov., 1978, p. 1.

6. *Ibid.*

7. Coal Basin, referring to the area, is two words, and Coalbasin, referring to the town is one word.

8. Olga Curtis, "Energy Boom," *Empire* (April 2, 1978), p. 10.

9. Edward Abbey, *The Journey Home* (New York: E. P. Dutton, 1977), p. 158.

10. *Ibid.,* p. 161.

11. *Ibid.,* p. 164.

Chapter 10

1. Robert Service, *Collected Poems of Robert Service* (New York: Dodd, Mead & Co., 1940), p. 4.

2. Alvin Steinel, *History of Agriculture in Colorado* (Fort Collins, Colorado: The State Board of Agriculture, 1926), pp. 504-05.

3. John D. Kiefer, *Autobiography* (1958), p. 55.

4. Mary Wilson, "We Move to Egeria Park," *The Colorado Magazine* (April 1963), p. 128.

5. David Lavender, *The Rockies* (New York: Harper and Row, Publishers, 1975), p. 331.

6. Minute Book of the Gunnison County Stockgrowers' Association, Gunnison, Colorado, I, Meeting of June 7, 1902, p. 45.

7. Wilson Rockwell, *New Frontier* (Denver: The World Press, Inc., 1938), p. 75.

8. John Rolfe Burroughs, *Where the Old West Stayed Young* (New York: Bonanza Books, 1962), p. 358.

Chapter 12

1. Norris Hundley, *Water and the West* (Berkeley, California: University of California Press, 1975), p. xi.

2. David Lavender, "Water and the Western Slope," Typescript, 1977, p. 2.

3. *Ibid.,* p. 4.

4. *Ibid.,* p. 7.

5. *Ibid.,* p. 8.

6. *Ibid.,* p. 11.

Farrington Carpenter

1. Farrington R. Carpenter, "Hayden's First Lawyer," *The Colorado Lawyer,* Vol. VIII, No. 2 (February, 1979), p. 213.

2. *Ibid.,* p. 217.

3. John Rolfe Burroughs, *Where the Old West Stayed Young* (New York: Bonanza Books, 1962), p. 340.

4. Personal Interview with Farrington Carpenter, Hayden, Colorado, May 28, 1979.

Chapter 13

1. Enos Mills, *The Rocky Mountain National Park* (New York: Doubleday, 1924), pp. 78 & 84.

2. Richard Beidleman, "The Black Canyon of the Gunnison National Monument," *Colorado Magazine* (July, 1963), p. 163.

3. "Hotel Colorado" (Glenwood Springs: 1909c), pp. 3, 4, & 14.

4. Ira Freeman, *A History of Montezuma County* (Boulder: Johnson Publishing Co., 1958), p. 115.

5. *Delta Independent,* Feb. 2, 1906, p. 1. *Montrose County Where Apple is King* (Montrose: Press Book, 1905), p. 17. R. Copeland Rohrabacher, *The Great San Juan of Colorado and New Mexico* (Durango: Durango Democrat, 1901), pp. 17-20.

6. *Weekly Chieftain* (Ignacio), Oct. 30 & Nov. 6, 1914, p. 1.

Chapter 14

1. *Polk's Grand Junction City Directory 1931-32* (Colorado Springs: R. L. Polk Directory Co., 1931), pp. 8-11.

2. Alan Pritchard, "The Walkers of Grand Junction," *Denver Westerners Brand Book* (1962), p. 218.

3. Mrs. W. N. Searcy to Norman Bawden, March 8, 1937. William Searcy Papers, Western Historical Collections, University of Colorado.

4. *Montrose Press,* July 26, 1939, p. 2.

5. *Durango Weekly Herald,* Dec. 26, 1940, p. 4.

6. J. G. Baragwanath to Henry Carlisle, Oct. 17, 1934, Henry C. Carlisle Collection, Western History Research Center, University of Wyoming.

7. *DeBeque Shale,* Jan. 19 (p. 1), 26 (p. 1), & June 1 (p. 1), 15, 1923 (p. 1).

8. "War Bulletin #1," Dec. 8, 1941, Box 24, Western Colorado Power Company Records, Center of Southwest Studies, Fort Lewis College.

9. The section on World War II and the Western Slope was taken from the following newspapers: *Montrose Press,* Dec., 1941; *Aspen Times,* Dec., 1941; *Gunnison Courier,* June, 1942; *Durango Weekly Herald,* April & Sept., 1942; *Glenwood Post,* April, 1943; *Pagosa Springs Sun,* July, 1943; *Meeker Herald,* Jan.-Feb., 1944; *Montrose Daily Press,* Jan. & May, 1945; *Craig Empire-Courier,* July-Aug., 1945. *Colorado Year Book 1945-1947,* pp. 577–598.

Chapter 15

1. David Lavender, *One Man's West* (Garden City: Doubleday, 1943), p. 3.

2. The preceding information was taken from Paul Proctor, et al., *Uranium: Where It Is and How to Find It* (Salt Lake: Eagle Rock Publishers, 1954).

3. *Colorado Yearbook 1945-47* (Denver: Bradford-Robinson, 1947), p. 267.

4. "25 Years Ago Column," *Empire-Courier* (Craig), Oct. 19, 1977.

5. Stephen McNichols, "A Basic Minerals Policy for Colorado," *Colorado Quarterly* (Summer, 1957), pp. 8, 10–12.

6. *Denver Post,* Dec. 25, 1977, p. 2.

7. *Denver Post,* Nov. 27, 1977, p. 33.

8. *Empire-Courier* (Craig), Sept. 14, 1977, p. 2.

Chapter 16

1. Robert G. Athearn, *The Coloradans* (Albuquerque, New Mexico: University of New Mexico Press, 1976), p. 334.

2. Neil Morgan, *Westward Tilt: The American West Today* (New York: Random House, 1963), p. 280.

3. David Lavender, *The Rockies* (New York: Harper & Row, Publishers, 1975), p. 371.

4. "Colorado: The Ultimate Fringe Benefit," Colorado Division of Commerce and Development, p. 47.

Chapter 17

1. Grace Lichenstein, "The Battle Over the Mighty Colorado," *The New York Times Magazine* (July 31, 1977), p. 11.

2. *Gunnison News Champion* and *Gunnison Republican,* March 17, 1938, p. 10.

3. Ex-Representative Wayne Aspinall of Palisade and Colorado's Fourth District and very powerful figure in the House of Representatives declared: "The original Gunnison-Arkansas Project was too large. . . . There just really has never been enough water for the . . . project." Letter from Wayne N. Aspinall to Duane Vandenbusche, November 9, 1978.

4. *Ibid.*

5. Marshall Sprague, *Colorado: A Bicentennial History* (New York: W. W. Norton & Co., 1976), p. 182.

6. David Lavender, "Water and the Western Slope," Typescript, p. 1.

7. Letter from Wayne N. Aspinall to Duane Vandenbusche, Nov. 9, 1978.

Wayne Aspinall

1. Personal interview with Wayne Aspinall, Gunnison, Colorado, July 22, 1977.

Chapter 19

1. John Gunther, *Inside U.S.A.* (New York: Harper & Brothers, 1947), p. 214.

2. *United Methodist,* Oct. 19, 1977, p. 1.

3. *Empire-Courier* (Craig), April 26, 1978, p. 1.

Bibliography

Books

Abbey, Edward. *The Journey Home.* New York: E. P. Dutton, 1977.

Allen, James B. *The Company Town in the American West.* Norman, Oklahoma: University of Oklahoma Press, 1966.

Annual Report of the Commissioner of Indian Affairs for the Year 1872. Washington: Government Printing Office, 1872, 1874.

Athearn, Frederic J. *An Isolated Empire: A History of Northwest Colorado.* Denver: Bureau of Land Management, 1976.

Athearn, Robert. *The Coloradans.* Albuquerque, New Mexico: University of New Mexico Press, 1976.

_____. *Rebel of the Rockies: The Denver and Rio Grande Western Railroad.* Reprint. Lincoln, Nebraska: University of Nebraska Press, 1977.

Backus, Harriet Fish. *Tomboy Bride.* Boulder, Colorado: Pruett Press, 1969.

Bailey, Stephen A. *L. L. Nunn: A Memoir.* Ithaca, New York: The Cayuga Press, 1933.

Baker, James and Hafen, LeRoy. *History of Colorado.* 5 vols. Denver, Colorado: Linderman, 1927.

Bartlett, John. *Familiar Quotations.* Boston: Little, Brown & Co., 1968.

Bartlett, Richard. *Great Surveys of the American West.* Norman, Oklahoma: University of Oklahoma Press, 1962.

Beardsley, Isaac. *Echoes from Peak and Plain*. Cincinnati: Curts & Jennings, 1898.

Bender, Henry E. *Uintah Railway; The Gilsonite Route*. Berkeley, California: Howell-North Books, 1970.

Berkman, Richard L. and Viscuse, W. Kip. *Damming the West*. New York: Grossman Publishers, 1973.

Black, Robert C. *Island in the Rockies*. Boulder, Colorado: Pruett Press, 1969.

Bollinger, Edward T. and Bauer, Frederick. *The Moffat Road*. Chicago: The Swallow Press, Inc., 1962.

Bolton, Herbert Eugene. *Pageant in the Wilderness*. Salt Lake City, Utah: Utah State Historical Society, 1972.

Bowles, Samuel. *Our New West*. Hartford: Hartford Publishing Co., 1869.

Brockett, L. P. *Our Western Empire: Or the New West Beyond the Mississippi*. Philadelphia: Bradley & Co., 1881.

Brown, Robert L. *Empire of Silver*. Caldwell, Idaho: Caxton Printers, 1968.

Burroughs, John Rolfe. *"I Never Look Back."* Boulder, Colorado: Johnson Publishing Co., 1967.

_____. *Steamboat in the Rockies*. Fort Collins, Colorado: The Old Army Press, 1974.

_____. *Where the Old West Stayed Young*. New York: Bonanza Books, 1962.

Bury, John and Susan, ed. *This is What I Remember, About the People of the White River Country*. Meeker, Colorado: Rio Blanco County Historical Society, 1972.

Chappell, Gordon S. *Logging Along the Denver & Rio Grande. Colorado Rail Annual*. Golden, Colorado: Colorado Railroad Museum, 1971.

Chappell, Gordon, Richardson, Robert, and Cornelius Hauch. *The South Park Line: A Concise History. Colorado Rail Annual*. Golden, Colorado: Colorado Railroad Museum, 1974.

Clark, C. M. *A Trip to Pike's Peak*. San Jose: Talisman Press, 1958.

Clifford, Peggy and Smith, John M. *Aspen: Dreams and Dilemmas*. Chicago: The Swallow Press, 1970.

Colorado: A Guide to the Highest State. New York: Hastings House, 1941.

Colorado Year Book. Denver, Colorado: State Planning Division, 1918–1961.

Conner, Daniel E. *A Confederate in the Colorado Gold Fields* Norman: University of Oklahoma Press, 1970.

Crampton, Frank A. *Deep Enough: A Working Stiff in the Western Mine Camps.* Denver: Sage Books, 1956.

Dallas, Sandra. *Vail.* Boulder, Colorado: Pruett Publishing Co., 1969.

Danielson, Clarence and Ralph. *Basalt: Colorado Midland Town.* Boulder, Colorado: Pruett Press, 1965.

Darley, George M. *Pioneering in the San Juan.* Reprint. Lake City, Colorado: Community Presbyterian Church, 1976.

Delaney, Robert. *The Southern Ute People.* Phoenix: Indian Tribal Series, 1974.

Doyle, Arthur. *Our Second American Adventure.* Boston: Little, Brown & Co., 1924.

Dyer, John. *The Snow-Shoe Itinerant.* Cincinnati: Cranston & Stowe, 1890.

Environmental Statement: Northwest Colorado Coal. 4 vols. Washington, D.C.: U.S. Department of Interior, 1976.

Ferrill, Mallory Hope. *Silver San Juan: The Rio Grande Southern.* Boulder, Colorado: Pruett Publishing Co., 1973.

Fetter, Richard L. and Suzanne. *Telluride: From Pick to Powder.* Caldwell, Idaho: Caxton Printers, Ltd., 1979.

Fiester, Mark. *Blasted, Beloved Breckenridge.* Boulder, Colorado: Pruett Press, 1973.

Fossett, Frank. *Colorado.* New York: C. G. Crawford, 1880.

Freeman, Ira. *A History of Montezuma County.* Boulder, Colorado: Johnson Publishing Co., 1958.

Gale, Hoyt. *Geology of the Rangely Oil District.* Washington, D.C.: Government Printing Office, 1908.

Gibbons, J. J. *Sketches in the San Juan.* Reprint. Telluride, Colorado: St. Patrick's Parish, 1972.

Goff, Richard and McCaffree, Robert H. *Century in the Saddle.* 4 vols. Boulder, Colorado: Johnson Publishing Co., 1967.

Gunther, John. *Inside U.S.A.* New York: Harper and Brothers, 1947.

Hafen, LeRoy. *Colorado and Its People.* 4 vols. New York: Lewis Historical Publishing Co., 1948.

_____, ed. *Mountain Men and the Fur Trade of the Far West.* 8 vols. Glendale, California: A. H. Clark Co., 1965–72.

Hall, Frank. *History of the State of Colorado.* 4 vols. Chicago: The Blakely Printing Co., 1889-1895.

Heap, Gwinn Harris. *Central Route to the Pacific.* Glendale, California: The Arthur H. Clark Co., 1957.

Helmers, Dow. *Historic Alpine Tunnel.* Denver: Sage Books, 1963.

Hundley, Norris. *Water and the West.* Berkeley, California: University of California Press, 1975.

Ise, John. *Our National Park Policy*. Baltimore: Johns Hopkins, 1961.

Jefferson, James, Robert Delaney, and Gregory Thompson. *The Southern Utes: A Tribal History*. Ignacio: Southern Ute Tribe, 1972.

Jocknick, Sidney. *Early Days on the Western Slope of Colorado*. Glorieta, New Mexico: The Rio Grande Press, Inc., 1968.

Kelly, Charles. *The Outlaw Trail*. New York: Bonanza Books, 1959.

Knight, MacDonald and Hammock, Leonard. *Early Days on the Eagle*. Eagle, Colorado: Knight and Hammock, 1965.

Kushner, Ervan. *Otto Mears: His Life and Times*. Frederick, Colorado: Jende-Hagan Bookcorp, 1979.

Lathrop, Gilbert. *Little Engines and Big Men*. Caldwell, Idaho: The Caxton Printers Ltd., 1955.

_____. *Rio Grande Glory Days*. San Marino, California: Golden West Books, 1976.

Lathrop, Marguerite. *Don't Fence Me In*. Boulder, Colorado: Johnson Publishing Co., 1972.

Lavender, David. *David Lavender's Colorado*. Garden City, New York: Doubleday Co., Inc., 1976.

_____. *One Man's West*. Garden City, New York: Doubleday, 1943.

_____. *The Rockies*. New York: Harper and Row, Publishers, 1968.

_____. *A Rocky Mountain Fantasy*. Telluride, Colorado: San Miguel County Historical Society, 1964.

Lipsey, John J. *The Lives of James John Hagerman*. Denver: Golden Bell Press, 1968.

Marsh, Barton. *The Uncompahgre Valley and the Gunnison Tunnel*. Lincoln, Nebraska: International Pub. Association, 1909.

McCarthy, G. Michael. *Hour of Trial*. Norman: University of Oklahoma Press, 1977.

Mills, Enos. *The Rocky Mountain National Park*. New York: Doubleday, 1924.

Morgan, Neil. *Westward Tilt: The American West Today*. New York: Random House, 1963.

Mumey, Nolie. *John Williams Gunnison*. Denver, Colorado: Artcraft Press, 1955.

Nash, Gerald D. *The American West in the Twentieth Century*. Englewood Cliffs, New Jersey: Prentice-Hall, Inc., 1973.

O'Rear, John and Frankie. *The Aspen Story*. New York: A. S. Barnes and Co., Inc., 1966.

Ormes, Robert M. *Railroads and the Rockies*. Denver: Sage Books, 1963.

Pierce, Neal R. *The Mountain States of America.* New York: W. W. Norton and Co., 1972.

Polk's Grand Junction City Directory 1931-32. Colorado Springs: R. L. Polk Directory Co., 1931.

Poor, Mac C. *Denver South Park and Pacific.* Denver: Rocky Mountain Railroad Club, 1976.

Proctor, Paul, et al. *Uranium: Where It Is and How to Find It.* Salt Lake: Bradford-Robinson, 1947.

Ransome, Frederick L. *Geology and Ore Deposits of the Breckenridge District, Colorado.* Washington, D.C.: Government Printing Office, 1911.

Raymond, Rossiter. *Statistics of Mines and Mining.* 4 vols. Washington, D.C.: Government Printing Office, 1870-73.

Report on the Ute Indians in Colorado, 1879. Washington, D.C.: Government Printing Office, 1880.

Rickard, T. A. *Across the San Juans.* New York: Engineering and Mining Journal, 1903.

Rifle Shots: The Story of Rifle, Colorado. Rifle: Rifle Reading Club, 1973.

Rockwell, Wilson. *New Frontier.* Denver: The World Press, Inc., 1938.

──────. *Uncompahgre Country.* Denver: Sage Books, 1965.

──────. *The Utes: A Forgotten People.* Denver: Sage Books, 1956.

The Rocky Mountain Directory and Colorado Gazetteer for 1871. Denver, Colorado: S. S. Wallihan & Co., 1871.

Rohn, Arthur. *Mug House: Wetherill Mesa Excavations.* Washington, D.C.: National Park Service, 1971.

Rohrabacher, R. C. *The Great San Juan of Colorado and New Mexico.* Durango: Durango Democrat, 1901.

Scamehorn, H. Lee. *Pioneer Steelmaker in the West.* Boulder, Colorado: Pruett Publishing Co., 1976.

Service, Robert. *Collected Poems of Robert Service.* New York: Dodd, Mead and Co., 1940.

Shoemaker, Len. *Roaring Fork Valley.* Denver, Colorado: Sundance Ltd., 1973.

Sibley, George. *A Crested Butte Primer.* Crested Butte, Colorado: Sibley & Sibley, 1972.

Sloan, Robert E. and Skowronski, Carl. *The Rainbow Route.* Denver, Colorado: Sundance, Ltd., 1975.

Smith, Duane A. *Colorado Mining: A Photographic History.* Albuquerque, New Mexico: University of New Mexico Press, 1977.

──────. *Rocky Mountain Boom Town: A History of Durango.* Albuquerque: University of New Mexico Press, 1980.

_____. *Rocky Mountain Mining Camps*. Bloomington: Indiana University Press, 1967.

Sprague, Marshall. *Colorado: A Bicentennial History*. New York: W. W. Norton, Inc., 1976.

_____. *The Great Gates*. Boston: Little, Brown & Co., 1964.

_____. *Massacre: The Tragedy at White River*. Boston: Little, Brown & Co., 1957.

Spurr, Josiah E. *Geology of the Aspen Mining District, Colorado*. Washington, D.C.: Government Printing Office, 1898.

Stegner, Wallace, ed. *This is Dinosaur*. New York: Alfred Knopf, 1955.

Steinel, Alvin. *History of Agriculture in Colorado*. Fort Collins, Colorado: The State Board of Agriculture, 1926.

Stevenson, Thelma V. *Historic Hahns Peak*. Fort Collins, Colorado: Robinson Press, Inc., 1976.

Taylor, Bayard. *Colorado: A Summer Trip*. New York: G. P. Putnam & Son, 1867.

Templin, J. Alton, et al. *The Methodist, Evangelical and United Brethren Churches in the Rockies, 1850–1976*. Denver: Rocky Mountain Conference, 1977.

Time-Life Books. *The Mountain States*. New York: Time-Life Books, 1967.

Torres-Reyes, Ricardo. *Mesa Verde National Park: An Administrative History, 1906–1970*. Washington, D.C.: Department of the Interior, 1970.

Ubbelohde, Carl, Benson, Maxine, and Smith, Duane A. *A Colorado History*. Boulder: Pruett Publishing Co., 1976.

Urquart, Lena M. *Glenwood Springs: Spa in the Mountains*. Boulder, Colorado: Pruett Publishing Co., 1970.

Vandenbusche, Duane. *Early Days in the Gunnison Country*. Gunnison, Colorado: B and B Printers, 1974.

Vandenbusche, Duane and Myers, Rex. *Marble, Colorado: City of Stone*. Boulder, Colorado: Golden Bell Press, 1970.

Vanderwilt, John, et al. *Mineral Resources of Colorado*. Denver, Colorado: Mineral Resources Board, 1947.

Wallace, Betty. *Gunnison Country*. Denver: Sage Books, 1960.

_____. *History With the Hide Off*. Denver, Colorado: Sage Books, 1964.

Wallace, William S. *Antoine Robidoux, 1784–1860*. Los Angeles: Glen Dawson, 1953.

Waters, Frank. *The Colorado*. New York: Holt, Rinehart & Winston, 1946.

Wentworth, Frank L. *Aspen on the Roaring Fork.* Denver, Colorado: World Press, Inc., 1950.

Woodard, Bruce A. *Diamonds in the Salt.* Boulder, Colorado: Pruett Press, 1967.

Woodruff, E. G. and Day, David. *Oil Shale of Northwestern Colorado and Northeastern Utah.* Washington, D.C.: Government Printing Office, 1914.

Wormington, H. M. *Prehistoric Indians of the Southwest.* Denver, Colorado: Denver Museum of Natural History, 1959.

Articles

"Anthracite Mine at Floresta." *Camp and Plant,* IV (August 8, 1903), pp. 78-80.

Bancroft, George. "Diversion of Water from the Western Slope." *The Colorado Magazine* (September, 1944), pp. 178-81.

Bartlett, Robert. "Aspen: The Mining Community, 1879-1891." *The Denver Westerners Brand Book* (1950), pp. 131-60.

Beidleman, Richard. "Black Canyon of the Gunnison National Monument." *The Colorado Magazine* (July, 1963), pp. 178-81.

_____. "The Gunnison River Diversion Project." *The Colorado Magazine* (July, 1959), pp. 187-201, 266-86.

Bollinger, Edward. "Middle Park Stage Driving." *The Colorado Magazine* (October, 1951), pp. 269-80.

Borland, Lois. "Ho for the Reservation: Settlement of the Western Slope." *The Colorado Magazine* (January, 1952), pp. 56-75.

_____. "The Sale of the San Juan." *The Colorado Magazine* (April, 1951), pp. 107-27.

Britton, Charles. "An Early Electric Power Facility in Colorado." *The Colorado Magazine* (Summer, 1972), pp. 185-95.

Brown, Robert L. "Animas Forks: The Life and Death of a Mining Camp." *The Denver Westerners Brand Book* (1965), pp. 203-18.

Butler, B. S. "Notes on the Unaweep Copper District, Colorado." *Contributions to Economic Geology.* Washington, 1915. pp. 19-23.

Carpenter, Farrington R. "Hayden's First Lawyer." *The Colorado Lawyer* (February, 1979), pp. 212-23.

Casement, Dan. "Pioneering the Unaweep." *The Colorado Magazine* (July, 1954), pp. 274-89.

"Coal Basin, Colorado." *Camp and Plant,* II (September 13, 1902), pp. 249-55.

Coberly, Carroll H. "Ashcroft." *The Colorado Magazine* (April, 1960), pp. 81-104.

Cole, Donald. "Transmountain Water Diversion in Colorado." *The Colorado Magazine* (May, 1948), pp. 49-65, 118-35.

Colwell, Raymond. "Lake City." *The Denver Westerners Brand Book* (1950), pp. 109-30.

"Crested Butte, Colorado." *Camp and Plant,* I (April 26, 1902), pp. 337-344.

Cummins, D. H. "Toll Roads in Southwestern Colorado." *The Colorado Magazine* (January, 1952), pp. 98-104.

Curtis, Olga. "Energy Boom." *Empire* (April 2, 1978), pp. 10-15.

_____. "Oil Shale — Miracle or Mirage." *Empire* (April 9, 1978), pp. 28-38.

Deets, Lee. "Paradox Valley — An Historical Interpretation of its Structure and Changes." *The Colorado Magazine* (September, 1934), pp. 186-98.

Dunbar, Robert G. "The Origins of the Colorado System of Water Right Control." *The Colorado Magazine* (1950), pp. 241-63.

Friggens, Paul. "Denver Digs 23 Miles for a Drink." *Reader's Digest* (April, 1961), pp. 189-96.

Haase, Carl. "Gothic, Colorado: City of Silver Wires." *The Colorado Magazine* (Fall, 1974), pp. 294-317.

Hafen, LeRoy. "Colonel Loring's Expedition Across Colorado in 1858." *The Colorado Magazine* (March, 1946), pp. 49-75.

_____. "The Coming of the Automobile and Improved Roads to Colorado." *The Colorado Magazine* (January, 1931), pp. 1-16.

_____. "Fort Davy Crockett, Its Fur Men and Visitors." *The Colorado Magazine* (January, 1952), pp. 17-33.

"Hard Coal Mine at Anthracite." *Camp and Plant,* III (January 28, 1903), pp. 73-74.

Harper's Weekly, XXVIII (February 16, 1884), p. 111.

Hastings, Homer. "Pioneers of the Uncompahgre Plateau." *The Colorado Magazine* (Winter, 1964), pp. 34-48.

Helmick, Ed and Kelley, Mike. "Carpenter: A Ghost Town." *The Colorado Magazine* (October, 1962), pp. 289-94.

Hill, Joseph. "Antoine Robidoux, Kingpin in the Colorado River Fur Trade, 1824-1844." *The Colorado Magazine* (July, 1930), pp. 125-31.

Hornbein, Marjorie. "Josephine Roche: Social Worker and Coal Operator." *The Colorado Magazine* (Summer, 1976), pp. 243-60.

Jackson, Helen H. "O-Be-Joyful Creek and Poverty Gulch." *Atlantic Magazine* (December, 1883), pp. 753-62.

Johnson, Jerome. "Murder on the Uncompahgre." *The Colorado Magazine* (Summer, 1966), pp. 209-24.

Johnson, John. "A Brief History of the Rocky Mountain Biological Laboratory." *The Colorado Magazine* (April, 1961), pp. 81-103.

Kaplan, Michael. "Otto Mears and the Silverton Northern Railroad." *The Colorado Magazine* (Summer, 1971), pp. 153-70.

——————. "The Toll Road Building Career of Otto Mears, 1881-1887." *The Colorado Magazine* (Spring, 1975), pp. 153-70.

Leckenby, Charles. "The Founding of Steamboat Springs and of Hahns Peak." *The Colorado Magazine* (May, 1929), pp. 92-97.

Lichenstein, Grace. "The Battle Over the Mighty Colorado." *The New York Times Magazine* (July 31, 1977), pp. 11-13, 25-30.

Lipsey, John J. "J. J. Hagerman, Building of the Colorado Midland." *The Denver Westerners Brand Book* (1954), pp. 95-116.

Look, Al. "John Otto, Fantastic Father of the Colorado National Monument." *The Denver Westerners Brand Book* (1960), pp. 180-248.

Mathews, Carl F. "Rico, Colorado—Once a Roaring Camp." *The Colorado Magazine* (January, 1951), pp. 37-49.

McCarthy, Michael G. "White River Forest Reserve: The Conservation Conflict." *The Colorado Magazine* (Winter, 1972), pp. 55-67.

McKee, Thomas M. "Early Discovery of Uranium Ore in Colorado." *The Colorado Magazine* (July, 1955), pp. 191-203.

McNichols, Stephen. "A Basic Minerals Policy for Colorado." *Colorado Quarterly* (Summer, 1957), pp. 5-14.

Mechau, Vaughn W. "Redstone on the Crystal." *The Denver Westerners Brand Book* (1948), pp. 37-54.

Mumey, Nolie. "John Williams Gunnison: Centenary of His Survey and Tragic Death." *The Colorado Magazine* (January, 1954), pp. 19-32.

O'Connell, Dan. "The Old Time Prospector," *Colorado Magazine* (March, 1924), pp. 103-08.

Pierce, Edward. "Telluride in 1900." *Pioneers of the San Juan*, vol. III (Durango: Durango Printing, 1952), pp. 27-33.

Pierce, Ellandean. "Early Days of Craig, Colorado." *The Colorado Magazine* (August, 1928), pp. 152-58.

Poor, Mac. "How Come, Why, and How I Wrote 'Denver South Park and Pacific.'" *The Denver Westerners Brand Book* (1965), pp. 333-56.

Pritchard, Alan. "The Walkers of Grand Junction." *The Denver Westerners Brand Book* (1961), pp. 181-246.

Pritchett, Lulita. "James H. Crawford's Winter in Burns Hole, 1880." *The Colorado Magazine* (July, 1955), pp. 191-203.

"Prospecting for Coal." *Camp and Plant,* V (January 30, 1904), pp. 53–62.

Rait, Mary. "Development of the Peach Industry in the Colorado River Valley." *The Colorado Magazine* (September, 1946), pp. 247–58.

Ranze, Dolores. "Permutations in Paradox Valley." *The Denver Westerners Brand Book* (1949), pp. 93–118.

Rizzari, Francis. "Railroads of the Crystal River Valley." *The Denver Westerners Brand Book* (1964), pp. 369–405.

Rockwell, Wilson. "Cow-Land Aristocrats of the North Fork." *The Colorado Magazine* (September, 1937), pp. 161–70.

_____. "The Fruit Utopia of the North Fork of the Gunnison." *The Colorado Magazine* (May, 1938), pp. 89–98.

_____. "Portrait in the Gallery, Otto Mears Pathfinder of the San Juans." *The Denver Westerners Brand Book* (1967), pp. 2–53.

Roller, Elizabeth. "Life in Montezuma, Chihuahua and Sts. John." *The Denver Westerners Brand Book* (1964), pp. 59–85.

Ronzio, Richard. "Fort Crawford on the Uncompahgre." *The Denver Westerners Brand Book* (1963), pp. 255–65.

_____. "The Uintah Railway: The Gilsonite Road." *The Denver Westerners Brand Book* (1959), pp. 37–54.

Root, George. "Reminiscences of White Pine, Colorado." *The Colorado Magazine* (May, 1936), pp. 112–17.

Scamehorn, H. Lee. "John C. Osgood and the Western Steel Industry." *Arizona and the West* (Summer, 1973), pp. 133–48.

Sharp, Verna. "Montezuma and Her Neighbors." *The Colorado Magazine* (January, 1956), pp. 17–41.

Shoemaker, Len. "The First Forest Ranger." *The Denver Westerners Brand Book* (1951), pp. 95–122.

Sibley, George. "The Desert Empire." *Harper's* (October, 1977), pp. 49–68.

Smith, Duane. "Colorado's Urban-Mining Safety Valve." *The Colorado Magazine* (Fall, 1971), pp. 299–318.

_____. "A Land unto Itself: The Western Slope." *The Colorado Magazine* (Spring/Summer, 1978), pp. 181–204.

_____. "Mining Camps: Myth vs. Reality." *The Colorado Magazine* (Spring, 1967), pp. 92–110.

_____. "Silver Coquette—The San Juans, 1860–1875." *The Denver Westerners Brand Book* (1969), pp. 307–36.

Suggs, George G. "The Colorado Coal Miners Strike 1903–1904." *Journal of the West* (January, 1973), pp. 36–52.

Taylor, Morris. "The Barlow and Sanderson Stage Lines in Colorado 1872–1884." *The Colorado Magazine* (Spring, 1973), pp. 142–62.

Thomas, Alfred. "Spanish Explorations into Colorado." *The Colorado Magazine* (November, 1924), pp. 290-300.

Thomas, C. S. "An Argonaut of the Roaring Fork." *The Colorado Magazine* (November, 1930), pp. 205-15.

Thompson, Thomas. "Early Development of Lake City." *The Colorado Magazine* (April, 1963), pp. 92-105.

Vandenbusche, Duane. "Man Against the Black Canyon." *The Colorado Magazine* (Spring, 1973), pp. 117-41.

_____. "Marble: Past to Present." *The Colorado Magazine* (Winter, 1969), pp. 16-39.

Walsh, Thomas. "Commencement Address." *Quarterly of the Colorado School of Mines* (July, 1908), pp. 3-18.

Wilson, Mary. "We Move to Egeria Park." *The Colorado Magazine* (April, 1963), pp. 121-27.

Wyman, Walker. "Grand Junction's First Year, 1882." *The Colorado Magazine* (May, 1936), pp. 127-36.

Newspapers

Aspen Times, 1925, 1941.

Craig Empire, 1916-1917.

Craig Empire-Courier, 1945

Daily Journal (Breckenridge), 1881-1888.

Daily Sentinel (Grand Junction), 1950, 1955.

DeBeque Shale, 1923.

Delta Independent, 1905-1906.

Denver Post, 1970-1979.

Durango Evening Herald, 1898.

Durango Herald, 1977-1979.

Durango Record, 1881-1882.

Durango Weekly Herald, 1940, 1942.

Empire-Courier (Craig), 1977-1978.

Engineering and Mining Journal (New York), 1866-1913.

Glenwood Post, 1925-1926, 1931, 1943.

Grand Junction News, 1882-1905.

Gunnison Country Times, 1975-1979.

Gunnison Courier, 1942.

Gunnison News-Champion, 1901-1979.

Gunnison Review, 1880-1882.

Gunnison Review-Press, 1882-1890.

Gunnison Tribune, 1891-1904.

Meeker Herald, 1912-1913, 1944.

Middle Park Times, 1908-1913.

Miner's Record (Tarryall), 1861.

Mining Record (New York), 1880.

Moffat County Bell (Maybell), 1919–1920.

Montrose Enterprise, 1897–1906.

Montrose Press, 1918, 1939, 1941.

Montrose Daily Press, 1945.

Pagosa Springs Sun, 1943.

Paonia Progressive, 1910.

Pueblo Chieftain, 1977-79.

Rangely Driller, 1955.

Rocky Mountain News (Denver), various issues 1859–1979.

Rocky Mountain Sun (Aspen), 1881–1899.

Shale and Oil News (DeBeque), 1920–1921, 1923.

Silver World (Lake City), 1875–1883.

Silverton Standard, 1893.

Solid Muldoon (Ouray), 1879–1892.

Steamboat Pilot, 1897–1922, 1929, 1933–1934, 1970–1979.

Summit County Journal (Breckenridge), 1906, 1917, 1919, 1926.

Telluride Daily Journal, 1897–1929.

United Methodist (Rocky Mountain Conference of Methodist Church), 1977.

Weekly Chieftain (Ignacio), 1914.

Weekly Sentinel (Grand Junction), 1916–1917.

Yampa Leader, 1923–1924.

Miscellaneous

Annual Report of the Denver & Rio Grande — 1886. Denver & Rio Grande Archives.

Armstrong, Gerald R. "Miss Josephine Roche, President the Rocky Mountain Fuel Company, 1927-1951." Annual Meeting of Shareholders, Rocky Mountain Fuel Company. April 14, 1975.

Aspen, Pitkin County, Colorado: Her Mines and Mineral Resources. Aspen: Daily Leader, 1892.

Aspen: Where and What it is and How to Get There. Aspen, np, 1892.

Aspinall, Wayne N. Gunnison, Colorado. Interview, July 22, 1977, and July 17, 1978.

Aspinall, Wayne N. to Duane Vandenbusche, November 9, 1978.

Black Canyon Region: Colorado Regional Profile. Boulder, Colorado: Business Research Division, 1975.

Carlisle, Henry. Collection, Western History Research Center, University of Wyoming.

Carpenter, Farrington. Hayden, Colorado. Interview, July 17, 1977, and May 28, 1979.

Colorado Energy Research Institute. "Future Energy Alternatives for Colorado." January, 1976.

Colorado: Mineral, Oil & Shale. Denver: State Board Immigration, 1930.

A Colorado Profile, The Western Slope: Dimension, A Colorado Perspective. Denver: The First National Bank Corporation, Inc., 1978.

Colorado: The Ultimate Fringe Benefit. Denver: Colorado Division of Commerce and Development, 1978.

Cummins, Densil H. "Social and Economic History of Southwestern Colorado, 1860–1948." Unpublished Ph.D. dissertation, University of Texas, 1951.

Dawson, Louise and Murray D. Keith, Compilers. "Colorado Coal Directory and Source Book." Resource Series 3, *Colorado Geological Survey.* Department of Natural Resources, Colorado, 1978.

Draft West Colorado Environmental Statement. 3 vols. U.S. Department of the Interior and Bureau of Land Management, 1978.

Goeldner, C. R. and Dicke, Karen. *Colorado Ski Industry: Characteristics and Financial Analysis.* Boulder, Colorado: Business Research Division, 1979.

Hyman, David M. "Romance of a Mining Venture." Manuscript. Western Heritage Center, University of Wyoming.

An Impact Study: Colorado Ski Country USA. Denver: Colorado Ski Country USA, 1976.

Lavender, David. "Water and the Western Slope." Typescript, 1977. In possession of Duane Vandenbusche.

Mayo, Clarence H. Letters. Henry E. Huntington Library.

Minute Book of the Gunnison County Stockgrowers' Association. Gunnison, Colorado, I. Meeting of June 7, 1902.

Montrose County Where Apple is King. Montrose: Press Book, 1905.

Northern Mountain: Colorado Regional Profile. Boulder, Colorado: Business Research Division, 1975.

Northwest Supplemental Report: A Supplement to the Northwest Colorado Coal Regional Environmental Statement. Bureau of Land Management, 1977.

The Plateau Region: Colorado Regional Profile, Region 11. Boulder, Colorado: Business Research Division, 1975.

San Juan: Colorado Regional Profile. Boulder, Colorado: Business Research Division, 1975.

Searcy, William. Paper: Western Historical Collections, University of Colorado.

A Survey of Skiing Among the Adult Population of Colorado. San Francisco: Field Research Corporation, 1978.

Tomboy Material, James D. Hague Collection, Henry E. Huntington Library.

Index

Montrose, Colo., 147, 201, 206, 210
Mora, Pedro, 16
Moran, Thomas, 31
Motion pictures, 257
Mount Emmons, 307
Mountain climbing, 255-56
Mug House, 10-11

N

National Radium Institute, 115-16
New Deal, 216-18, 219
New Jersey Zinc Company, 240, 241
Newspapers, 71-73, 224
North Fork Valley, 148, 149-50, 127-28
Norwood, Colo., 291
Nucla, Colo., 152, 189

O

Oak Creek, Colo., 133, 134
O'Connell, Dan, 54
Oil, 227, 236-38, 293
Oil Shale, 220-21, 238-39, 242-43
Orchard Mesa, 190
Osgood, John, 128-29
Otto, John, 200-01
Ouray, Colo., 79, 108, 164, 169, 202, 233, 291
Ouray, Ute leader, 78-79, 80

P

Pabor, William, 150
Paepcke, Walter, 247-48
Pagosa Springs, Colo., 202
Palisade, Colo., 150
Palmer, Bruce, 250
Palmer, William Jackson, 84, 85, 86, 87, 88, 91

Panic of 1893, 65, 90, 97, 105-06, 140-41
Paonia, Colo., 148, 149, 211
Perins, Colo., 125
Philibert, Joseph, 19
Pike, Zebulon, 76
Pike's Peak Gold Rush, 35-36
Pinchot, Gifford, 159
Pitkin, Colo., 175
Pitkin, Frederick, 68, 306
Politics, 67-68, 216, 218, 224, 279-81, 303, 306
Pollution, 43, 46, 67, 113, 130, 135, 136, 183, 240-41, 242, 243, 300, 302, 308
Population patterns, 67, 197-98, 307
Porter, Colo., 124
Powell, John W., 261, 271
Prior Appropriation Doctrine, 182, 274-75
Progressivism, 207-08
Prohibition, 208-09, 213-14
Prostitution, 64, 73, 174
Public domain, federal regulation, 161
Pueblo culture, 9, 10

R

Radio, 223-24
Railroads, 83-84, 103, 170, 222-23, 285. *See* Denver and Rio Grande and other individual lines
Raine, William, 202-03
Ranching, 144, 146, 153, 154-56, 157, 158-60, 161-62, 173, 194, 195. *See also* Sheep
Range wars, 156, 157-58
Rangely, Colo., 227, 236, 237, 293
Ransome, Frederick, 113-14
Reclamation. *See* Water, Environment

Tourism, 46-47, 54, 64-65, 68, 176-77, 198-204, 224, 253, 254, 255, 256-57, 294-95, 300-01

U

Uintah Railway, 102
Uncompahgre Valley, 185-86, 187
Unions, 110-11
Upper Colorado River Basin Compact, 267-68
Uravan, Colo., 219
Urbanization, 53-54, 56-57, 66, 67, 211, 284
Ute Mountain Ute Park, 4
Utes, 12-13, 14, 15, 16, 43, 44, 45, 47, 53, 60, 72, 75-81, 144, 147, 153, 164, 198

V

Vail, Colo., 249-50
Vanderhoof, John, 306

W

Wade, Sam, 148, 149
Waite, Davis, 68, 306
Walsh, Thomas, 111-12
Water, 172, 181-82, 294-95. *See also* specific chapters

Water projects: Animas-La Plata, 269-70; Colorado-Big Thompson, 263-64; Dallas Creek, 270; Dolores, 188, 270; Fryingpan-Arkansas, 265-66; Gunnison-Arkansas, 264, 267; Taylor Park, 294-95
Werner, Buddy, 252
Western Colorado Chamber of Commerce, 206
Western Federation of Miners, 110-11
Western Slope Historical Association, 206
Western State College, 212-13, 214
Weatherill, Richard & Al, 12
Wheeler, George, 30, 32
Wheeler, Jerome, 61
White Pine, Colo., 57
Whitman, Marcus, 25
Wiik, Sven, 252
Williams, Bill, 26
Winter Park, Colo., 248-49
Women, 40-41, 46, 58-59, 71-73, 81, 107, 198, 212, 225
Women's suffrage, 107
Wood, David, 139-41
Woodstock, Colo., 94
Wootton, Richens, 21, 26-27
World War I, reaction to, 209-10
World War II, reaction to, 224-28